THE UNTOLD STORY OF
LUBY'S
CAFETERIAS

Including

**Joseph Owen Luby Sr.'s
Original Cookbook**

LAWRENCE P. LUBY

Copyright © 2022 by Lawrence P. Luby

All rights reserved. Except as permitted under the U.S. Copyright Act of 1976, no part of this publication may be reproduced, distributed, or transmitted in any form or by any means, or stored in a database or retrieval system, without the prior written permission of the publisher.

Proper credit, when available, has been provided for all images. All images copyrighted or owned by other sources have been cited and used with permission of the owner. No images used were owned by Getty images at the time of this publication.

HIS Publishing Group
4310 Wiley Post Rd., Suite 201D
Addison, TX 75001
info@hispub.com

ISBN-13:   978-1-7352651-9-3 *paperback*

Library of Congress Control Number: 2021949980

Printed in the United States of America

10 9 8 7 6 5 4 3 2 1

Division of Human Improvement Specialists, llc.
www.hispubg.com | *info@hispubg.com*

CONTENTS

Preview..5

Walk Down Memory Lane 7
The Early Years 1911 – 1946.. 11
Joe O. Luby Sr. Dallas Luby's Founding Partner 23
Joe O. Luby, Lt. (jg) D-V (G) USNR,
Commanding Officer of LCI (G) 340............................. 33
Expansion of Luby's by the Dallas Group After WWII 37
Luby's Cafeterias in North Texas..................................... 55
Colorado Expansion 77
Changing Times 85
The Decline of Bob Luby's Branch of Luby's Cafeterias............ 101
The Winds of Change and Darkness Settles................. 107
Parting Words... 121
Favorite Luby Stories 123
Joseph Owen Luby Sr.'s Original Cookbook................. 127

Addendum A 457

PREVIEW

THE HISTORY OF A FAMILY legacy. How does one set out to write the truth? By relating the factual events that defined that legacy and forever sealed the heritage for generations to come. We live in a society today that deviously rewrites history to fit selfish narratives. The truth is deceptively altered just enough to make that narrative believable. *The Untold Story of Luby's Cafeterias* lifts the veil from the past and introduces the factual history about how Luby's Cafeterias came into existence. You will be introduced to Joseph Owen Luby Sr. (Joe O. Luby), my father, a founding partner of Luby's, who was instrumental in laying the foundation for growth that helped Luby's become one of the most revered food service establishments of the 20th century.

Joe O. Luby's name was intentionally deleted from the current entity's history for reasons that will be revealed later. Because of family division and his untimely diagnosis of lung cancer that led to his death in 1977, the history was easily edited so that credit could be given to others.

This book is dedicated to Harry Luby, my cousin, who unified Luby family members and provided them with an opportunity to build successful lives. Harry's character was such that he would want *The Untold Story of Luby's Cafeterias* to be told. The story begins in Illinois when Harry, who had lost his father at the age of four, teamed up with his cousin, both of whom had tremendous entrepreneurial spirits. The two of them would eventually move to Dallas, Texas, where their story would spring to life and the company roots would be established.

WALK DOWN MEMORY LANE

I CAN STILL REMEMBER WALKING into my father's cafeteria in the Inwood Village Shopping Center in 1959; I was six years old. The cafeteria was located on the south side of the Inwood Shopping Center. I recall how much fun it was to watch a movie at the Inwood theatre and then walk south down the enclosed walkway to our cafeteria. As customers entered the front door and looked to the right, they would see Ms. Inez playing a baby grand piano. She was the Dallas crown jewel of music and created an invigorating atmosphere.

As I approached, she would look up at me and the creases of her lips would break into a bright smile. I still remember the warmth I felt from the vibration of the notes emanating from her tender fingers on the keys. Beyond her was the walkway along the west wall that led to the food line. Continuing with culinary expectation, the serving ladies with hair nets carefully set in place always offered me a welcoming smile.

"Mr. Larry, I do believe you've grown since you last came in."

Of course, as the owner's son, I was afforded a king's treatment. But to me the experience was just as normal as riding my bike through our neighborhood and waving to the neighbors. Normal in the sense that there was an outpouring of love. We were family, and there was no indication that one family member was better or more important than any other.

See and Hear
MISS INEZ
...at the Organ
KRLD-TV • Channel 4
Every Sunday Afternoon 3:15-3:30 P.M.
Courtesy of all Luby's Cafeterias

My mouth would water as I moved from the salad section with all the colors of the rainbow glistening from the various greens and fruits to the meats. My eyes were always bigger than my stomach.

Delighting my palette were the savory scents rising from the fresh baked entrees to the puffs of steam billowing from the pans containing a variety of delectable goodies. My favorite being the chicken fried steak made with lean cutlet meat lathered in buttermilk and seasoned flour and then fried to a golden-brown perfection. Mind you in the 1960-1970s, Luby's had the best chicken fried steak to be found in Dallas.

Many reading this book will remember dining at Luby's and will reminisce about their own experiences. Please join me on a journey through time where the sight of ladies with hairnets and the aroma of roast beef and fresh baked breads awaits.

THE EARLY YEARS
1911 – 1946

IN 1929, THE GREAT DEPRESSION hit our nation, and by that time Joseph (J.E.) and Jerusa (Louise) Luby had birthed twelve children, losing one during childbirth and another due to a sports injury. The remaining six boys and four girls would all find success in life.

Picture of the Luby boys taken at the family reunion in 1918.
Frank, Clyde, George, Mack, Ralph, and Earl (L to R)

REUNION GIVEN FOR SON—

Ralph Luby departed for Camp Taylor Tuesday after spending a five-day furlough with his parents, Mr. and Mrs. J. E. Luby. A family reunion was held Sunday at the home of his parents, 2421 DeWitt avenue in his honor. At the noon hour an excellent dinner was served. All members of the family were present, except one, Mrs. Hazel Stone of Livonia, Ind. A picture was taken of the family group and also one of the six brothers, Sunday afternoon. In the evening ice cream, cake and frozen fruits were served.

Those present, besides the guest of honor, were Mr. and Mrs. George Luby and son, George David, of Palestine; Mr. and Mrs. M. S. Luby and daughter, Rosanna, of Danville; Mr. and Mrs. C. V. Luby and children, Dorothy, Donald and Lois, of Paris; Mr. and Mrs. C. E. Johnson and son Charles Jr., Miss Fannie Purkiser, Miss Helen Luby, Miss Opal Luby, Earl Luby and Edward Brumleve, of Mattoon.

Article from the Journal Gazette, June 19, 1918, Mattoon, IL.

The Luby girls shown with parents Joseph Emerson and Jerusa Paradise Rosanna. Opal, Hazel, Helen, and Lola (L to R)

Born on May 28, 1855, in Ohio, J.E. Luby was four years old when his father died. His mother moved the family to Illinois where they settled in Mattoon. He died December 8, 1932. Louise was born in Ohio on October 2, 1859. They were happily married for fifty-three years and left behind ten children and seventeen grandchildren. Louise preceded J.E. in death on October 16, 1931.

Like J.E., their cousin Harry, lost his father when he was four years old. It was a tough time for Harry and his family. Harry lived a short distance from Mattoon, Illinois, where he eventually would bond with his ten first cousins. Harry had a vision after eating at a diner in Chicago, and he would later turn that vision into a reality: New England Dairy Lunch, the predecessor to Luby's Cafeterias.

Harry had a tremendous work ethic and proved to be a blessing to his family. Like everyone moving from the dust bowl in Texas to the Midwest in hopes of finding employment, Harry moved from Chicago to Decatur, Illinois, in 1909 and opened a millinery store.

> **Pana News Notes.**
>
> Harry M. Luby of Chicago has rented the south room at the Grand opera house building and he and Mrs. Luby will open a millinery store in the room the first of March.

Article from the Decatur Herald, Friday January 29, 1909

In a book titled *House of Plenty*, the authors incorrectly list Harry's birthdate as 1887 and mis-identify his store as a *Men's Haberdashery* located in Springfield, Missouri. The book has other inaccuracies, which is surprising considering it was published by a reputable establishment. Harry was born on December 12, 1884 and lived a long and full life. He died in San Antonio, Texas, at the age of ninety-four on August 24, 1978. He and his wife Julia are buried in a mausoleum at Sunset Memorial in San Antonio.

I have not been able to determine why Harry ventured into making women's hats except that his wife had great influence in his life. While visiting Chicago, he ventured into a restaurant called The Dairy Lunch. The concept caught his attention, and upon his return, he discussed the concept with his wife who was an excellent cook in her own right. One year later, Harry made the decision to sell his millinery store and move to Springfield, Missouri. Julia was experiencing health issues at the time, and Harry thought Springfield might be a better location for her.

> SELLS HIS MILLINERY.
> Harry M. Luby has sold his millinery stock and will leave shortly for western Missouri, where he expects to locate for the benefit of his wife's health, she being afflicted with nervousness.

Daily Review in Decatur, Illinois, Thursday February 10, 1910

In 1911, Harry's first venture into the restaurant business was a small restaurant named The New England Dairy Lunch.

Julia had been preparing a New England style roast stew with a variety of vegetables. Harry thought her stew would make a splash and would be easy to keep fresh, hot, and ready to serve. He opened his second restaurant in Springfield, Missouri, a year later and ventured to St. Joseph, Missouri, in 1914, changing the names of his establishments to New England Cafeteria.

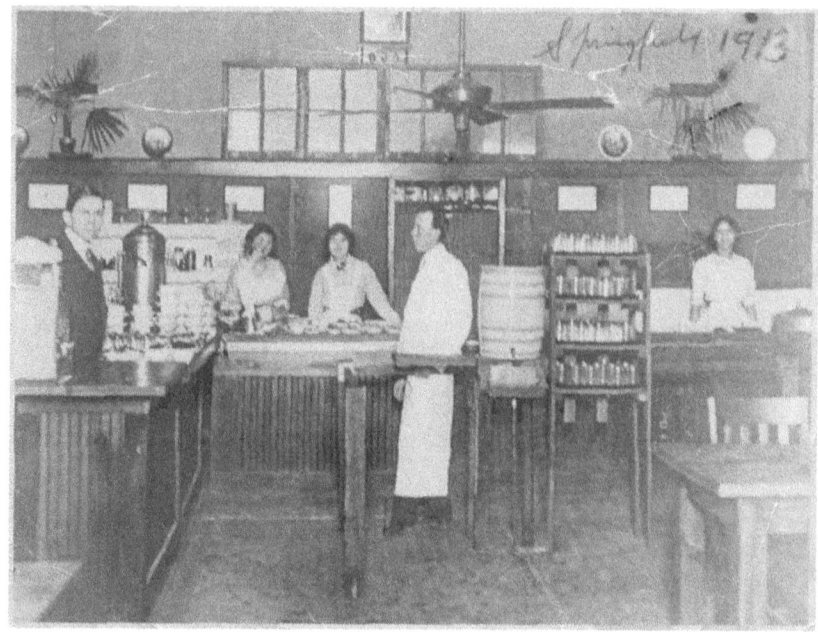

Around this time, his cousin and my uncle, Earl Luby, joined him, and the two of them began a quest that would eventually lead them to Dallas, Texas. Ultimately, the next generation, including Earl's brother, Ralph Luby, my father, Joe O. Luby Sr., his brother George Luby Jr., and their cousin, J. Pat Luby, would partner with Earl and carry on the legacy. Harry laid the foundation for many of Earl's brothers and sisters who joined him and Harry in the cafeteria business, ultimately, providing Harry's son, Robert (Bob) Luby, a springboard to launch his own division of the Luby's Cafeteria chain in San Antonio in 1947.

Like the final leg in a relay, Bob took the baton, ran faster than anyone else in the family, and eventually built one of the most respected cafeteria chains in the country, Luby's Cafeterias Incorporated. By the 1980s, Luby's had over one hundred locations, was debt free, and owned the real estate under many of their locations.

The story could end there, and it would be a nice ending, but the story has a lot of internal parts. To understand the success of the Luby's Cafeteria chain, we must go back in time and look at the untold story of Luby's. The Luby boys were a strong and resourceful bunch, and like many families their personalities showed signs of strengths and weaknesses.

Frank, the oldest was a strong personality and provided stability for his brothers and sisters. Frank joined his sisters, Hazel, Helen, and Lola and opened the cafeteria that was located at 1006 Main Street, in downtown Dallas, Texas.

One of the brothers in particular played a major role in Harry's success. His name was Clyde, the second oldest of the eight Luby sons. Like Harry, Clyde was smart and had a strong work ethic. He was instrumental in laying the foundation for Luby's in smaller Texas towns during the 1920s and 1930s. Like everyone in the family, Clyde started out in Dallas, but he was instrumental in opening several Luby's cafeterias in Houston, Lubbock, Abilene, San Angelo, and Amarillo. He ultimately put down roots in San Angelo where he owned and operated a Luby's. Clyde and his son, Don would eventually play a significant role in the future of Luby's Cafeterias Incorporated, but you will read very little about their involvement in the current Luby's history.

Next in the line was my grandfather, George Sr., who was tough as nails. Rumor had it that during his amateur boxing career he once sparred with Max Baer.

THE EARLY YEARS 1911 – 1946

A fun story my dad liked to tell was the day that Earl borrowed one of George's new suits. George walked in the front door as Earl was descending the stairs. George walked up and hit him square in the nose and then looking down at him said, "Never wear one of my suits again."

George met the love of his life, Jennie Cochonour, and after they married, they settled in Palestine, Illinois, where he enjoyed a long career with the railroad. He was the sole Luby brother that didn't care to venture into the restaurant business. However, he played a major role with Earl in birthing the concept.

Mack was a self-starter and a hard worker. Like his brother George, he began his career with the railroad. Later, he joined Harry and Earl in Dallas. Eventually, he joined his brother Clyde and operated his own cafeteria in San Angelo, Texas.

Ralph was close to his brother Earl but was less than admired by others within the family. In 1922, Ralph moved from Denver where he had been living and joined Earl in Muskogee, Oklahoma. The two of them eventually continued their relationship in Dallas. Ralph proved to be a turncoat to two of his cousins, my father Joe O. Luby Sr. and J. Pat Luby, Earl's adopted son. More on that subject later.

Earl was the youngest of the Luby boys and had a mind for marketing that eventually led him to partner with Harry and build the initial foundation for Luby's Cafeterias. Earl approached my grandfather, George Sr., whom he admired, and asked his advice about joining their cousin Harry in business. After hearing about the concept, George asked him how much money he needed. Earl replied, and George made him a loan. No one in the family seems to recall if Earl ever paid his brother back, but knowing my grandfather, he was probably not expecting anything in return. If it had not been for my grandfather, Earl would probably not have entered the restaurant business.

Harry and Earl had become close, and Harry knew he needed help. The restaurant business was tough, and the hours were long. A normal day started around six and didn't end until well after the dinner hour, and they were open seven days a week. By 1915, Harry operated two locations in Springfield, one in St. Joseph, Missouri, and one in Joplin, Missouri. Earl entered the scene in 1919 and opened a cafeteria in Muskogee, Oklahoma. Earl proved to be a smart businessman, and along with Harry, they began to lay an incredible foundation.

THE EARLY YEARS 1911 – 1946

The Ku Klux Klan didn't like the idea that Earl and Harry employed "colored people." Separating black and white back then, as it is now, was only a means to achieve an evil agenda. The reality is neither is a color; they are both void of color. The only color that we all share is red, the color of our life blood. The Luby family understood this concept better than most at the time. They knew by using the talents of all their employees they could provide the best quality food and service to their customers. Some had more talent than others in certain areas of the establishment.

The real talent was with their black employees who were by far the better cooks. In fact, they knew more about cooking than either Harry or Earl, and the cafeterias would not have survived without their input. The Klan approached Earl and demanded that he join their organization, or they would shut down his cafeteria.

After discussion with Harry, Earl determined that the fight would have to play out somewhere else because neither of them were about to join a group hell bent on suppressing minorities. They absorbed the loss and closed the Oklahoma establishment. The two of them then embarked on the next chapter of their careers and moved south to Dallas, Texas. That one decision was foundational and was also a blessing that helped their business grow and flourish.

Earl, his brothers, and his sisters were in the prime of their lives. They all had needs and wanted to provide for their families. They were looking to build fortunes. Together, they had survived the Great Depression; rather than giving up, they fought. Harry and Earl provided an opportunity and put the sisters and brothers to work in the cafeteria business.

The concept of hiring family members was popular, so they were at the right time and place. All family members, except Ralph, received their initial training in a Downtown Dallas location owned by Earl. The Luby kids exhibited greatness and became pioneers and leaders in the food industry.

Few people realize that the cafeteria concept was birthed out of a desire to provide fresh food in the shortest amount of time. In the early 1900's, people didn't take long lunch breaks, so there was a need for a restaurant where hot meals could be enjoyed within the limited time employees were given for the noon meal. With the food pre-prepared, people could get in and get out in record time. Most importantly, they could enjoy a gourmet-style meal that was healthy and filling. The cafeteria became the grandfather to the fast, casual dining concepts we enjoy today.

JOE O. LUBY SR. DALLAS LUBY'S FOUNDING PARTNER

My father, Joseph (Joe) Owen Luby Sr., was born in Palestine, Illinois on July 12, 1919. His father worked for the railroad, and his mother stayed at home and raised him and his older brother George Junior.

George Jr. on the left, my father on the right

JOE O. LUBY SR. DALLAS LUBY'S FOUNDING PARTNER

Grandfather Luby, father, and George Jr.

My father played football and other sports in high school. Mother told the following story: "One game your father suffered a gash over his eye. The doctor on the sideline stitched it up, and he went back in the game." I remember thinking he must have had a high tolerance for pain. My father never confirmed the story, maybe out of humility. He is number nineteen in the image with his teammates. They were mostly farm boys who were sorry on the eyes but tough and scrappy.

In 1942, with the country joining the war effort, Joe now twenty-three years old and a graduate of the University of Illinois with a degree in accounting enlisted in the Navy Reserves and was sent to the USNR Midshipmen's School at Northwestern University in Chicago, Illinois.

On December 23, 1942, while stationed in Chicago, he married Betty Jane Prather, and they enjoyed a one-night honeymoon. My mother loved to tease my father by saying, "I couldn't believe your mother called us at 9:30 the next morning and woke us up—I could have shot her."

PRINCETON, INDIANA, MONDAY, JANUARY 4, 1943

Recent Marriage Is Announced

Mrs. Joe O. Luby

Announcement has been made of the marriage of Miss Betty Jane Prather, daughter of Mr. and Mrs. J. H. Prather of Palestine, Ill., to Ensign Joe O. Luby, son of Mr. and Mrs. George Luby, also of Palestine, which was solemnized December 24, in Chicago, Ill. An impressive single ring ceremony was performed at 3:30 o'clock in the John Timothy Stone chapel of the Fourth Presbyterian church on Lake Shore Drive by the Rev. Kenneth N. Hildebrand before an altar of chrysanthemums and candelabra.

Only the immediate families of the bride and bridegroom were present.

The bride wore a light victory blue wool suit with matching hat and accessories of alligator and a corsage of orchids.

Following the ceremony, dinner was served at the Sherman hotel.

Mrs. Luby formerly attended Indiana university and is a member of Kappa Kappa Gamma sorority.

Mr. Luby is a graduate of the University of Illinois, class of '42, and received his commission in the U. S. navy on the date of his wedding.

Ensign and Mrs. Luby left January 1 for Norfolk, Va., where the former was to report for duty on January 4.

Mrs. Luby is the granddaughter of Mrs. Nora Milburn of Patoka.

The next day, they traveled to the naval base in Norfolk, Virginia, where he received orders that he had been assigned to the U.S.S. LST 391 which was a tank landing ship. In June of 1943, he was transferred to the Amphibious Training Base, Solomons, Maryland, as Prospective Executive Officer for an LCI (L), Crew #1348. LCI stood for Landing Craft Infantry and were several classes of seagoing *amphibious* assault ships.

On June 9, 1944, he was reassigned as the Executive Officer on the U.S.S. LCI (L) 340, and in September 1944, he assumed command of the ship that had been converted to an LCI (G). The ship had been retrofitted with larger guns and rocket launchers. Some of his battle incident reports refer to the ship as an LCI (R) 340. Their ship was tasked with clearing the beaches and landing Marines. The USS LCI 340 earned eight battle stars for its service during WWII.[1]

---

1   http://www.navsource.org/archives/10/15/150340.htm

Image taken off Leyte, 20 October 1944

The USS fleet of LCIs was given the nickname "Water Bug Navy." Lore has it that an Admiral was looking down from his battleship at a task force of LCIs darting back and forth and said, "They look like a bunch of water bugs." From that point on, the nickname became part of WWII history.

The men serving on the LCI's were put through intensive physical training. The ships worked close to shore where they strafed the beaches with machine gun fire and plummeted the shoreline with rockets ensuring that our troops and their equipment had the best opportunity for a safe landing. They didn't receive the same recognition as some of the larger ships in the Navy, but they were instrumental in carrying out land invasions. In doing so, they suffered many casualties.

After my father joined the Navy, he and my mother did not see each other for three years. He served with the Seventh Fleet in the Southwest Pacific Area (SWPA) under General Douglas MacArthur.

JOE O. LUBY, LT. (JG) D-V (G) USNR, COMMANDING OFFICER OF LCI (G) 340

I INCLUDE MY FATHER'S WAR history to show the intense situations he, like so many of our young men at the time, endured during World War II. These experiences prepared these men for life. My father's war record, when added to his work in the cafeterias growing up and his accounting background, provided the preparation needed in 1946 when he partnered with his Uncle Earl Luby and took over the operational reins of Luby's Cafeterias in Dallas. His leadership and dedication in those early years were instrumental in laying the foundation for all Luby's cafeterias that came after.

After his death, I was fortunate to find several of my father's confidential activity reports sent to the task commanders and to the Commander of the Seventh Fleet in the South Pacific. These reports include the only stories he told me when I was growing up, and they also give a timeline of his ship's activities during several crucial sea battles in our Navy's efforts to stop Japan's expansion in the Pacific.

As in any war, men who served in WWII didn't talk much about their experiences. My dad was no exception. His experiences during this time were not good memories, and he didn't like reliving them. Addendum A at the end of the book shows a portion of those reports and describes the operations in more detail.

The first story I remember was how one of his gunners scored a direct hit on a Japanese dive bomber, and the pilot parachuted from the cockpit. The crew later rescued a lone Japanese survivor who they expected was the same pilot. My father said that he and the crew were more scared of the pilot than he was of them. They had witnessed crazy kamikaze pilots flying into ships and feared he might have an explosive device hidden on his body. Telling the story, my father would laugh and say, "We proceeded to strip him and checked every hole he had." He was proud of his crew that day.

Another story was told in a more somber tone. One night, they entered Mariveles Harbor, and his ship, along with several others, took on heavy fire. Several LCIs were sunk, and his ship, though damaged, managed to escape. He knew the men on those sunken ships and said he lost a lot of friends that night. It's hard to understand in war how some are spared. Is it luck or divine intervention?

On one occasion, when his ship was under enemy fire, he was stationed on the brig with one of his men. The man didn't have his helmet on and took a bullet to the head. I never asked how he was able to process that event, and he didn't offer an explanation. I have often wondered what long-term effect that event had on my father. Although, I don't remember him struggling with the memory, I was left thinking, "How does anyone go about dealing with death in battle?"

Years later, I learned from my mother that one of his crew contacted him on a regular basis. Evidently, my father was one of the few people who could calm him down. The man had what we know now as post-traumatic stress disorder (PTSD), a condition that wasn't diagnosed until the 1970s. Mother received a call after my father passed away from the man's wife saying he really needed to speak with my father. I never learned what became of the man, but I hope he was able to find the peace he was searching for.

The last story he told was about an encounter he had a few years after the war. Close friends had asked my mother and him to dinner. They were entertaining out-of-town guests, and the husband had served on a ship in the South Pacific. They felt my father and their guest might have something in common. As the night progressed, the two men shared stories about their service during the war. The man related that the aircraft carrier, CVE 73, that he served on had been sunk, and he and many of the crew were rescued by an amphibius landing craft. He recalled how many of the men drowned, and some had been eaten by sharks. Shocked, the two discussed the events surrounding the rescue and determined that it had been my father's LCI-340 that had saved his life along with many of his crewmen. The world was truly small to the two of them on that night.

EXPANSION OF LUBY'S BY THE DALLAS GROUP AFTER WWII

Lt. Joseph Owen Luby received orders to return home on November 1, 1945, with a fifty-four day leave until the expiration of active duty which took effect on December 24, 1945. Once discharged, he weighed one hundred and twenty-two pounds and was diagnosed with tuberculosis. Mother traveled to San Francisco where the two of them reunited after three long years. She was excited to see him, but shocked to see how thin and weak he was.

After a time of recovery, they traveled home to Palestine, Illinois. He was joined by his brother George Jr. who had just returned from the war, where he served on an aircraft carrier. Earl, who their father, George Luby Sr., had loaned money to showed up at the house. Earl asked if he could meet privately with Joe and George Jr. After the meeting, Earl walked out of the room, passed my mother, looked at my grandmother Luby, and said, "Well Jenny, I just got both of your boys." Mother never cared for Earl.

My mother and father at the train station with his parents George Sr. and Jenny

Earl had offered Joe and George a lucrative ownership position in all his Dallas cafeterias and shared his plans for expansion. It was agreed that they would relocate to Dallas and take over the management of the Browder Street cafeteria in downtown Dallas and lay the groundwork for expansion into the suburban areas of Dallas. At the time, Earl and his brother Ralph had a majority ownership in three cafeterias located in downtown Dallas.

*My mother and father in the middle,
Earl and his wife to the right*

George was a congenial sort and drawn to the front of the house, where my father was a bolder personality and excelled in the back of the house. Father's acumen in the kitchen had become well known during his days working in the Dallas locations during high school, but now he provided the added benefits of an accounting background and several years military experience.

Traveling to Dallas in 1946 was a pioneering move for my parents. Their first home was a rented apartment near the intersection of Hillcrest Road and Northwest Highway. The complex was just north of the N.W. Hi-Way Drive-In Theatre which was built in 1941 at the corner of Hillcrest Road and Northwest Highway in North Dallas.

Their idea of an inexpensive date night was to sit on the balcony with their next-door neighbors and watch the movies (which they couldn't hear) playing on the big screen. They related that those were some of the happiest times in their marriage. The names of the couple next door were Bill and Louise McAfee who became lifelong friends.

Bill would later become Vice President of Purchasing for Sedco Inc., the oil drilling equipment firm founded by former Texas Gov. William Clements. He and my father loved to tell the story how they met. One morning my father was shaving in front of the medicine cabinet mirror in their bathroom. You may remember there were hinges on the mirror, and when opened, they revealed a few shelves for toiletries and a small horizontal slit for discarding razor blades. He overheard the couple next door, so he opened the cabinet and speaking through the small razor slit said, "Good morning." Surprised, Bill returned the greeting, and their conversations became a ritual carried out most mornings.

Dallas, Texas, was a great place to live after World War II. It was a big city, but small in comparison to many cities across the country. My parents settled in Dallas and began building a life. Father went to work at five every morning, and Mother raised their children and forged their social relationships. They were one of the families who fifty years ago founded a dance club that still meets in Dallas at a private Country Club. Over the course of their marriage, they developed a tremendous number of friendships.

The Dallas Morning News Thursday, November 8, 1951

Coterie Club Sets Dance For Dec. 17

Dallas' newest dinner dance organization, the Coterie Club, has announced Dec. 17 as the date for its first dance.

The affair will be at the Preston Hollow Country Club. Other dances are planned for February, April and May.

Charter members are Mr. and Mrs. Birch Budd, Mr. and Mrs. Jack Ford, Mr. and Mrs. Gene Roderick, Mr. and Mrs. William Moore, Mr. and Mrs. Mark Meyers, Mr. and Mrs. Don Wagner and Mr. and Mrs. Joe Luby.

The club was organized by Mr. and Mrs. Budd and is patterned after one they belonged to in Atlanta, Ga.

My father left the house around 4:30 every morning and head to the farmers market in downtown Dallas. Farmers from around the state would set out fresh produce and sell to the brokers early in the morning. Later, residents of Dallas would visit the market to buy the freshest vegetables in town. Dad developed relationships with the farmers and would get there before the brokers and purchase the best produce for all the cafeterias.

Source: Farmers Market, Hayes Collection, Dallas Public Library Historic Photograph Collection

Seldom would he return home before 8 or 9 at night. Sixteen- and seventeen-hour days were not uncommon at the time. He had no choice because there was no one else willing to dedicate that kind of time in the operations. Earl was getting older, and George didn't have the necessary culinary experience.

Mother love to tell the story about getting a call from my father one morning. As usual, he had been at the cafeteria for a few hours, and she was at home with Joe Junior. Dad knew that she needed a break and had called a neighbor to come over and babysit. He then called mother to say he was short of help and needed her to come downtown to assist.

When she arrived, he took her to the bakery department and asked her to cut the pies once they got out of the oven. Of course, the first pie she cut was a disaster with the filling running off the plate. Dad, took the knife from her hand and cut the next pie in four swift motions, lifted each piece, and put them on separate plates—eight perfectly sliced pieces. He handed her back the knife and said, "That's all there is to it." They both laughed when she realized he had cut a pie that had already cooled.

In late 1946, our cousin Robert (Bob) Luby, the son of Harry, contacted my father and shared his plan to relocate to San Antonio where his parents were living at the time. San Antonio was the only large city in Texas where Bob could acquire the name rights to Luby's Cafeteria. Earl's older brother Clyde and his son Don owned the name rights in Houston as well as Waco and San Angelo. Another relative, Elbert Lavender, who had trained in one of the downtown Dallas locations, had helped Clyde open a cafeteria in West Texas. Soon after he made the decision to move to Fort Worth where he would ultimately open four Luby's.

My father discussed the move with my mother, and she was in favor. She knew that Bob was a good businessman but lacked skills in the back of the house. She and my father discussed, that though they had similar personalities, a partnership between them might not be a bad idea. My father asked if his brother George Jr. could join them, but Bob was adamant that the invitation extended only to my father. Being a loyal family man, my father could not in good conscience join forces with Bob and leave his brother behind. He declined Bob's offer. This was the first time a Luby had been rejected within the family business.

Back row: Second from left Joe, Earl, unknown, George Jr., George Sr., unknown
Front row: Mother third from the left and Grandmother Luby fourth from the right

Earl was relieved that my father declined Bob's offer and soon realized that he was a foundational gift for the organization they were forming. Considering there were no more family members to draw from, Earl and my father knew they would need to come up with a management incentive plan to lure top talent for future expansion. My father approached Earl with an idea in 1946 as they were planning the Lomo Alto and Inwood locations in the Dallas suburbs. The plan dictated that they would finance, build, and supply each cafeteria. They would also be responsible for all capital expenditures. Any large purchases of any kind would need their approval. From day one the management team would share in the profits sixty-forty, the owners would of course get the larger share of the profits. This incentive plan would later be adopted by the owners of other Luby's cafeterias that were managed solely by non-family members.

EXPANSION OF LUBY'S BY THE DALLAS GROUP AFTER WWII

Luby's treated the people running their restaurants as business executives not just managers. One fun story my father liked to tell was about a decision presented by one of those executives. The executive manager of our Richardson location had been to a food show where he had seen a presentation on a commercial washer and dryer. At the time Luby's contracted with a linen company to supply tablecloths, napkins, aprons, and kitchen towels. The manager put in a request to purchase a commercial washer and dryer showing the amount of savings that could be generated by doing laundry in house.

My father declined his request, so the manager invested his own money, bought the commercial equipment, and had them installed. He determined that he and his management team stood to make back the investment and earn a substantial gain with their 40% share of the profits. Unfortunately, his plan backfired. Joe Campisi, who owned the Egyptian restaurant on Mockingbird Lane in Dallas and was rumored to have ties to the New Orleans mafia, called my father. My father always respected Joe and considered him a friend. They also maintained a respectful relationship from an industry perspective. Mr. Campisi said, "Joe one of your managers cancelled their linen contract, and I thought I should warn you that rumor has it that a car rigged with explosives is parked in your lot. You might want to warn your staff."

My father managed a slight laugh and thanked him for the heads up. I'm not sure how things were handled, but the next morning, we learned that a car had exploded in the parking lot late the night before. I think our manager decided the washer and dryer might not have been such a good idea after all. Although this plan failed, it was an indication of the loyalty of the managers Luby's employed and the entrepreneurial spirit Luby's instilled in its people.

Joe and Earl admired how Harry had offered ownership positions to the various family members interested in the cafeteria business. They also were aware that over time Harry phased out his ownership position and allowed the family members to be the sole owners of those cafeterias. Harry's ownership program had served him well over the years until his retirement in 1923 at the age of thirty-nine. Bob, his only son was only thirteen years old at the time. Harry, the consummate family man stayed in touch with the family members helping to promote the Luby brand.

By 1953, Earl, Joe, and George Jr. owned seven cafeterias in the Dallas market and were drafting plans to open additional Dallas locations and cafeterias in Denver, Colorado. At the time Ralph, Earl's brother had an ownership interest but played a minor role in the operation of the units.

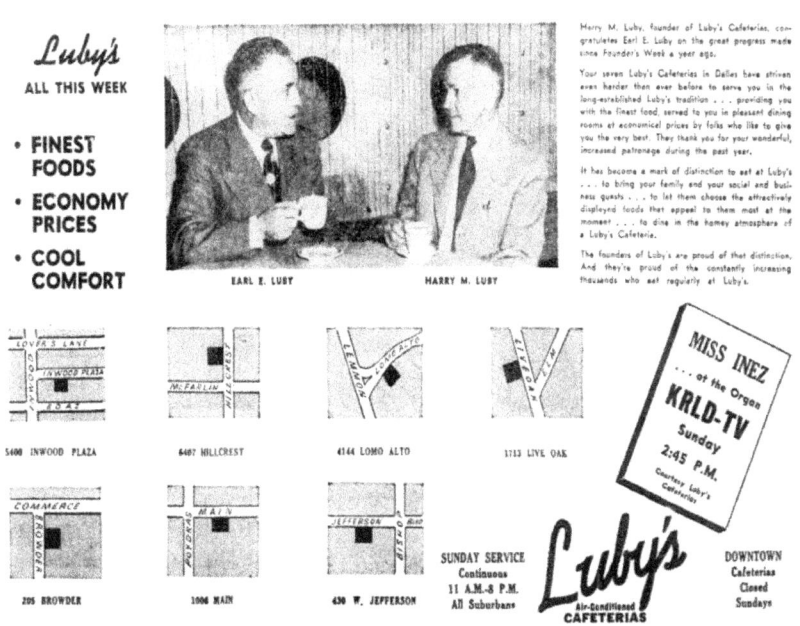

Earl and Harry, Dallas Morning News 1953

Matchbook showing Dallas locations

The current Luby's branch of the family credits Bob for developing the management incentive program, but Bob didn't really begin his expansion until late 1950. He had opened a cafeteria in El Paso in 1939, but upon joining the war effort, he turned over the daily operations to one his ownership partners who managed the unit. He also sold his interest in the Live Oak location in Downtown Dallas before the war.

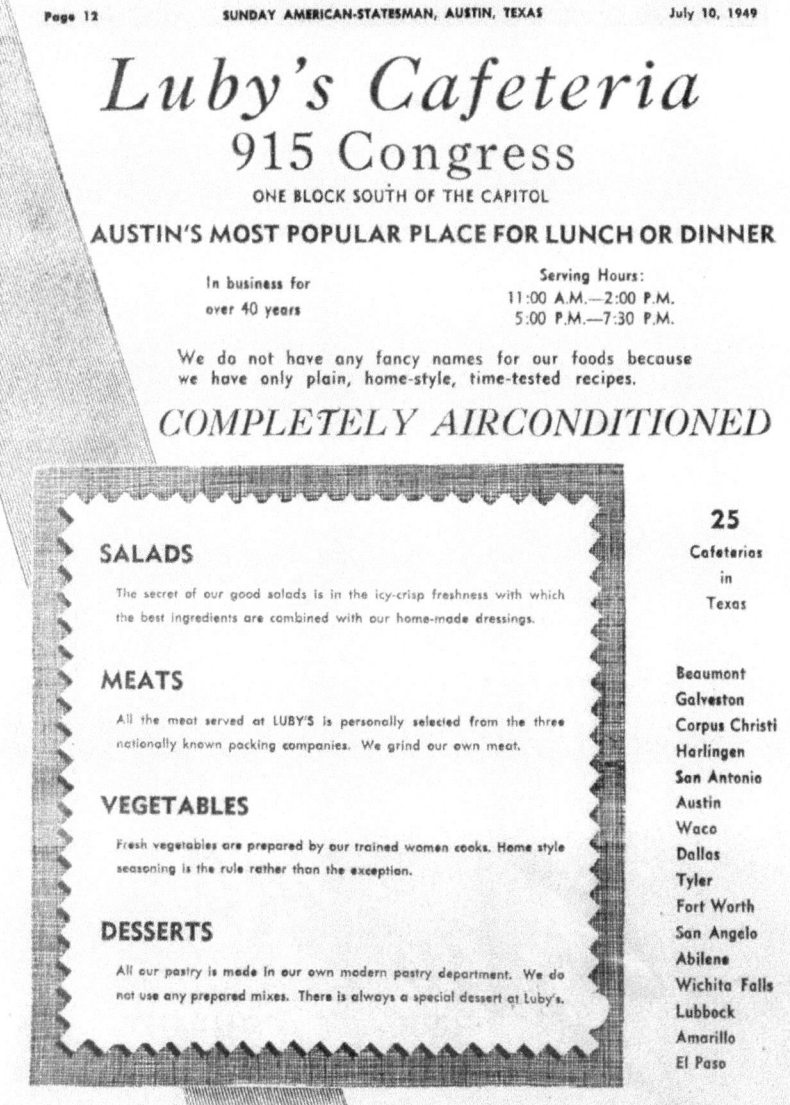

Ad in the Austin American Statesman, July 1949

98   THE LUBY STORY

APPENDIX F
Cafeteria Opening Dates and Managers

CAFETERIA	DATE OPENED	MANAGERS
EL PASO #1 *(moved)*	12/5/39	R.E. Ragland, Bess Ragland, George H. Wenglein
SAN ANTONIO #1 *(closed 8/31/79)*	1/28/47	Norwood W. Jones, John A. Lee, Jr.
SAN ANTONIO #2	9/8/48	George H. Wenglein, John A. Lee, Jr.
TYLER #1 *(moved)*	6/14/49	George W. Evans, William C. Smith
HARLINGEN #1 *(moved)*	11/6/50	Kenneth I. Weaver, John W. Cunningham, Jr.
EL PASO #1 *(relocation)*	12/18/51	Arthur S. Kidd, Leslie Dandridge
SAN ANTONIO #3	7/20/54	Tommy H. Griggs, Virgil T. Hill, Asa Hubbard, Jr.
BEAUMONT	12/6/55	Virgil T. Hill, Asa Hubbard, Jr.
SAN ANTONIO #4	2/19/57	Porter Woliver, E. R. Gipson
EL PASO #2	5/14/57	George W. Evans, Milton B. Haehnel
HARLINGEN #1 *(relocation)*	11/10/57	Kenneth I. Weaver, John W. Cunningham, Jr.
CORPUS CHRISTI #1	3/2/60	Gerald W. Lee, Bill M. Lowe
SAN ANTONIO #5 *(moved)*	3/23/60	Bernie J. Cypert
PORT ARTHUR #1	4/27/60	Alan J. Tanner, Harlen E. Tinker
SAN ANTONIO #6	9/23/60	Don M. Goudge, Tom H. Glimp

Page taken from The Luby Story, a book published for Luby Cafeterias, Inc., showing Bob's early openings

    Upon review of these two images, you will see that the cafeterias listed in the July 10, 1949, advertisement were already in existence before Bob's offshoot of Luby's Cafeterias was birthed in 1947 in San Antonio. The units listed in 1949 were owned by other Luby fam-

50

ily members including my uncle Earl, my father Joe, and my uncle George Luby Jr. The fact remains that Bob didn't open a cafeteria in Beaumont until December 1955. History should never be rewritten to serve certain individuals or promote one's own narrative.

For example, in the book mentioned previously, *House of Plenty* on page 116 the author incorrectly titled an image *Beaumont Luby's*. The correct title should have been *Austin Luby's* that my father and his brother opened.

The author borrowed the image from my uncle George Luby Jr. and made a copy. The original image shown on the next page has not been touched up and is in my possession. To support my claim, I have included the correct image of the Beaumont opening on the page following the Austin image. The correct Beaumont image can be found in the book, *The Luby's Story*. I can't identify all the individuals in the Austin image, but I can most certainly name my mother's family members who traveled from Illinois and Indiana for the opening. None of my mother's relatives attended the Luby's Beaumont opening.

Personal family photo from the opening in Austin, Texas Caption: From left to right on the first row: Marge Luby, my mother Betty Luby, my grandmother Almyra Prather (Betty's mother), Georgia Luby (holding baby), unknown, unknown, unknown, the manager of the Austin location (name intentionally not disclosed, but he was married to a cousin). Second row: Marcia Adams (Betty's sister), Gertrude Johnson, unknown, Earl Luby, George Luby Jr., Robert (Bob) Luby, my grandfather Harold Prather (Betty's father), unknown. Third row; Charles Johnson, three unknown men, unknown, George Wenglein.

Helping celebrate the opening of the Beaumont cafeteria in December 1955 were (from left) Boyd Morrow, Tommy Thompson, Mrs. Carrie Louise Bennett, Asa Hubbard, Mrs. Phyllis Wenglein, Mrs. Gerald Lee, Gerald Lee, Harlen Tinker, Mrs. Pat Tinker, Mrs. Levine Morrow, Mrs. Rhea Lathrop, Mrs. Hazel Stone, Mrs. Helen Blodgett, Virgil Hill, Mrs. Helen Lee, John Lee, Mrs. Gertrude Johnston, Charles Johnston, Mrs. Georgia Luby, Robert Luby.

Image from The Luby Story - Beaumont opening in 1955

LUBY'S CAFETERIAS IN NORTH TEXAS

Foundational for Luby's strong reputation and future growth

YOU MIGHT FIND IT HARD to believe that at one time there were three cafeterias in downtown Dallas. Dallas was always considered a well-organized, but small city. Before the growth to the suburban areas, most activity remained in the middle and just north of the downtown area. On the following pages are images of our Browder Street Cafeteria located in the Southland Life Building circa 1959.[2] Notice the white tablecloths. The Dallas Luby's always promoted excellence in their cafeterias and had a reputation for quality food and service.

---

2   Squire Haskins Photography, Inc. Collection, University of Texas at Arlington Libraries. "Southland Life Insurance building, downtown Dallas, Texas." UTA Libraries Digital Gallery. n.d. (https://library.uta.edu/digitalgallery/img/20006710)

Southland Life Building with Luby's sign at bottom left

Interior of the Luby's located in the Southland Life Building

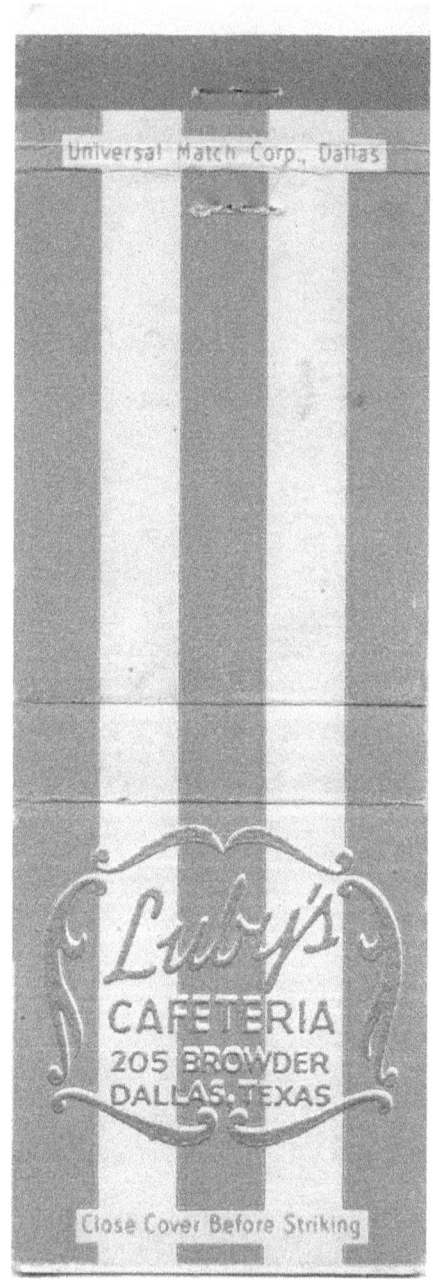

Matchbook from the Browder location

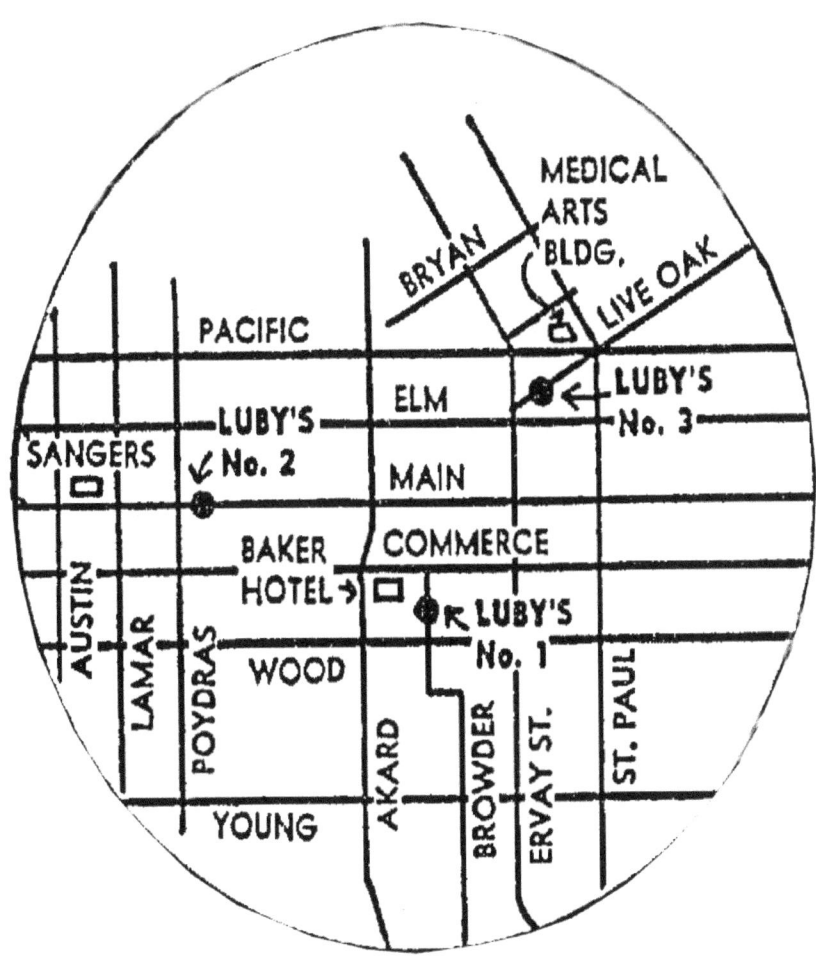

Downtown locations shown on a map insert from one of our ads placed in the Dallas Morning News.

In 1946 Joe O. Luby began working on redesigning the serving lines with Dallas fabricator, Huey Philips. The designs would become the standard to be incorporated into all future Luby's Cafeterias. He and his partners hired interior designers to enhance the dining experience. In the image on the next page notice the white tablecloths and the tailored uniforms worn by the staff.

Birthday celebration for my mother

The first move to the suburbs beginning in 1947 included the following locations:

Hillcrest in Dallas, TX
Oak Cliff (Jefferson) in Dallas, TX
Inwood in Dallas, TX

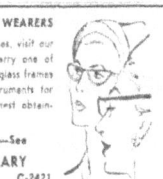

Ad from the Dallas Morning News, 1950

From 1951 – 1968 the following cafeterias were added to Luby's Dallas Group:

Lomo Alto in Dallas, TX
Lochwood in Dallas, TX
Wichita Falls, TX
Ft. Smith, AR
Jonesboro, AR
Fayetteville, AR
Colorado Springs, CO
Lakeside in Denver, CO
Preston Forest in Dallas, TX
University Hills in Denver, CO
Westland in Denver, CO
Hoffman Heights in Denver, CO
Cherry Creek in Denver, CO
Ft. Collins, CO
Irving in Dallas, TX
Richardson in Dallas, TX
Hampton in Dallas, TX
Belaire in Hurst, TX
Town House in Greenville, TX
Denton in Denton, TX

Ad from the Dallas Morning News 1969

Our Lomo Alto cafeteria was located south of Highland Park where the current Whole Foods Store is on Lomo Alto just north of Lemon Avenue. This was the first cafeteria I ever worked in. We had a young man running the unit, and my father gave him free reign to discipline me if necessary. My first task was filling the salad line with shaved ice. Later I was introduced to the dish washer, who became my new boss.

Lomo Alto location prior to opening

LUBY OPENS LOMO ALTO CAFETERIA

Luby's Lomo Alto Cafeteria, 4144 Lomo Alto, is pictured here. This new restaurant is opening for business Tuesday and will be the seventh in the Luby chain of cafeterias in Dallas. There are twenty-five Luby cafeterias in Texas. Earl, Joe and George Luby, with members of their families and close friends, operate the chain. Earl Luby said Monday the Lomo Alto Cafeteria is completely air-conditioned and up-to-date in its kitchen equipment and dining facilities.

Joe O. Luby shown on the right sitting next to his father George Sr., 1951

Lomo Alto remodel in 1957

Across the street from the Lomo Alto cafeteria was another Dallas institution, Strictly Tabu. Members of North Texas

University Lab bands were frequent players as well as many of Dallas' best jazz musicians.

The cafeteria was once robbed by a shotgun bandit who pointed the barrel at the manager. Our managers were trained not to offer resistance, and fortunately, no one was injured. Evidently, the thief had been robbing several establishments in the area, and after robbing Luby's, he tried his luck one too many times at a nearby store and was arrested.

Welcoming the last Luby son, the Dallas group invited J. Pat Luby, Earl's wife's son whom he had adopted to join their group. My mother and father pretty much raised Pat due to the tenuous relationship he had with Earl. As a result, my father and Pat were extremely close, and so were our families. Pat would later be tasked with managing the newly added Lochwood Village cafeteria.

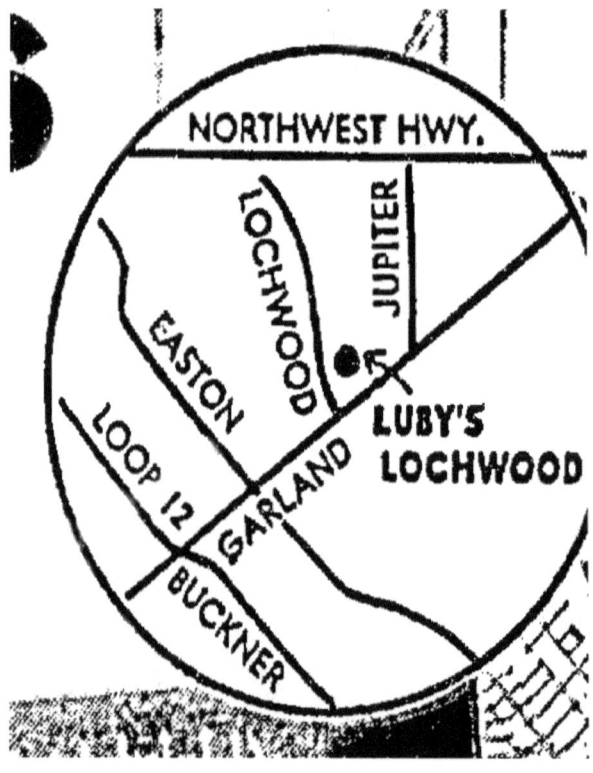

Matchbook from the Lochwood Village location

By 1956, the group had added cafeterias in Wichita Falls, Texas, and Denver, Colorado (Lakeside Shopping Center). In 1960, Luby's opened the most celebrated cafeteria to date in Dallas' premier Preston Forest Shopping Center.

The shopping center owned by George Mixon was located just east of the current Whole Foods Market on the southeast corner of Preston Road and Forest Lane. In the same shopping center were several well-known Dallas businesses: Wyatt's Grocery, Preston Forest Pharmacy, Preston Forest Bowling Center, and Holiday cleaners.

NOW OPEN

AT THE CROSSROADS OF DALLAS NORTH
PRESTON ROAD and FOREST LANE

DALLAS' NEWEST, MOST MODERN SHOPPING CENTER IS NOW COMPLETE. FINE RETAIL STORES, A MODERN BOWLING ALLEY, MEDICAL FACILITIES AND BEST OF ALL, ADEQUATE PARKING. NO EXPENSE HAS BEEN SPARED TO BRING DALLAS NORTH A REAL FINE SHOPPING CENTER.

WE ARE PROUD OF THE SELECT GROUP OF TENANTS AND EXTEND TO YOU AN INVITATION TO JOIN IN THE GRAND OPENING CELEBRATION OF THESE STORES.

Wyatt's
Luby's Cafeteria
Morgan & Lindsey Variety Store
Top Value Redemption Center
Fair of Texas
Preston Forest Pharmacy
Preston Forest Bowling Center

Humble Station
Artha Garza, Realtor
Preston Shoe Service
Stotts Shoppe
H. B. Eberhart Barber Shop
L. W. McCarley
Holiday Cleaners

Wilson's Drive-In Grocery
Searls Builders Hardware
Housley-Hansen, Inc.
Dan Drain Jewelry
Alfonso's Beauty Salon
Stauffer-Ziegler System
Medical Offices : . . Dental Offices

PRESTON FOREST SHOPPING CENTER
GEORGE F. MIXON SR., President
GEORGE F. MIXON JR., Vice-Pres.
305 PRESTON ROYAL Shopping Center EM 1-6635

BUILDERS AND DEVELOPERS OF
PRESTON FOREST SHOPPING CENTER
NORTHWOOD HILLS ADDITION
PRESTON ROYAL SHOPPING CENTER
PARK FOREST SHOPPING CENTER

As you faced the cafeteria the lease space to the right was available, so my father came up with an idea to rent the space and add a Luby's Takeout. I guess it might be a stretch to claim that my father pioneered the full meal take out industry, but Luby's was most certainly a pioneer of the concept in Dallas, Texas. The takeout offered a smaller variety than what was available in the main dining room. However, you could purchase any of the food that was offered in the main cafeteria. There was a door connecting the takeout facility to the kitchen area of the main cafeteria so they could easily fill orders.

★
YOU CAN TAKE IT WITH YOU

One of the most unusual features of the new Luby's Preston Forest operation is the Luby's Take-Out Service, housed in a separate room next door to the cafeteria proper.

The "take-out" food service will offer hot foods, such as meats, vegetables and pastries, available by telephone order for persons who wish to drive by to pick up special orders or complete family meals.

Matchbook from the Preston Forest location

The Preston Forest cafeteria was decorated by a well-known Dallas designer, William F. Lowder, who came up with the idea for an eighteenth-century look. The cafeteria had two serving lines, three dining rooms, and seated over 500 people. The main dining room was a contemporary design and could hold 232 patrons. The second dining room as seen in the in the picture on the next page had a beamed ceiling, was a French Provincial design, and seated 168 patrons. The third dining room with sliding doors and often used for private functions, was English by design and seated another 108 patrons.

The cafeteria had custom chandeliers, custom carpet with the Luby crest, and meticulously placed art for the walls. Mr. Lowder was allowed to add many additional custom accents, such as Italian mosaic tile, antique mirrors, a wall mural depicting an English fox hunt, custom designed draperies which provided fire protection, hand finished walnut and ash wall panels, and special ceiling tiles with sound absorbing material. There was a combination of chair designs for each room. The French room had traditional chairs and booths covered with raw silk and vinyl. The English room was furnished with captain chairs. The kitchen equipment was provided by Huey Philip Company and was state of the art. The back drops and line were made from custom fabricated stainless steel.

The location was originally managed by Ken Wright and Jimmy Rushing. Ken was transferred from the Lomo Alto cafeteria and had been with Luby's for ten years, and Jimmy had been a manager with the company for twelve years. Both were experienced food and beverage managers well-trained in the Luby's style of management.

All Luby's cafeterias in the Dallas market had contracted with Oak Cliff Music Company to have Conn Organs installed in each of the units. Dick Workman was an accomplished pianist in Dallas at the time and was hired to provide regular entertainment at the Preston Forest location. A fun story was told about Dick. Over a few weeks' time, Dick was concerned that his skin had turned red, and he couldn't understand why. He had not been in the sun. Upon inspection, the managers discovered the lighting above the piano had tanning bulbs and were providing Dick with a nice tan. Everyone got a good laugh at Dick's expense, but being a good-natured fellow, he just smiled and took the ribbing in stride.

DINING COMFORT AND BEAUTY

English Room of Luby's Preston Forest is depictive of beauty and comfort afforded in the three dining areas, seating up to 508 persons. Features are the Luby crest in carpeting, captain's chairs, beamed ceiling, mural of fox hunt. Room at right is French Provincial. Front room is in contemporary decor.

Our Congratulations to *Luby's* Beautiful New Preston Forest Cafeteria

We are proud to have been selected to furnish the all-stainless-steel kitchen equipment and supplies for this newest Luby's Cafeteria . . . designed to prepare and serve top quality foods in the traditional Luby manner. Below are shown representative sections of this spacious, modern kitchen.

HUEY & PHILP COMPANY
Manufacturers and Distributors of Food-Serving Equipment and Supplies
DALLAS ★ HOUSTON ★ FT. WORTH

Congratulations to LUBY'S PRESTON FOREST CAFETERIA

DINE AT THIS NEWEST MEMBER of the famous LUBY family of line eating establishments. As at other Luby Cafeterias, you may enjoy wonderful music played on the CONN ORGAN while partaking of Luby's delicious foods.

DICK WORKMAN —presides at the console of the CONN ORGAN at Luby's Preston Forest Cafeteria. Extra Conn Leslie tone cabinet, provide lovely music for the three spacious dining rooms.

 MISS INEZ —at Luby's Inwood Village Cafeteria this lass plays your favorites on the CONN ORGAN. She has been organist for the Dallas Rangers for many years.

 MISS ALTA FAYE —brings added enjoyment on the CONN ORGAN to your dining at Luby's Hillcrest Cafeteria. She is also organist for Northside Westminster Church.

 JOHN BATTEN —you'll enjoy JOHN'S music on the CONN ORGAN at Luby's Jefferson Cafeteria in Oak Cliff. JOHN is also organist for Bethany Christian Church.

 DENNIS ALLEN —dines at Luby's Lockwood Cafeteria while DENNIS plays beautiful melodies on the CONN ORGAN. Dennis is electronics minded and supervised Conn Organ installations in several of Luby's Cafeterias.

 VIVIAN ARGO —is heard playing the CONN ORGAN at Luby's Loma Alta Cafeteria. She is also organist for the Oak Cliff Rotary Club.

 GAIL BONNER —presides at the console of the CONN ORGAN at Luby's Downtown Cafeteria, 306 Browder Street. Hundreds of busy shoppers and downtown workers enjoy her music daily.

Lend an ear to the CONN ORGAN you hear at Luby's. Discover the noticeable difference in a CONN ORGAN. Listen to the pure, rich tones. You can enjoy the same quality of performance in home, church or public auditorium for a lot less than you think.

Millions heard the CONN ORGAN over television and radio during the Republican National Convention in Chicago last month. Drop by one of our stores soon. See— Hear — Play the CONN ORGAN.

CONN ORGAN STUDIOS
6127 BERKSHIRE LANE   EM 1-4550
IN PRESTON CENTER

OAK CLIFF MUSIC CO.
612 W. JEFFERSON   WH 8-7341

At the north end of the shopping center was the Preston Forest Bowling Alley. In May of 1968, two brothers, Carl and Don Finch were managing the Preston Forest location. One night after closing, they exited the building and proceeded to their vehicles. As Don was walking to his car, which was located in a different area than Carl's, he noticed two men approach Carl with a shotgun. The robbers shoved the barrel of the shotgun in the back of Carl's head and forced him back inside to open the safe.

There were no cell phones in 1968, and the only business open close by was the bowling alley. Don ran to the bowling alley so he could alert the police. The night watchmen, Richard King, sprang into action running along with Don back to Luby's in hopes of thwarting the burglary. As Richard pulled his pistol out of its holster, he dropped the gun and shot a pedestrian in the arm. Fortunately, they were able to get her to Methodist hospital where she survived. Carl was not harmed, but the burglars got away with the day's proceeds.

Shotgun Bandits Take $4,600 in Two Holdups

By JOHN RUTLEDGE

Bandits used shotguns to hold up an Oak Cliff grocery and a North Dallas cafeteria in separate raids Friday night.

A bystander, Miss Meryetta Vaughn, 18, of 2128 Royal Crest, was accidentally wounded in the right arm by a bullet from a watchmen's pistol near the scene of one stickup.

Raided were:

Bill's Silver Dollar Grocery & Market, 2200 Cedar Crest, where a bandit whacked a butcher on the head with a shotgun barrel while his two companions, wearing women's clothes, forced a grocer to hand over about $1,000.

Luby's Cafeteria, Preston Road at Forest Lane, where manager Carl D. Finch was forced to open the safe at shotgun point by two men after closing time and surrender about $3,600 from the safe.

AT THE GROCERY STORE, owner Charles Roark, 33, told detectives Gus Rose and Eugene Lipe that three men entered through the back door of the grocery.

One man clubbed butcher James Wilbanks on the head with a sawed-off shotgun. His two companions forced him at pistol point to surrender the money from the cash register. All three escaped in a waiting auto.

Cafeteria manager Finch told police he and his brother, Don Harold Finch, 27, a student manager, had closed the restaurant in the Preston Forest Shopping Center and were walking toward their car near the back door about 8:50 p.m.

DON FINCH SAW two men, one leveling a shotgun, hurry around a corner toward them. He ran. The bandits caught Carl Finch, forced him to reopen the cafeteria, lead them to the safe inside, open it, and hand over the money. They ordered him to lie on the floor. They escaped.

Meanwhile, Don Finch, police said, sprinted through the shopping center, yelling "Help, Robbery! Police!" In the bowling alley, according to police sergeant Jim Wright, Don Finch found watchman Richard Eugene King, a uniformed guard of the Greater Dallas Patrol, sipping coffee. King and Finch raced outside to head off the stickup man.

KING, PULLING his pistol as he ran, accidentally dropped the weapon. It struck the pavement, went off, and sent a bullet drilling into the upper right arm of Miss Vaughn.

She was treated at Methodist Hospital. By the time the younger Finch arrived at the cafeteria's rear door, the robbers had made good their escape.

Detective Capt. Will Fritz, detectives P. M. Parks and B. B. Norris were investigating to determine if the bandit team held up the cafeteria was involved in the grocery store stickup.

COLORADO EXPANSION

by the Luby's Dallas Group

Lubys began began expanding in Colorado, and my father was personally tasked with overseeing the openings. He hired Dub Radford as our regional manager. By 1965, with the addition of the Denver locations, we had ten cafeterias outside of Texas.

Joe O. Luby in Denver, 1957

COLORADO EXPANSION

Denver.   Restaurants.   Luby

$180,000 Luby restaurant opens in Lakeside shopping center.   Post Dec. 11, 1956 p.53
Second of four Luby Cafeterias for Denver area at University Hills Plaza Shopping Center.
                    RMN March 16, 1962 p.111
Luby's Cafeteria will open its third Denver area dining spot in Westland Shopping Center.
                    RMN Mar. 7, 1963 p.48
Five more cafeterias planned for Denver area.
                    Post Jul. 26, 1964 p.35

Source: Denver Library archives

Denver Lakeside

Source: Denver Cherry Creek, Denver Library archives

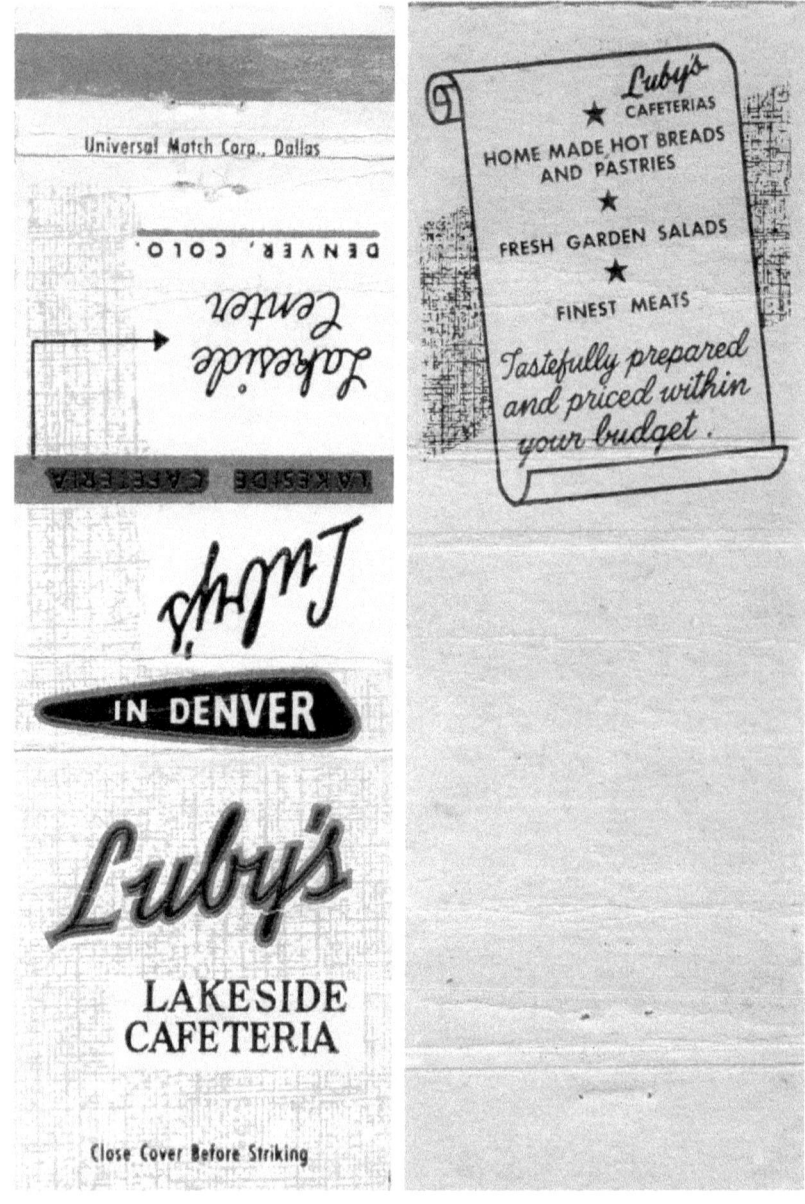

Matchbook from the Lakeside location

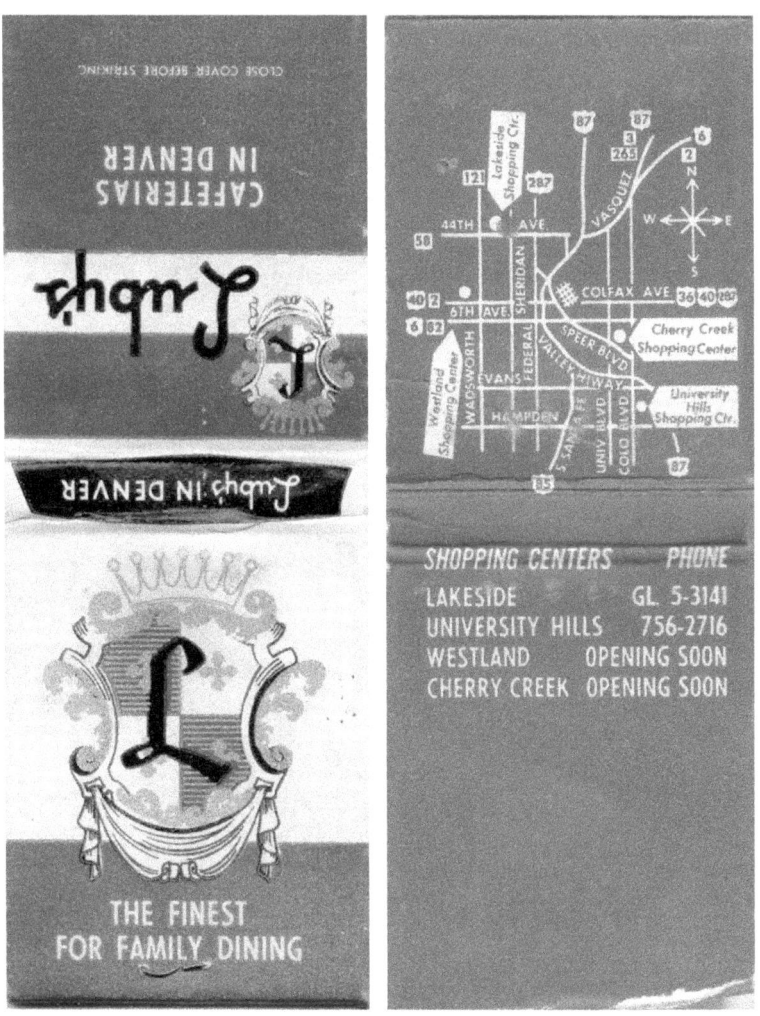

Matchbook showing some of the Denver locations

In 1964, our Cherry Creek location was attacked by an arsonist causing over $450,000 in damages. Unfortunate occurrence, but the unit was remodeled and was open for business a year later. There are many pitfalls in owning restaurants, and one of the most difficult is the constant strain of being open seven days a week. The company was dependent on those sales to pay the bills and provide for the employees.

COLORADO EXPANSION

```
         Denver.    Restaurants.    Luby's cafeteria

$450,000 fire destroys cafeteria in Cherry Creek Shopping
Center Wednesday.     Post Sept. 2, 1964 p.1
Arsonist admits setting $450,000 Luby's Cafeteria fire.
                  Post Sept. 15, 1964 p.2
```

Source: Denver Library archives

    I don't remember my father being stressed by the unfortunate occurrence, but I do remember that the unit was remodeled and was open for business a year later. As the saying goes, "The show must go on."

    When we opened a cafeteria in a newly remodeled Hoffman Height Development, Harry Luby, at the age of seventy-seven, attended the opening. In the image on the next page, he is shown talking to Sal Dichter, the developer. Just shows how much class Harry had—always ready to support the brand and assist his relatives. Harry had a burning desire to preserve family unity.

Denver Hoffman Heights

Denver Public Library Digital Collections P1996.13391 (Circa 1967)
Figure 14.
Sol Dichter, the person on the left side of the image, speaks to Harry Luby of Luby's Cafeteria. The restaurant was added to the Hoffman Heights Shopping Center in 1964 as part of Dichter's $400,000 remodeling project called "Operation Facelift". His office for the Ace Realty Corporation was located at 750 Peoria Street.

Source for images: Denver Library archives

COLORADO EXPANSION

In the summer of 1965, I was invited by my father to travel with him to Denver and work at the reopening of the Cherry Creek location. Driving from Dallas to Denver, we passed our billboard.

I still remember several of the life lessons he shared with me on the trip.

- "Son, you never want to date any of our employees."
- "If anyone asks how much you are making, remember they are being curious to see if you are making more than they are."
- "People are watching how you act and will respect you when you take charge and share the workload."
- "Practice what you preach, and people will listen to you."
- "Don't live with a member of the opposite sex prior to marriage."

As I got older, and the head on my shoulders started thinking correctly, I missed his counsel and was sad that I could no longer seek his advice.

CHANGING TIMES

Prior to the 1970's Dallas was void of the many theme restaurants that would soon burst upon the culinary scene, such as TGI Friday's, Bennigan's, and Steak and Ale. Besides Luby's, Dallas had many mom-and-pop diners, several drive-in restaurants, and different cafeteria concepts: Furr's, Wyatt's, Highland Park, and Jay's. Then there were the fine dining establishments of Arthus, Chateaubriand, Cattleman's Steak House, and the French Room at the Adolphus.

There were only a handful of Mexican food restaurants to choose from. Some of the better knowns were El Fenix, El Chico, and Casa Dominguez on Cedar Springs. Dad mentored Pete Dominguez in the restaurant business, and they became close friends. Pete's initial restaurant was on Cedar Springs across from where the Crescent development is currently located. The strip center was destroyed by fire. Pete also enjoyed success at his restaurant located in Highland Park Village near the current *Mi Concina*. Casa Dominguez was always one of my families' favorite places to eat.

Pete Dominguez in the center speaking to my father, Joe O. Luby on the right

By 1965, the Dallas branch of Luby's Cafeterias consisted of the following locations: Lochwood, Jefferson, Hillcrest, Wynnewood, Inwood, Lomo Alto, Austin, Preston Forest, Wichita Falls, Irving, Richardson, two in Arkansas, and five in Colorado. The cafeteria in Wichita Falls was owned and operated by Leroy Daniels. Leroy was a fine Christian man that my father admired and respected.

My father was an avid pilot and owned two airplanes during his lifetime. The first was a Cessna 150B, which was a four-seat model. He and my mother made several trips to see family in Illinois. Flying was an activity that they both enjoyed. Mother decided that she would take flying lessons just in case anything happened to my father, and she had to land the plane. Her instructor was out of Addison airport in north Dallas. Addison, now a very populated suburb of Dallas, was mostly farmland back then so driving to the airport was considered to be a ride through the countryside.

1962 Cessna 150B with my mother standing by

Two years later, my father decided he needed to upgrade to a larger plane with more power. He purchased a six-seat Cessna 210-5. The plane would be used to make the out-of-town restaurants more accessible. He also knew the importance of getting his instrument rating. I remember him studying for the test and telling me after completion that it was one of the most difficult tests he had ever taken.

One of my many fond memories of flying with my father was the day he asked me to go out to Addison airport, saying he needed to check on the plane. Unknown to me, the plane had been fueled and was sitting outside the hanger ready for flight. We jumped in and flew to Oklahoma City, had lunch, and then returned. I flew the plane all the way to Oklahoma. I still remember breaking through the clouds and looking down at a sea of white clouds and above only blue sky. My father told me that he was impressed by the way I kept my eyes glued to the instruments. Of course, I did so more out of fear more than awareness. I later took some lessons, but they ceased once he became ill.

1963 Cessna 210-5

Earlier I shared an image of our Austin location. I intentionally didn't disclose the name of the manager in the picture so not to bring judgement on him or his family. He caused the demise of that particular location because of a gambling addiction. He was stealing money from the cafeteria and betting on the horses. In an attempt to hide his addiction and hoping to pay back the money, he marked vendor invoices as being paid. The books he kept looked fine until the overdue bills started mounting up.

My father tells the story how he received a call from one of their primary vendors asking why they were in arrears down in Austin. Upon traveling to Austin, Joe and his partners uncovered the scheme, but not until large sums of money had been lost. There were no computers or fax machines during those times, and Austin was a good distance from Dallas. They never thought that someone married to one of their family members would steal from them. Out of ignorance, they learned a valuable lesson.

Bob and Charles Johnson both attended the Austin opening in the late 1950s. Before the day of the opening, my father had called Bob to propose a merger of all the Luby's cafeterias. My father had a friend who was a well-respected financier in Dallas who approached him with an offer. An investment group out of Florida wanted to take Luby's public; however, they had one major condition: all the cafeterias had to be unified under one umbrella. My father knew that this could be an incredible opportunity and provide the necessary funds for expansion, but he needed Bob to come on board. He and Bob met and decided the time was right to combine all the cafeterias under one corporate umbrella. They both felt they could get Don who was operating in Houston and the other Luby cousins to join with them. Bob held a surprise meeting and proposed the idea to his partners. Charles Johnson was not happy because he preferred their current operations.

A closer look at those attending the Austin opening

Unknown to my father at the time was the fact that Earl had previously experienced financial issues and had covertly sold part of his interests to M. O. "Red" Leggett and William B. Lowder. Red was an employee with one of our vendors in Dallas and Lowder was our interior designer. Red and Bill learned that Earl needed money and approached Earl about investing.

Earl proposed bringing the two into the Dallas operation. I remember my grandfather Harold Prather was visiting at the time. Being a savvy businessman and very intuitive, he warned my father saying, "Joe, you need to watch your back around Red. He is up to no good." Dad was not fond of any outsiders having a say in running their operations, and along with his brother and J. Pat they objected to bringing in Red and Lowder.

Mother's father, James Harold Prather

Earl had been instrumental in the development of Luby's and was ready to retire but wanted to remain as the figure head. My father was running the overall operation, and it had been agreed that Earl would handle the marketing. Earl didn't like the fact that everyone agreed that my father was to run the day-to-day operations. He was incensed that his adopted son, J. Pat had been the one to offer the primary objection to his continued leadership.

Earl's attitude had begun to sour. Dub Radford, our regional manager in Colorado, called my father one day and said, "Joe, you need to rein in Earl and Red. They came into Lakeside today and reversed many of the decisions we implemented. They are under minding our Colorado operations." I remember my father telling Dub to ignore their changes and keep running his operation as agreed.

My father had bigger plans and didn't have the time to deal with Earl's personality.

Joe O. Luby Sr. on the right

When my father first approached Bob about unifying, he knew he would need the approval of his Dallas partners. The primary owners at the time were Earl and his brother Ralph, J. Pat, George Jr., and my father. Having raised J. Pat through the years, he and my father were very close. None of Earl's other investors held voting stock, so Dad knew that having his brother and J. Pat on his side, Earl and Ralph would not have the votes needed to block the merger with Bob.

What my father didn't anticipate was his older brother's jealousy. George Jr. was not a natural restauranteur like Joe. His natural talent was in sales. He harbored resentment toward my father knowing that his leadership role would be reduced if the merger was completed. He cast a dissenting vote, thereby splitting the company. His decision would prove to be the beginning of the end of the Dallas based Luby's Cafeteria chain.

Earl's relationship with Red and Lowder further alienated Joe and J. Pat. I don't include George because he was too ashamed by what he had done to his brother. He knew the decision to vote against the merger destroyed everything they had worked so hard to accomplish.

When Bob learned that Earl, Ralph, and George had objected, he was not happy. Bob made it clear that he wanted nothing to do with Earl and offered his condolences to my father. From that day forward, the unity that had existed in the family for over seventy years ceased. This was a dark period for my father, but his hands were tied.

Bob was never the unifier that his father Harry was. When he moved to San Antonio, he did so with his own agenda, not a unifying family agenda. Some insight to Bob's true nature was made clear from comments made in the following article,

> "The company's official history makes much not just of Harry's limited ambitions but of his affability, and it clearly implies that Bob Luby differed significantly from his father in both respects. 'My mother was kind of mean,' Luby says, in what may be a joke. 'I think I got some of her.' (At first, Cafeterias Inc. called some of its cafeterias "Romana" because a few cities already had competing cafeterias called

"Luby's"--relics from Harry Luby's day. The company changed its name to Luby's in 1981.)³

"The truth is Bob never cared for Earl because of an earlier expansion project they attempted in San Francisco. Luby's Cafeteria's Inc. recording of history claims the decision was Earl's, but what they failed to acknowledge was that Earl had three cafeterias in Dallas at the time and had his hands full managing those units. Earl provided the monetary and operational support for Bob and in 1935 they opened a Luby's in the Sutter Hotel located in downtown San Francisco. The cafeteria failed miserably, and Earl abandoned Bob financially. Bob desperately held on for the next two years until finally he had to close the unit. Harry had retired in 1927 and moved to San Antonio. Bob was on the outside of Luby's looking in; he had no ownership position in any of the cafeterias at the time.

He moved to Dallas, leveraged the equipment, and borrowed money from his father Harry to open his own cafeteria on Live Oak Street. Two years later in 1939, Bob partnered with one of his cousins and his son-in-law and opened a unit in El Paso. As stated earlier in the book, when the war broke out, Bob turned the management of the El Paso unit over to his cousin and sold the Live Oak cafeteria to none other than Earl. The animosity he had for Earl was always floating just under the surface, so when the merger fell apart, no one could really blame Bob for harboring a resentment toward the Dallas group.

Bob followed through with the proposal he had made to his partners and implemented the plan that he and my father had crafted. In order to fund expansion, Bob and his partners incorporated on February 4, 1959, under the name Cafeterias, Inc.

The San Antonio group owned only nine units at the time. Over the next ten years they would add another eight units bringing the total number of stores to seventeen.

---

3   *Rewriting History by Bob Luby*, Barrier, M. 1991. "First in Line at the Cafeteria." Nation's Business 79 (2): 29

In 1969 Bob realized they were stagnated and to continue their growth he needed the support from the other family members who owned nine cafeterias. They entered into an agreement to place those units under Bob's umbrella via a fifteen-year operating agreement. At the end of that time frame, the company could exercise an option to purchase those units.

Bob made no such offer to my father or his partners because of Earl. This further demonstrated Bob's animosity toward the Dallas group, which consisted of twenty-three units. These units would have been extremely valuable to Bob's expansion plans, but he wasn't ready to forgive Earl. So, with the additional cafeterias, the total number of units under the San Antonio group came to twenty-six. Unknown to anyone at the time, they had just laid the foundation on which Luby's would flourish for the next twenty-seven years.

Earl had done permanent damage to his partners, and the Luby family members in Dallas would forever be separated from their southern cousins because of his greed. When we opened our Preston Forest location in 1960, Earl falsely stated in several advertisements that he was the president of a newly formed corporation, and the other participants were his vice presidents. Neither Bob nor Charles was listed because they were forging ahead with their own plans in San Antonio. The article listed my father and J. Pat as vice presidents, and they were not pleased.

Earl, threatened by my father's independence tried to exercise control, and in 1965 to his discredit, almost signed Luby's death wish. He wanted to roll out an "All You Can Eat" program in hopes of increasing customer counts. My father was adamantly against the idea. Luby's had always been perceived as an upscale cafeteria. Wyatt's and Furr's, two primary competitors in the Dallas area, were known as value cafeterias. Their food was not on the same quality level as Luby's, and their prices were lower. The customers that Luby's enjoyed didn't mind paying extra for the quality of product Luby's offered.

I remember my father saying, "When you go to an all you can eat format you are attracting a different clientele. Not a Luby's clientele. They want as much food for the least amount of money and will sacrifice quality for price." Earl insisted, and George Jr. once again acquiesced. Ads were run and the program was rolled out in four Dallas locations.

Earl's failed promotion

The four locations suffered, and it became obvious the promotion was a failure. My father cancelled the initiative and ran television ads in the Dallas market returning to their roots, "Good food at good prices." Though the mistake cost the restaurants, they were able to rebound and in so doing everyone learned a valuable lesson.

Dad and J. Pat had their own plan for expansion that didn't include Earl and they opened cafeterias in Richardson and in Irving. Additionally, they signed a tentative agreement with the owners of the property located on the Southwest corner of LBJ Freeway and Midway Road. Plans were being drafted, and they were getting ready to build a new cafeteria. Today the property is occupied by an *In and Out Burger*.

In 1967 my father received a call from a good friend who was also his banker at Preston State Bank. Dad learned that Earl had several loans with Preston State Bank that he was not servicing properly. His friend said the bank let Earl know that if he borrowed money from any other institution, they would call his loans, which would also put my father's loans in jeopardy.

Earl acting in defiance took out a loan with another bank and finally the atmosphere changed for good. J. Pat and my father saw the situation with the bank as an opportunity. They knew Preston State did not want to call their loans so they offered an ultimatum—buy us out, or we will buy you out. George, once again sided with Earl and blocked a deal in either direction.

J. Pat suggested that he and my father leverage the threat by Preston State Bank and offer an alternative solution to Earl, Ralph, and George. They agreed they would sell all the cafeterias.

Dad had a very good relationship with the remaining Dallas cafeteria chains and had been approached previously by Wyatt's Cafeterias. Wyatt's catered to more of a blue-collar clientele and wanted to purchase Luby's in hopes of improving their image in the North Texas market. Wyatt's was a large chain with a food commissary operation and the financial ability to make Luby's a sizeable offer. Furr's Cafeterias also indicated that they had an interest in some of the Dallas locations.

As fate would have it, in 1968 my father became ill, and all the plans he and J. Pat had for expansion were put on hold. Dad negotiated a deal with Wyatt's on three conditions; Hillcrest, Lochwood, and Wichita Falls would remain independent Luby's cafeterias. Dad knew J. Pat would need to generate a steady income, Dub Radford along with his brother, who was a doctor, wanted to buy the cafeteria on Hillcrest, and Leroy Daniel had no interest in selling the Wichita Falls location.

After closing the deal in 1970, the majority of Luby's in North Texas, Arkansas, and Colorado came under Wyatt's ownership.

Wyatt buys 17 Luby Cafeterias

Seventeen Luby Cafeterias, including the one in Fort Collins, have been sold to Wyatt Cafeterias, Inc.

The sale was announced by Emery L. Blachly, president of the Dallas-based firm. He said that with the additional Luby Cafeterias and those under construction, Wyatt's will be operating 75 units this year.

The cafeterias involved in the sale will continue to operate under the Luby name until operational systems and remodeling at some locations can be completed.

Luby Cafeterias also were headquartered in Dallas and began operation in 1929. Wyatt Cafeterias began 39 years ago.

Included in the sale were five Luby Cafeterias in Denver, six in the Dallas area and several individual operations in Fort Smith, Fayetteville and Jonesboro, Ark., and Denton and Hurst, Tex.

Wyatt's had only one condition to the sale, Joe O. Luby had to sign a five year non-compete agreement. They didn't require any of the other owners to sign the non-compete. My brother was attending SMU law school at the time and counseled him against the idea for tax purposes. Dad's mind was made up, and he wanted no more to do with Earl and George.

A couple years after the sale I was standing in our kitchen when the phone rang. I answered and it was J. Pat on the line asking to speak to my father. Pat anxiously said he had received a call from a Luby's attorney. He threatened Pat that if he didn't sell the name rights in the Dallas market that Luby's were going to build cafeterias all over Dallas and run him out of business. Well, so much for that strong Luby family loyalty. My father listened patiently and said, "The heck with him, you own the rights. They aren't going to do anything." I was proud of my father that morning.

The truth was Pat was a great guy, and everyone loved him. He had conquered an issue with alcohol, married the love of his life, and spent most of his time sailing on Lake Ray Hubbard. He just wasn't passionate about expansion after my father died. At the time, his Lochwood Cafeteria was running fine and generating a good income for him and his family. To his credit, he took my father's advice and told their attorney to go fly a kite, he had no intentions of letting go of his name rights.

Luby's had a cafeteria in the Romana Shopping Center in San Antonio, and when Luby's decided to open a cafeteria at the intersection of Meadow Road and Central Expressway in Dallas, they named it Luby's Romana Cafeteria. Everyone wondered why Luby's had opened under a different name, but the San Antonio group wasn't about to disclose the true reason: Pat owned the Luby name rights in the Dallas area. On page 93, the quote from *Rewriting History by Bob Luby* makes reference to this fact, but incorrectly states, "relics from Harry Luby's past."

Harry had no interest in the Dallas group's cafeterias.

Luby's did the same thing in Houston where another Luby family member owned the name rights. Over time, Luby's presence hurt Pat's business, and in 1983 he finally gave in and sold the name rights. Luby's agreed he could change the name of his cafeteria to Pat Luby's Cafeteria.

Pat operated the location in Lochwood Village until a fire destroyed the cafeteria a year later. Dub Radford had invested in Pat's operation in 1981 and was managing the location along with Jerry Rhodes another long time Luby manager. After the fire Pat and Dub took over a failed Wyatts cafeteria and reopened Pat Luby's Cafeteria in Casa View shopping center, but the location could not support the concept and they closed in the late 1990's.

The same year they sold the Dallas group's cafeterias my father learned that he had lung cancer. The following year, he had his right lung removed. You may be thinking that this sounds like a sad ending, but the Lord's hand was at work. My father and mother spent the next five years managing their farms and traveling. They didn't spend a day apart from one another until he passed away in 1977.

We were told that more people attended his funeral at Restland Funeral Home than any in recent memory. Our guest book has over 250 signatures. Bob and his son-in-law, George Wenglein, offered their condolences by sending flowers. To his credit, Charles Johnson who had partnered with Bob in San Antonio, attended the funeral. Bob's branch of the Luby's Cafeteria chain was in full throttle by 1977. Luby's would later become a publicly held company on the New York Stock Exchange. They continued to capitalize off the foundational reputation my father, his partners, and the other family members had established in North Texas and beyond.

THE DECLINE OF BOB LUBY'S BRANCH OF LUBY'S CAFETERIAS

BOB RESIGNED HIS OPERATIONAL CONTROL in 1971, handing the reins over to his brother-in-law, George Wenglein. George retired as CEO in 1983 and chairman in 1988. John Lahourcade, who was formerly with the CPA firm Bielstein, Lahourcade & Lewis took over for George as CEO in 1983. The saving grace from the decision to replace George with a financial guy such as John was the fact that Henry Jones was named COO. Having opened the Houston market in 1965, Jones was one of the first operational vice presidents in 1972. Jones knew what it took to operate a cafeteria day in and day out.

Following Jones was Ralph Erben who was also entrenched in the operations and had helped Luby's to achieve operational balance with the changes in top leadership. Erben took over as president and COO in 1988. Ralph was a manager in El Paso in 1965 and was promoted to area manager/area vice president in the mid 70's. Erben was well respected by the managers and understood what it took to run a cafeteria on a day-to-day basis. To Lahourcade's credit, his financial background helped Jones and Erben expand Luby's.

The cafeteria segment of the restaurant industry is a phenomenon. Luby's (1911), Morrisons (1920), and Piccadilly (1934), to name a few, survived the ups and downs of the U.S. economy for over seventy years. Many would like you to think the cafeteria segment of the foodservice industry is dead and will not survive, yet the segment held on like the energizer bunny. Morrisons sold to Piccadilly in 1998 for $46 million. Luby's made their founders wealthy. Piccadilly didn't cash flow as well as Luby's but enjoyed a similar success over the years and is still in existence.

> Piccadilly, based in Baton Rouge, La., has 101 units from Florida to Arizona and has no plans to expand outside the region. During the financial year ending June 30, 1984, the chain compiled $8.4 million in net income on revenues of $173.8 million. It is similar to Luby's in that each manager buys his own food, and it uses no prepared mixes or centrally distributed materials. However, the average manager makes only about $65,000, just a little more than half of what the average Luby's manager earns.[4]

The cafeteria segment is at its lowest point. Luby's has only thirty-two stores, Morrisons only one, and Piccadilly has just thirty-three stores remaining. Time will dictate what the next chapter will be. Personally, I believe the segment could be strong again, but it will take innovation and money to make it happen.

The chain restaurants are being surrounded by local specialty restaurants, and the younger generation prefers the latter. They want celebrity chefs, fancy menus, enticing surroundings and are willing to pay for those features. It is not unusual for a couple to spend in excess of one hundred dollars on a casual night out. The same couple might pay two hundred dollars or more for a more luxurious night out. At a cafeteria, you can receive comparable quality at a much lower price, but you will

---

4   "Why They're Lining Up at Luby's," *New York Times* in the August 18, 1985, Section 3, Page 11)

not enjoy the same atmosphere or be able to compliment your meal with wine or alcohol.

Growing up and working in the business was an incredible experience. Out of college, I entered TGIF's manager training program. At the time it was considered the boot camp for restaurant training. Everything was made from scratch, and the managers learned how to generate profit and loss statements on a weekly basis. Fridays, like many of their contemporaries, patterned their operations after Luby's in terms of training. However, those restaurants didn't provide the autonomy Luby's afforded their managers. They all adopted a salary plus bonus compensation program. As a result, you didn't see an ownership mentality exhibited in their establishments.

Operators who own their establishments are in constant survival mode knowing that every day is critical to the bottom line. Rents are through the roof, food costs have skyrocketed, and labor poses more of a challenge than ever before. They have to be tough and innovate to grow sales and cut costs.

The bonus program my father, Joe O. Luby, developed in 1946, in essence, created that owner/manager mentality, and many of their managers went on to make six figure incomes. The managers had control over their potential earnings. In my father's era, the Luby's management team didn't earn a paycheck until everyone else had been compensated.

Bob Luby and George Wenglein later introduced a base pay to compliment the shared profit bonus program. Doing so was more out of necessity to enhance recruitment. However, the introduction of a base salary was counterproductive to the mentality that Luby's needed their managers to have. Many of the older managers who had worked so hard for the majority profit share began to put more and more pressure on the junior managers and spent less time on the floor with customers.

How did Luby's lay its foundation? When World War II ended, Luby's entered a new era. My father and his partners laid their foundation on a trinitarian base. The three sides of the triangle were the company, the employee, and the customer. By keeping the triangle in balance, the operations ran smoothly, and everyone profited. Harry had instilled these principles early on, and beginning in 1946, the next generation of the Luby family was poised to expand the concept.

Running a cafeteria was a unique business challenge. The operation required sourcing real estate and negotiation, design and build, recruiting, training, purchasing, manufacturing, service, marketing, and accounting. Managers had to be properly trained in every area for the cafeteria to be successful. My father, along with all the family members whom Harry had employed started in the kitchen, were trained in every area before venturing out on their own to open a cafeteria.

Dallas Luby's drew from a program that had been developed during war called "Training Within Industry." Though the TWI program is not found anywhere in the Luby's history, Luby's success was founded on the program's principles, which were inbred within the walls of every Luby's cafeteria, and their effectiveness provided the life blood for a thriving company.

Several major corporations, at their own expenses, had loaned their training executives to the U.S. Government War Department to create a special training program to put several million people into skilled positions to ramp up production to meet the demands of war.

> Walter Dietz of Western Electric came to Washington in August 1940 as the Associate Director of the Training Within Industry Service (TWI). He worked with the Director and the assistant directors, without compensation, in planning operations and setting national standards. The Associate Director was in charge of "development and research" and was responsible for the development of the various TWI programs, the gathering and correlation

of statistical information and operating reports, and the preparation of TWI publications.[5]

TWI consisted of three primary sections: Job Instruction (train the trainer), Job Relations (Solve People Problems), and Job Methods (Improve processes and timing while increasing quality).[6]

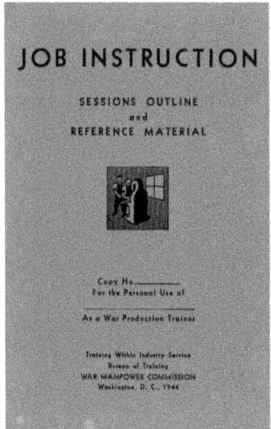 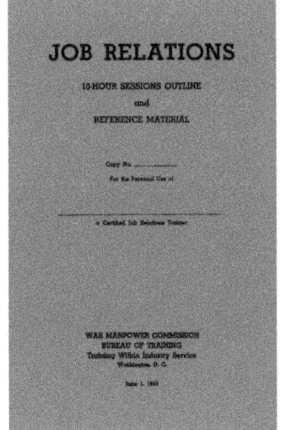 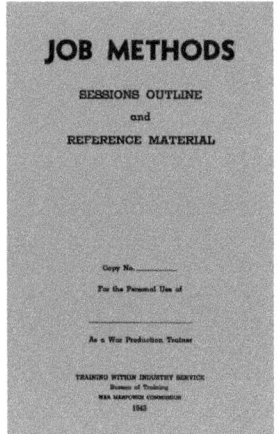

These three sections worked in harmony with one another, and as a result over 1.7 million workers in over 16,500 plants received a certification.[7]

The triangular balance was shifting as Luby's slowly drifted from its roots and the principles the original founders had established. Senior managers were spending more time in the office while junior managers worked in excess of seventy hours a week. Executive management became out of touch with the daily

---

5   National Archives Catalog U.S. National Archives and Records Administration

6   Manuals JI, JR, and JM open source and available to the public

7   "War Production Board, Bureau of Training, Training Within Industry Service," September 1945, *The Training Within Industry Report: 1940-1945*, (Washington D.C.: U.S. Government Printing Office), p 126.

operations when the reins were taken up by the financial managers within the company. The design of the cafeterias were stale and gave the impression of institutional dining establishments that lacked entertainment value. These facts, along with future events that were about to unfold, would prove to be catalyst for change that would disrupt the foundational balance Luby's had been built on.

THE WINDS OF CHANGE AND DARKNESS SETTLES

OCTOBER 16, 1991, AN EVIL act of violence was perpetrated on the customers of Luby's cafeteria in Killeen, Texas. To this day, no one knows why a lone gunman choose Luby's to inflict his venom. He entered the restaurant that was filled with people and began shooting. Twenty-three people were killed and another twenty-five were wounded. The heartless coward then turned the gun on himself and took his own life. That day would forever hang a cloud over Luby's as being the worst mass shooting in the country's history at the time.

Sadly, people today are still impacted by the grief of lost loved ones from that terrible day. No one could have anticipated the events of that day, and no blame can be applied. Luby's embraced the community, and many people came and rallied around those effected. The Killeen fatality was a turning point in the future of Luby's.

Four years later, Ralph Erben tendered his resignation. Erben had been put out with the board's plan to purchase twenty Wyatt's cafeterias from Triangle Foodservice Corporation. The board saw Erben's discontent as an opportunity to take over operational control.

Erben had groomed John E. Curtis Jr. to take his place; he treated him like a son. In January 1996, the board announced that John E. Curtis Jr. would replace Erben as the next president

THE WINDS OF CHANGE AND DARKNESS SETTLES

and COO. John would be the first COO not to have come out of operations to lead Luby's. The board also announced in January 1996 they had signed a joint venture agreement with the owners of Waterstreet, a seafood concept out of Corpus Christi.

The Wyatt's purchase ended up costing fourteen million, and Luby's management spent another five million to get the units up and operational. Luby's and Wyatt's were alike only in the sense that they were cafeterias. Wyatt's management, though competent, did not embrace the ownership mentality that the founders of Luby's had instilled in their managers over the years. As mentioned earlier in the book, Wyatt's catered to a different clientele than Luby's. All the founding fathers must have been turning in their graves.

In 1995 Luby's had generated $419,024,000 in revenue with net income of $37,015,000. Luby's had a total of 187 stores, owned the real estate under 133 of those locations, and most importantly, had no long-term debt. Luby's had thrived with John Curtis as chief financial officer and Ralph Erben as COO.

Unknowingly, John Curtis was about to be thrown to the wolves. He had no idea that he was about to inherit an operational nightmare created by the board that was having an erosional effect on a once thriving company providing excellent value to its employees, customers, and shareholders.

In March of 1997, Curtis took his own life. Many believed he did so because he realized Luby's was on the brink of a financial collapse. Personally, I never knew John, but his brother and I attended the same fraternity at Texas A&M University. When the news broke, we both suspected foul play. He supposedly left a note that indicated he had, in fact, taken his own life. However, everyone who knew him said that he was a strong Christian and extremely knowledgeable of the Luby's operations, and the employees had tremendous respect for him. One can only speculate about what really happened. I am sure he is safe in heaven, his family will join him one day, and the truth will be revealed.

Once the shock of John's death abated, the board named fellow board member John E. Lahourcade as interim chairman to assume Curtis's role. He was also asked to assume the CEO role but declined. Instead, another board member, David Daviss, was appointed to assume Erben's role. Daviss did not come up through the operational ranks, like Lahourcade. Instead, he was a CPA and had headed the audit committee for a number of years. The financial minds were in complete control.

The following facts are taken from a Proxy Statement presented at the 2001 Annual meeting of Shareholders.[8] They paint a clear picture of the cause and effect leading to the demise of Luby's that would ultimately put over 11,000 jobs at risk.

> "Luby's has paid legal fees to the law firm of Cauthorn Hale Hornberger Fuller Sheehan & Becker (Cauthorn Firm), of which James R. Hale, former Secretary of Luby's, is a member. The legal fees were as follows: 1999 ($475,000), 1998 ($416,000), 1997 ($584,000), 1996 ($563,000), 1995 ($439,000). For five (5) years, Luby's paid legal fees to the Cauthorn firm, which averaged out to $41,284 per month. On March 24, 2000, Mr. Greenberg wrote to Mr. Daviss, Chairman of the Board, asking (1) if and when Luby's last conducted an audit of the aforesaid legal fees and (2) when Luby's last 'shopped the market' with respect to the cost of legal services being provided. On March 27, 2000, Mr. Daviss forwarded a non-responsive reply."

> "Since at least 1996, Luby's has employed a director (former officer of Luby's) as a 'consultant' and paid that director $7,083 per month. His original contract was to expire in 2001. Prior to January 1998, another director and previous officer of Luby's received

---

8 https://www.sec.gov/Archives/edgar/data/16099/000112481200500016/fullprox.txt

'consulting fees' of $10,417 per month. The nominees, if elected to the BOD, would advocate that, in order to avoid potential conflicts of interest, any person serving as a director not, also, receive compensation from Management."

The following, which showed exceptional insight on the behalf of the shareholders, was also included in the filing.

"A conflict of interest occurs when one is required to be loyal to two masters at the same time where the interests of the masters oppose one another. There are situations at Luby's where conflicts of interest might occur."

"The resignation of Ralph "Pete" Erben, 66, as chairman of the company followed only four days after the suicide death of his protege, Luby's president and chief executive, John E. Curtis Jr. Board member John B. Lahourcade, 72, a former chief executive and chairman of Luby's, was elected to fill temporarily both Erben's chairman slot and Curtis' chief executive post."[9]

When David B. Daviss, took over as Chairman of the Board in 1997, he hired Barry J. C. Parker from the County Seat Clothing chain thinking the company needed an outsider to effectively evaluate the next chapter in Luby's history. Daviss in his operational ignorance stated at the time of Parker's hiring,

"Barry Parker is a retail executive accustomed to working in a large, multiunit service environment," Daviss said. "He has strong credentials

---

9   Nation's Restaurant News. 1997;31(13):3

in marketing, merchandising and finance, attributes that will be of value to Luby's." Daviss added that Parker's background in retail was what attracted him to the board. "We believe," Daviss said, "the outside perspective he will bring to our industry will be a significant advantage to Luby's as we face the future."

Barry Parker took over as CEO in October 1977, and Luby's was generating slightly more revenue than the previous year at $495,446,000 even though the number of stores had increased by forty-two. The chain consisted of 229 stores, and Luby's owned the real estate under 135 locations. Net revenue, however, decreased to $28,447,000 and the long-term debt ballooned to $84,000,000.

By the time Parker exited the scene in October 2000, Luby's was generating less in revenue at $493,384,000 with a total of 231 stores. Net income had declined to $9,125,000. Most importantly, Luby's was now strapped with $116,000,000 in long-term debt and on the verge of bankruptcy.

The County Seat Clothing chain that Parker headed had filed for bankruptcy in October 1996, a year before he joined Luby's. Why would Luby's board think that someone from outside of Luby's who was leading a failed clothing chain could be the savior of a cafeteria chain in the volatile foodservice industry?

The logical answer to that question will never be known because there is no logical answer. The financial wizards were draining the company of its vast resources, and when the bleeding began there were not enough bandages to stop the hemorrhaging.

Barry Parker's biggest failure at Luby's was shown by his ignorance of the founding principles that had defined Luby's. Parker saw the pile of money Luby's was paying their management teams and was quoted by one of the longest standing General Managers as saying, "We can find all the managers we need at $90,000." After restructuring the pay like David Daviss stated, 15% of Luby's seasoned managers immediately threw their keys onto the desk and quit the company. What Daviss didn't say is that when the dust had settled ninety senior managers had retired.

> "The young manager can expect to earn big bucks fast. Last year, the average Luby's manager earned $116,000 - one made $200,000- under a compensation plan whereby the store manager retains 40 percent of his unit's operating profit, out of which he pays his assistant managers, and splits the rest, 65-35, with his second-in-command."[10]

One other important fact Daviss and Parker failed to disclose was that the junior managers who were working seventy plus hours a week for the carrot dangled before them started vacating the company as well. However, the virus that Parker had injected didn't stop at the operational level but spread to the corporate level as well.

> "In 1998, the compensation plan was adjusted on three (3) occasions with the result that the former '60/40' compensation plan no longer exists, and that Unit Manager compensation was substantially reduced…As an example of the impact of the change, the compensation of top managers was reduced by 40% to 50%."[11]

> "But the two moves that most enraged store managers and caused many to leave were its decision to outsource … and restructuring management compensation." (HC, 10/28/00) "Over the past 12 months, 15 percent of the

---

10 Why They're Lining Up at Luby's," *New York Times* in the August 18, 1985, Section 3, Page 11
11 https://www.sec.gov/Archives/edgar/data/16099/000112481200500016/fullprox.txt

company's top managers have resigned," Daviss said.[12]

"Managers chafed under increasing directives from corporate headquarters that seemed to have no connection with store-level reality. The company that kept managers for decades by giving them freedom and paying them well had become one that sent rules down from above and brooked no argument." (HC, 10/28/00)[13]

"Anderson Advertising announced that it was giving up the Luby's account that it had held for about 20 years. .... Also, on Tuesday, Luby's announced that Bob Burke, senior vice president of marketing, has resigned. His resignation 'is really coincidental,' Bishop said." (SAEN, 5/24/00)[14]

"In or about March 2000, Luby's commenced the employment of a Vice President, General Counsel and Secretary. In October 2000, she tendered her resignation. Also, in October 2000, Ms. Laura Bishop, Senior Vice President - Chief Financial Officer, and Ms. Sue Elliott, Senior Vice President - Human Resources, resigned. 'They were not asked to leave,' Daviss said of Bishop and Elliott. (SAEN, 10/27/00) Earlier, in 2000, the Vice President - Equipment, and Vice President - Construction and Design resigned."[15]

---

12   ibid
13   ibid
14   ibid
15   ibid

Those managers jumping ship were a devastating blow to a company that had always cooked everything from scratch. Parker was forced to make another monumental mistake by redefining the back of the house operations (the kitchens). Luby's began to outsource production of food, a move that impacted the overall quality customers had enjoyed for years. Eating at Luby's had always been like going to your grandmothers for dinner where you would become intoxicated by the scents of fresh baked pies. There was always more food than you could possibly eat, and every dish was cooked from scratch with the freshest ingredients.

> "Under a "long-term strategic plan" conceived and implemented by Mr. Parker, Luby's switched from its food preparation process of 'made-from-scratch' to the use of outsourced food."[16]

Further proof that Parker had no business running restaurants came in 1999, three years after Luby's had invested in the seafood concept, Waterstreet. Luby's divested themselves from the concept, and Parker cited the reason, "Our skill set is really in the limited-service restaurant business."[17]

Real restauranteurs know that every concept must identify and build on its own DNA. If Luby's didn't have the skill set, then Parker should have divested Luby's of the concept much earlier and focused on the real problem at hand—the demise of an incredible foodservice concept that had weathered the storms of change for many years.

Cafeterias were built on high volume and low margins. People were efficiently moved through the line to a beautiful dining room where they could gather as a family and enjoy a nutritious meal. Gourmet quality food pre-prepared was the only way to accomplished this.

---

16 https://www.sec.gov/Archives/edgar/data/16099/000112481200500016/fullprox.txt

17 (Ruggless, Ron. 1999. "Luby's Sells Joint-Venture Interest in Water Street Seafood." Nation's Restaurant News 33 (51): 11)

Many people in the Dallas market will remember the lines running down the sidewalks near the entrances to Luby's cafeteria. The Preston Forest location had two serving lines to accommodate customers. Luby's didn't have waiters, but they always had personnel working the floor refilling drinks, running food, communicating with customers, and keeping tables bussed and clean. The dining rooms were designed by local designers with grand pianos to entertain guests.

Luby's had always prided itself on locating cafeterias in smaller communities whether in the boundaries of a larger city like Dallas or Denver or in the many small towns around Texas. Luby's was part of the heartbeat of those communities. They catered to the schools and hospitals, they were active in community service, and their take-out programs were a great success in those markets. The founders of the Dallas branch of Luby's understood the importance of joining in and working with the local communities. They listened to their customers and responded to their needs.

Parker and his team implemented a redesign and attempted to rescale the cafeterias. Unfortunately, they had no real eye for design in accordance with what the public wanted. The problem with their analysis at the time: their older clientele who were now the new seniors had matured. They still wanted a good meal, but they wanted to dine in a nicer more upscale environment.

During these years, the restaurant industry was exploding with new concepts. Anyone doing research should have determined that the public was demanding a change to the traditional food service they had been engaged in growing up. People would tell you how much they loved Luby's and share their experiences of growing up with Luby's. They would also tell you that the current Luby's dining rooms reminded them of assisted living dining rooms. Luby's obviously had ceased listening to their customers.

Instead of taking ownership for his failed leadership when he resigned from Luby's, Barry C. Parker blamed Luby's demise on the economy by stating, "The senior population is dying." Funny how history has a way of repeating itself. Just like he did with County Seat, Parker left Luby's on the verge of bankruptcy.

THE WINDS OF CHANGE AND DARKNESS SETTLES

Parker was correct that an older senior population was dying out, but they were being replaced by a new senior population, and in the Southwest area of the country, the new senior population had all grown-up eating at Luby's. Luby's didn't predict this very important paradigm population shift.

> "In 2011, the oldest baby boomers—Americans born between 1946 and 1964—will start to turn 65. Today, 40 million people in the United States are ages 65 and older, but this number is projected to more than double to 89 million by 2050. Although the 'oldest old'—those ages 85 and older—represent only 15 percent of the population ages 65 and older today, their numbers are projected to rise rapidly over the next 40 years. By 2050, the oldest old will number 19 million, over one-fifth of the total population ages 65 and older."[18]

Parker and the other Luby's executives at the time didn't have a clue about what drove the Luby's brand. As shown earlier in this writing, a brand that didn't start in 1947 like Luby's Incorporated would have everyone believe, but actually started in 1911 in a small town in Missouri by a much-loved man with a vision.

I don't fault Barry Parker because he was in a no-win situation. Without brand knowledge and the expertise of former senior operational leadership, I don't think there is any way he could have turned Luby's around.

I do fault my cousin Bob Luby and his brother-in-law, George Wenglein, for not being visionaries. Bob exited the board in 1982 when the company was thriving. The biggest mistake that Bob Luby made was defined for him before he retired. A prominent designer at the time told him that if he didn't upgrade Luby's image, the

---

18   Linda A. Jacobsen et al., "America's Aging Population," Population Bulletin 66, no. 1 (2011

franchise would be on the verge of death in ten years. Bob was not interested in what she had to say because at the time, all the signs showed success. However, by the time he and George exited the operations of Luby's, the foodservice industry was beginning to change. The designer was off by a few years, but considering the events that took place in 1996, she was not off by my much.

If they had been more focused on what was going on in the industry, they would have realized that a new generation of theme concepts were springing up. Those new concepts borrowed the best practices from Luby's but wrapped themselves in new skins to attract the customer who was longing for a better experience. Further the fast casual segment that was getting ready to explode on the scene could be likened to Luby's grandchildren. They serve pre-prepared food with limited service taking advantage of Luby's ability to turn tables quickly and operate at high volumes with reduced labor costs.

In 1965, Alan Stillman opened his first TGI Fridays in New York. In 1971, he sold a franchise in Memphis, Tennessee, to a group of businessmen. One year later, Dan Scoggin and his investment group bought the rights for eight states opening their first unit in Dallas, Texas, on Greenville Avenue. With an intriguing and eclectic atmosphere Fridays captured the hearts of their customers. Scoggins was known to say, "We were taking money to the bank in suitcases." The rest is history, and the theme segment of the restaurant industry began to dominate.

In 1966, a restaurant industry icon, Norman Brinker, opened a casual steak house concept in Dallas, Texas, called Steak and Ale. He sold the chain in 1976 to Pillsbury and took over leadership of their restaurant group. While at Pillsbury he was the brainchild behind the Bennigan's chain and led Burger King as they surpassed rival McDonalds in sales for the first time with the famous advertising campaign crafted by Ron McDougal called the "Battle of the Burgers."

During this time, Norman realized that customers wanted something more. He began his research by asking clients what they desired in a dining experience. Norman discovered customers

THE WINDS OF CHANGE AND DARKNESS SETTLES

wanted a casual dining experience in a more upscale atmosphere. In 1984, he made an investment in a small Dallas burger chain named Chili's that had been founded by Larry Lavine. Norman brought in his team from Steak and Ale and some other industry heavy weights. In 1984, Goldman Sachs took them public, and Norman built a company that would become one of the largest restaurant holding companies in the world, Brinker International.

Restaurateur Phil Romano opened the first Eatzi's Market and Bakery in 1996 in Dallas, Texas. His vision was to offer gourmet prepared foods to an upscale clientele. He saw the need to create various stations where customers could order sandwiches, salads, beverages, and desserts. He also predicted that his clientele, being more sophisticated, would appreciate the fine wines they stocked. Romano also opened Fuddruckers in 1979 and Romano's Macaroni Grill in 1988.

In 1977, Houston's opened in Dallas on Walnut Hill Lane a block away from Presbyterian Hospital. Almost immediately it became one of Dallas' most popular restaurants. Granted, it was a member of a more upscale segment of the restaurant industry than Luby's. However, when you approached the restaurant, the exterior décor lured you in, and upon entering you experienced a warm and inviting atmosphere, one that was vibrant and full of energy. Luby's, on the other hand, had turned into an institutional dining concept. The décor was dull and unexciting.

In 1976, Paradise Bakery was birthed and later adopted a similar line to Luby's by serving prepared foods in an upscale and much more pleasing atmosphere. Customers would take a tray and move down a line making selections or ordered from the soup, sandwich, and salad stations. Ultimately, the customers ended up at the cashier where they would pay and then find their places to sit in the dining room.

In 1980, Au Bon Pain Co. Inc began expanding. They became what is now known as Panera Bread which too used a similar set up as Luby's.

One of the most popular fast casual restaurants opened in 1983, La Madeliene French Café. As in Luby's, customers formed a line and selected gourmet food that was already prepared. Patrick Esquerré, from France's Loire Valley choose a location on Mockingbird Lane across from Southern Methodist University. Patrick loved to tell the story about when he was negotiating the lease. Frustrated that he was not communicating effectively to get the best deal, he dialed his friend Stanley Marcus. Stanley patiently listened as Patrick explained his dilemma and then said, "Put them on the phone." Marcus negotiated the lease for Patrick over the phone, and another iconic brand was launched.

PARTING WORDS

CUSTOMERS WERE ENTERING A NEW era of expectation and wanted to combine their dining experience with an exciting night out, but there were not a lot of affordable options for a family. Luby's was poised to meet this need but failed to respond. To avoid the death sentence, Luby's should have been redefining their approach years before.

In the mid 1980's, Luby's had grown to one hundred locations and employed about 8,000 people. Management could have initiated an incredible campaign to solicit their employees' ideas as well as their customer's ideas. The campaign would have been a brilliant advertising move. It would have been the occasion to travel the country and research concepts that were being established and the clientele they were attracting. Listening carefully, it is possible they could have initiated a corporate redevelopment that would have been unparalleled at the time.

Luby's was positioned to redesign the concept of the future. It had plenty of square footage and the most up-to-date kitchens. Luby's had an opportunity to get away from the standard "cafeteria line" and create a renewed dining experience with an enticing ambience. Luby's served all the products at the time, but they didn't canvass their customers to see what they wanted in a dining experience. If they had, quite possibly Luby's might have been more than the grandfather to the fast casual segment and continued as a leader within the foodservice industry.

Today, wherever I go people ask me if I am part of the Luby's Cafeteria family, I hold my head high and proudly say,

PARTING WORDS

"Yes, my father was one of the founding members." It is a wonderful heritage, and I am forever grateful for the lessons learned over the years.

FAVORITE LUBY STORIES

ONE OF OUR DOWNTOWN DALLAS cafeterias did not have a rear entrance, so employees and delivery men used the front door. Every morning after the front line was set up, the employees would convene in the dining room for a smoke and cup of coffee. In the early 1940's, everyone smoked cigarettes.

One morning, the boyfriend of one of the women cooks was scheduled to arrive after the line had been set up. She had learned that he was having an affair. She casually slipped a butcher knife under her apron and positioned herself so that he would have to pass by her upon arrival. At the time, several customers were out front waiting for the cafeteria to open.

The boyfriend showed up right before opening time and as he neared, she drew the knife and slashed his thigh, obviously aiming at a section of his anatomy that I dare not comment on. My father and several of the men carried him into the kitchen. Dad tied a trinket on his thigh and informed him to pray because he wasn't about to drag him bleeding through the dining room in the middle of their lunch rush. They managed to get him to a hospital after the rush, and he made a full recovery.

Another story my father liked to tell involved two women in the kitchen. Two of his cooks got into an argument and one picked up a butcher knife threatening to kill the other. I asked my father, "How did you break up the fight?"

He laughed, "Well, we turned the hot water hose on them. One of them had a wig that flew off, and she was so embarrassed she ran out the back door."

He went on to say, "Men will threaten, but the women will act."

I believe that still holds true today; strong women are a force to be reckoned with.

On another occasion my father told me about one of his cooks who always boasted about how strong he was. Number ten cans were packed four to a case and stacked near the back door. One day, my father removed two of the cans from one of the cases and resealed the case. He told the cook, "I'll bet you a dollar I can put my fist through that case without hurting my hand."

The cook responded, "Mr. Joe, I'll take that bet because there is no way you can punch through that case."

Father said he reared back and slammed his fist through the case with ease. The cook had an amazed look on his face and said, "Mr. Joe, if you can do it, I know I can do it."

So, he bet another dollar that he could do the same. The cook reared back and slammed his fist into one of the full cases. There was no real damage to the man except his ego and they all had a good laugh at his expense. Father said the man was a little less boastful afterward.

Dad and a few of the managers were sitting at a table in the dining room around closing. When one of the lady cooks sauntered through the dining room, my father watched her go by and then did a double take. He called her and said, "Ida, lift up your apron." His suspicions were confirmed: she had a ham strapped to the inside of her thigh. I remember my father laughing as he told the story, "Amazing how creative people are when trying to steal from you."

One morning, I was in the kitchen at home when Dad got a call from the Dallas police letting him know they caught the thief who had broken into our restaurant on Lomo Alto the night before. The young man had used a sawed-off shotgun to force the manager back into the restaurant after closing and forced him to open the safe. I asked my father, "What would you have done if that had been you?" He smiled, "Well, he'd have to shoot me, I don't know the combinations to any of our safes."

Shortly after the signing of the Civil Rights Act of 1964 my brother was working at one of our restaurants and witnessed a conversation our father had with a man sent from the NAACP. The man said, "We are sending one hundred of our members this Sunday for lunch. If you choose not to serve us, we will boycott and shut you down."

Our father just looked at him and asked, "Will your money be green?"

The man looked confused and said, "Yes, why do you ask."

Dad responded, "Because green is the only color I care about."

One day, I was working at the Preston Forest Cafeteria. The manager's office was near the main entrance to the kitchen on the north side of the cafeteria. Suddenly, the doors flew open, and a repairman came running yelling, "She's going to kill me!" Hot on his heals and waving a butcher knife was Big Mama one of, if not, our best cooks at the time. Big Mama wasn't physically big, but she was big in character and let everyone know who was boss. The repairman had entered her space without permission and shown her disrespect. I guarantee from that point on, he asked permission. Fortunately for me, Big Mama and I always got along.

JOSEPH OWEN LUBY SR.'S ORIGINAL COOKBOOK

THE FOLLOWING RECIPES COME FROM a three-ring binder four inches thick that my father owned. I personally scanned each page and cleaned them up to the best of my ability. Some of the recipes will be familiar as you reminisce about your own experiences eating at the Luby's. Others will be fun to read because of their origin and ingredients. If you are so inclined, feel free to break them down and reproduce for your own enjoyment. Luby's was always about family, and if you grew up eating at a Luby's Cafeteria, well, you are considered family.

WHAT EMPLOYEES LOOK FOR IN EMPLOYMENT WITH A SUCCESSFUL ORGANIZATION

1. Recognition as an individual.
2. Job security.
3. Freedom from discrimination. (Equal consideration for all employees)
4. Opportunity to advance.
5. Meaningful tasks. (Importance of each little job for successful operation)
6. Genial associates.
7. Satisfactory working conditions.
8. Fair wages for work performed.
9. Discussions about things that effect them. (Let them express themselves)
10. Competent leadership.

WHAT WORKERS EXPECT FROM THEIR BOSSES

1. Recognition for work well done.
2. Provide good leadership.
3. Give constructive criticism. (The why and how expected)
4. Follow chain of command.
5. Compliment and thank employees for work well done on heavy days and when cooperation is necessary when due to employees being off for sickness, etc.
6. Have confidence in their work abilities and them.
7. Take responsibilities and do not pass the buck.
8. Make good decisions.
9. Be loyal and respectful to all employees.
10. Train employees well.
11. Delegate authority when earned.

CHAPTER I

SALADS AND SALAD DRESSINGS

VEGETABLE SALADS	Page	JELLO SALADS WITH VEGETABLES	Page
Avocado Variations	1-44	Lemon Variations	34-32a
Beans		Lime Variations	34
Green, Variations	1	Orange Variations	34
Green, Sweet Sour	2	Coleslaw Salad (Jello)	35
Kidney, Salad	3	Lime Salad	35
Lima, Salad	2	Tomato Aspic	14-34
Lima, Summer Salad	2		
Slaw, Calico Bean	3	FRUIT SALADS	
Beets		Ambrosia	23
Pickled	4	Apple	
Salad	3	Variations	24
Spiced Pickled	4	Baked	24
Cabbage		Delight	43
Variations (Health Salads)	4-5	Whole Cooked Fresh	24
Harlequin Slaw	6	Salad	24
Old Fashioned Slaw	6	Apple-Celery Variations	23
Salad	5	Apricot Variations	24
Shredded	5	Banana Variations	26
Shredded Salad	6	Cantalope Variations	26
Carrot		Cherry, Bing, Salad	26
Variations	7-8	Cranberry, Creamy Relish Salad	25
Turnip and Carrot Slaw	7	Fruit Salad	
Cauliflower		Combinations	22
Variations	8	Fresh, Compote	22-23
Salad	21	Salad	23
Celery, Stuffed, Variations	8	Polar Bear Salad	43
Combination Salad	11	Grapes	26
Corn Salads	9	Grapefruit Variations	27
Cucumber Variations	9	Mandavin Delight	25
Garnished Plate (Various)	19-20	Peach Variations	27
Green Salad		Pear Salad	27
Variations	9-10	Pineapple	
with Croutons	21	Variations	27
Guacamole Salads	1	Pineapple-Date Salad	28
Hominy		Pineapple-Grapefruit Salad	28
Variations	11	Prune Variations	28
Salads	11	Raisins, Stewed	28
Lettuce		Raisin-Cheese Salad	28
Variations	10	Tangerine or Orange Variations	29
Romaine Variations	10	Waldorf Salad	29
Mixed Vegetable Salads	12-35a		
Mustard Green Salad	11	JELLO SALADS WITH FRUIT	
Pea-Salad Variations	12-13	Cherry Variations	30
Pickles, Sweet	14	Lemon Variations	30
Potato Salad Variations	13	Lime Variations	31
Relish Plate or Bowl	14	Orange Variations	31
Spinach Variations	10-11	Strawberry Variations	30-32a
Tomato		Other Variations	31
Variations	14	Fruit Congeal	33
Aspic	14-34	Grapefruit Surprise	33
Salad w/cream cheese dressing	19	Lime Jello Congeal Salad	32
Turnip Salad	14	Lime, Frosted Congeal	32
Italian (Wop)	10	Pineapple-Avocado Souffle Salad	33
		Royal Fruit Gelatin-Self-Layering	32

FRUITS (COOKED)	Page
Apples, Dried	29
Fruits, Dried	30
Peaches, Dried	29
Prunes	30
Raisins, Stewed	28
Rhubarb	29

CHICKEN SALADS
Chicken Salad	15
Chicken or Ham Salad	15

COTTAGE CHEESE
Variations	18-19
Cottage Cheese	19
Cottage Cheese Special	19

EGGS
Egg Salad	16
Egg and Olive Salad	16
Eggs, Deviled	16
Eggs, Whole Boiled	16

FISH SALADS
Variations	16-17
Tuna and Shellroni	17

MACARONI SALADS
Variations	15
Shellroni Salad w/Vegetables	15

MEAT SALADS	Page
Frank Salad	15
Meat Salad	15

SALAD DRESSINGS	
Anchovy Dressing	36
Anchovy Sauce	36
Avocado Dressing	42
Cardinal Dressing	36
Celery Seed Dressing	37
Cream Cheese Dressing (Orange)	38
Cream Cheese Dressing (Honey)	38
Creole Dressing	37
French Dressing	37
French Dressing (1 Gal.)	37
Fruit Salad Dressing	39-42
Fruit Topping	41
Garlic Oil Dressing	39
Italian Wishbone Dressing	44
Lemon-Lime Dressing	38
Mayonnaise - 4 Gallon	39
Orange Cream Mayonnaise	38
Pineapple Dressing	39
Poppy Seed Dressing	40
Roquefort Cheese Dressing	40
Salad Dressing	38
Shrimp Cocktail Sauce (1 Gal.)	40
Sour Cream Dressing	38-40-44
Sweet Cream Dressing	40
Tartar Sauce	41
Thousand Island Dressing	41
Vinegar Dressing	41

LIST HERE new recipes:

Hot Potato Salad	13a
Italian Potato Salad	13a
Calico Bean Salad	13a
Shrimp Salad	17a
Green Goddess Dressing	17a
Strawberry Congeal	32a
Spinach Congeal	32a
24 hour vegetable Salad	35a

AVOCADO VARIATIONS

1. Avocado, tomatoes, green onions, salt & pepper, mayonnaise.

2. Avocado, cubed, tomatoes, green onions, salt & pepper, mayonnaise.

3. Avocado, diced, chopped celery, eggs, salt & pepper, mayonnaise.

GUACAMOLE SALAD

Cream 6 avocados. Add onion (chopped fine), ripe tomato (pulp), Tobasco sauce, Worchestershire sauce, lemon juice, salt to taste. Serve on slice of tomato and lettuce leaf. Garlic, green hot peppers.

GUACAMOLE SALAD

Peel and dip in lemon juice 18 (8 + 12 oz. Florida avocados). Cream and add 1 tb. grated onion, 1 tb. very fine chopped garlic, 2 cups ripe tomato pieces (cut fairly small pieces) 2 tb. Evangeline hot sauce, 1 tb. Worchestershire sauce, 2 tb. level salt.

This may be served on tomato slices as individual salads.

GREEN BEAN VARIATIONS

1. Wash and drain No. 10 can (1 gal.) can of green beans; about 10 medium cooked carrots, diced; chopped celery; minced onion to taste. Vinegar oil dressing.

2. No. 10 can washed and drained; chopped celery, whole kernel corn, drained; green pepper, chopped; diced tomatoes.

3. Green beans washed and drained, onion rings, black pepper, salt, vinegar oil dressing.

4. Green beans, onion rings mixed with sour cream dressing - 1 box sour cream, 1 sour cream box full of mayonnaise. 1 tsp. prepared mustard. Salt and pepper.

SWEET SOUR GREEN BEANS

4 cups cooked green beans
1 large onion (sliced paper thin)
1/2 cup cider vinegar
1/4 cup water
1/2 cup sugar
2 tbsp. salad oil
  salt and pepper to taste
1/2 tsp. Accent

Heat vinegar, water and sugar together until mixture boils. Remove from heat, add salad oil, and pour over green beans and onions. Season with salt and pepper and accent, and toss gently. Cover and chill several hours or overnight.

Helen Blodgett thought recipe better when the amount of vinegar and water was doubled.

LIMA BEAN SALAD

Cooked lima beans (5 lbs. Fordhook limas) cooked in 6 cups water and drained, chopped celery, chopped pimento, chopped green pepper, 10 cooked carrots, diced; little onion, chopped very fine may be added.

SUMMER LIMA SALAD

Lima Beans, cooked (10 lbs.)
Chopped celery
Sliced radishes
Chopped green onions (tops and bottoms)
Diced dill pickles
Diced American cheese

Cook and drain and chill thoroughly the lima beans. Combine all ingredients with sour cream dressing and mix lightly. (Mix in enough crumbled bacon to taste.) Mix bacon in sour cream.

SOUR CREAM DRESSING

3 cups sour cream
1 tb. prepared mustard
1 ts. salt

2 tb. vinegar
White pepper
Bacon pieces

Chapter I   Page 2

KIDNEY BEAN SALAD

1 Gal. Kidney beans (washed and drained)
Sliced boiled eggs (lots of eggs)
About 3 cups sweet relish
4 cups fine chopped green onions (tops and bottoms)
Salt and white pepper
About 5 cups chopped celery
Chopped pimento for color.

Mix lightly with mayonnaise.

KIDNEY BEAN SALAD (Makes one large bowl)

Wash and drain 5 No. 2 cans kidney beans, 10 hard boiled eggs, coarsely diced; chopped celery; generous amount chopped sweet pickles, well drained; chopped pimento (enough to color); very little onion, minced. Do not add tomatoes or vary this recipe.

CALICO BEAN SLAW

2 cups cooked large dry lima beans
1 cup canned red kidney beans
8 slices bacon
1 large onion (red preferred)
2 cups shredded cabbage
6 thinly sliced red radishes
3/4 c. mayonnaise
3 tablespoons vinegar
Salt and pepper and small lettuce leaves.

Drain and chill beans. Fry bacon crisp, drain. Slice onion into paper thin slices and separate into rings. Combine limas, kidney beans, cabbage, onion rings and radishes and top with broken up bacon. Mix mayonnaise and vinegar. Pour over salad and toss lightly. Season with salt and pepper, if needed. Serve on small lettuce leaves.

BEET SALAD

Sliced spiced beets. Mix with sliced onion rings. Use vinegar and oil.

Chapter I

PICKLED BEETS

Cook, peel and slice beets. 2 parts vinegar to 1 part sugar. Pinch salt. (2/3 cup pickling spice optional.) Bring vinegar and sugar to boil. Let boil about 10 minutes. Pour over beets.

SPICED PICKLED BEETS

Cook, peel and slice 1 bu. beets. Put in large crock.
1 1/2 gal. vinegar to 3 gal. sugar (gal. meas.)
Pinch salt
1/4 cups pickling spice in cloth bag and put in pan with vinegar, sugar and salt. Let boil about 10 min. Pour over beets while hot.

CABBAGE SALADS

HEALTH SALADS:

1. Equal parts chopped cabbage and carrots. About 2/3 as much chopped fresh spinach as carrots. Mix with mayonnaise, and salt to taste.

2. Use garnished plate and put a small mold (use ice-cream dipper) of each of chopped carrots, chopped cabbage, and chopped spinach. Each vegetable should be mixed with a little mayonnaise and salt.

Mix these with mayonnaise and salt to taste:

1. Plain slaw - chopped cabbage. Mix with mayonnaise and little vinegar oil dressing. (Add a little sugar if cabbage is strong.)

2. Chopped cabbage, drained, crushed pineapple, diced marshmallows. Garnish top with chopped pecans.

3. Chopped cabbage, drained diced pineapple; seedless green grapes cut in halves.

4. Chopped cabbage, unpeeled red apples, diced small; drained diced pineapple; raisins (soaked in hot water 20 min.)

5. New York Slaw: Chopped or shredded cabbage, diced tomatoes. Garnish top with very thin slices of dill pickle (or above plus: vinegar oil dressing and black pepper).

6. Chopped cabbage, cooked diced carrots, chopped green pepper.

7. Chopped cabbage, drained kidney beans, diced tomatoes, finely chopped onion, chopped pimiento.

8. Chopped cabbage, chopped sweet pickle, finely chopped onion, diced tomato.

Chapter I   Page 4

CABBAGE SALADS (CONT'D.)

HEALTH SALADS: (CONT'D.)

9. Spanish Slaw: 16 cups finely shredded cabbage
   6 cups hand chopped celery
   1 med. onion, chopped fine
   2 large green peppers, chopped fine
   Chill all ingredients. Just before serving, moisten with mayonnaise. Add 1 cup chili sauce and 40 sliced stuffed olives.

10. Chopped cabbage, halved (purple - red) diced, unpeeled apples, Pecans.

11. Shredded cabbage, drained green beans, diced tomatoes, chopped celery. Mix with salt and mayonnaise.

CABBAGE SALADS:

1. Chopped cabbage, shredded carrots, mayonnaise and garlic salt.

2. Chopped cabbage, chopped onions, bell pepper, tomatoes and mayonnaise.

3. Shredded cabbage, sweet cream dressing.

4. Shredded cabbage, shredded carrots, sweet cream dressing.

5. Shredded cabbage, sliced carrots, onion rings, pepper rings, vinegar, oil, salt & pepper.

CABBAGE SALAD

1 Dishpan coarse shredded cabbage
1/2 Gal. broken pineapple pieces
1 Large bunch Tokay grapes (halved and seeded).

Mix with mayonnaise, little salt. Garnish top with pineapple pieces

---

SHREDDED CABBAGE

1 Dishpan coarse shredded (on slicer) cabbage
  Sliced eggs
  Salt

Mix lightly with mayonnaise to which a little prepared mustard has been added. No garnish.

Chapter I

SHREDDED CABBAGE SALAD

Cabbage, shredded
Radishes, sliced
Onions, sliced
Celery, chopped coarsely
Tomatoes, diced

Season with salt and pepper and mix with vinegar and oil.

OLD FASHIONED SLAW

1/4 Cup vinegar
1½ Tsp. salt
1 Tbs. sugar
1 Tbs. butter or margarine
  Dash black pepper
3 Eggs
3 Cups crisp, shredded cabbage

Scald vinegar with salt, sugar and pepper. Add butter. Beat eggs and slowly stir in vinegar mixture, stirring constantly. Cook over hot water until creamy. Pour over cabbage and toss until mixed. 2 tbs. heavy cream may be added to dressing just before mixing with cabbage.

HARLEQUIN SLAW

12 cups shredded cabbage
 6 cups coarse shredded carrots
1 1/8 cups lemon juice
1 cup diced canned pimento
3/4 cup minced parsley
6 tbsp. minced onion

6 tsp. salt
2½ cups light cream, top milk
  or evaporated milk
6 tbsp. catsup
3 tbsp. prepared mustard
1/4 cup vinegar

Sprinkle pepper and paprika to taste. Add a dash of cayenne.

Combine cabbage, carrots, lemon juice and toss well. Add pimento, parsley, onion and salt. Combine remaining ingredients and blend. Pour over slaw and toss lightly.

CARROT SALADS

(Mix with mayonnaise and salt to taste)

1. Chopped carrots, chopped celery.
2. Shredded carrot; diced, unpeeled apple, diced pineapple. Sprinkle with coconut.
3. Shredded carrot; diced, unpeeled apple, raisins, (soaked in hot water 20 min.)
4. Shredded carrot, raisins (soaked in hot water 20 min.) drained crushed pineapple.
5. Shredded carrot, diced pineapple, seedless green grapes, halved.
6. Chopped carrot, chopped cabbage, diced unpeeled apple, diced pineapple.
7. Chopped carrots and raisins, mayonnaise.
8. Shredded large or small carrots with raisins and mayonnaise.
9. Shredded carrots, pineapple and mayonnaise.
10. Shredded carrots, apples, dates and marshmallows. Mayonnaise.
11. Carrots, pineapple and marshmallows. Mayonnaise.
12. Carrots and dates. Mayonnaise.

TURNIP AND CARROT SLAW

3 C. shredded turnips
1½ C. shredded carrots

Mix with:

1/4 C. sour cream
1/4 C. mayonnaise
1/4 Tsp. prepared mustard
   Salt and pepper. Garnish with pickle slices.

---

2   C. cooked carrots, sliced
2/3 C. cooked beets, sliced
2/3 C. green onions, sliced
2/3 C. Cooked peas
   Salt, pepper, French dressing and mayonnaise mixed.

Sliced carrots, radishes, green onions, green pepper, celery and tomatoes. French dressing.

Chapter I   Page 7

CARROT SALADS (CONT'D.)

2/3 C. grated carrots
2/3 C. grated cabbage
2/3 C. chopped celery
1/2 C. cucumber
1/2 Bunch radishes
   Mix with Thousand Island Dressing

CAULIFLOWER VARIATIONS

1. Cauliflower, sliced radishes, celery, green onions, sweet pickles, bell peppers, mayonnaise.

2. Cauliflower, onions, celery, pimentoes, bell pepper, dill pickles, tomatoes, mayonnaise, salt and pepper.

3. Cauliflower, onions, celery, pimentoes, sweet pickles, American cheese, mayonnaise, salt and pepper.

STUFFED CELERY VARIATIONS

1. Celery sticks, cream cheese and pecans.

2. Celery, cream cheese with pineapple.

3. Celery, cream cheese, horseradish.

4. Celery, American cheese, pimentos.

5. Celery, American cheese, sweet relish.

STUFFED CELERY

Soften one 3 oz. package of cream cheese and mix with it 1/4 cup drained Dole "Crisp Cut" crushed pineapple and 1 tsp. horseradish. Stuff crisp green celery.

STUFFED CELERY

Cream well together:
1/2 lb. grated American cheese
1/2 cup chopped sweet pickle
1/4 cup chopped pimento

Use a little pickle and pimento juice to soften cheese for mixing. This will mix easier if allowed to reach room temperature.
Stuff celery hearts and arrange on large garnished plate.

Chapter I   Page 8

CORN SALAD

1 gal. No. 10 can - whole kernel yellow corn, drained; chopped green pepper, chopped pimento, diced tomato (1/3 the amount of corn) diced celery - same amount as tomatoes.

CORN SALAD

Corn drained, green peppers (chopped) pimento, tomato diced.

CUCUMBER VARIATIONS

1. Cucumbers, salt, pepper, vinegar, oil, tomatoes, bell pepper and onions.

2. Cucumbers, tomatoes, green onions, vinegar dressing. Carrots may be added sometimes for color.

3. You may use any of the following with cucumbers: onion rings, bell pepper rings, sliced carrots, sliced radishes, sliced celery.

    Use vinegar and oil.

GREEN SALAD VARIATIONS

(Serve without any dressing unless stated)

1. Lettuce, coarsely chopped, chopped celery, diced tomatoes, very thinly sliced, radishes and carrots, chopped endive, finely chopped onions.

2. Lettuce, coarsely chopped, diced tomato, sliced hard boiled egg, chopped spinach. Toss lightly with a little mayonnaise.

3. Lettuce, coarsely chopped, very thin sliced radishes and carrots, green pepper rings, cut thin and broken, diced tomatoes. Fill bowl about half full of lettuce. Cover with layer of diced tomatoes, sliced carrots and radishes, and few broken pepper rings. Fill bowl with more lettuce and cover top with more tomatoes, radishes, carrots and pepper rings.
   This may be varied by mixing chopped endive with lettuce.

4. Follow same recipe as above except use Romaine lettuce for half of lettuce.

5. Spinach: Coarsely cut fresh spinach. Add very thin sliced onion rings. Salt. Toss lightly with vinegar oil dressing.

6. Mixed green: Coarsely cut lettuce, Romaine lettuce, endive, fresh spinach. Toss lightly with garlic oil dressing.

GREEN SALAD VARIATIONS (CONT'D)

7. Wop Salad: Fill Casite bowls full of combination salad (No. 1). on top of each bowl of salad arrange 1 slice hard boiled egg, 1 ripe olive, 1 slice tomato, 1 Italian pepper and 1 anchovy.

8. Arrange on large plate or in bowl: celery hearts, carrot sticks, green pepper rings, fresh green onions, whole radishes, sliced cucumber rings. Place ice flakes over top to keep crisp.

WOP SALAD

Lettuce, tomato, celery, sliced carrots, sliced radishes, onions, endive. Put in wooden bowls. Serve with 1 slice of hard boiled egg, one olive, 1/2 slice tomato, Mexican pepper. Anchovy.

LETTUCE VARIATIONS

1. Lettuce, tomatoes, shredded American cheese, mayonnaise.

2. Leaf lettuce in layers with tomatoes and cream cheese. Top with French dressing.

3. Leaf lettuce, boiled eggs, vinegar, sugar, oil, drained bacon pieces.

4. Lettuce, eggs, tomato wedges, sliced carrots, green onions, sliced celery, bacon pieces and mayonnaise.

5. Lettuce, tomatoes, eggs, onions, Roquefort or French dressing.

ROMAINE LETTUCE VARIATIONS

1. Romaine, garlic oil and vinegar. Top with croutons or toasted cubed bread with garlic salt.

2. Romaine, endive, cucumbers with French dressing.

3. Romaine, small amount shredded carrots, green onions.

SPINACH VARIATIONS

1. Spinach, lettuce, tomatoes, garlic dressing.

2. Spinach, lettuce, onion rings, eggs, mayonnaise.

3. Spinach, lettuce, tomatoes, eggs and Roquefort dressing.

Chapter I

SPINACH VARIATIONS (CONT'D)

4. Spinach, small amount shredded cabbage, sliced radishes, sliced celery. Mix with small amount French dressing and a small amount of horseradish.

5. Spinach, Romaine, tomatoes, vinegar, oil and salt.

6. Spinach, Romaine, celery tops, purple cabbage and leaf lettuce. Any dressing desired.

7. Spinach, Romaine, lettuce, endive. Celery seed dressing.

8. Spinach, lettuce, tomatoes, avocado with garlic dressing.

COMBINATION SALAD

Chopped lettuce, tomatoes, carrots, green peppers, radishes and red cabbage for color.

MUSTARD GREEN SALAD

Wash and pick curly leaf mustard greens. Chop coarse. Add small onion rings and sprinkle with vinegar - oil dressing and Evangeline hot sauce. (1 tsp. hot sauce to a 10 oz. ice-tea glass.)

HOMINY SALAD VARIATIONS

1. Hominy, bell pepper, onions, dill pickles, celery, pimentos, tomatoes, mayonnaise, salt & pepper.

2. Hominy, diced American Cheese, bell peppers, green onions, pimentos. 1 tablespoon Roquefort dressing, mayonnaise, salt and pepper.

HOMINY SALAD

1 gallon yellow hominy
4 pkgs. Fordhook limas
1 head cauliflower chopped coarse
  Celery, diced
  Tomatoes, diced (just enough for color)
  Salt. Mix with Roquefort cheese dressing.

As a change - cheese diced, onion, pimento, dill pickle, Roquefort cheese and mayonnaise.

Chapter I   Page 11

MIXED VEGETABLES

Tomatoes, bell pepper, sliced large onions, vinegar, salt and pepper.

1½ C canned lima bean	1½ C kidney beans
1½ C cooked, diced carrots	1½ C green beans
1½ C diced celery	1½ C sliced green onions
1½ C. English peas	3 chopped pimentos

Thousand Island or mayonnaise

Lima beans, hominy, green beans, peas, tomatoes, celery, dill pickles, onions and pimento. Mayonnaise.

Put in layers green beans, peas, lettuce hearts, cut up beets. Top with sliced eggs and French Roquefort dressing.

MIXED VEGETABLE SALAD

Cooked lima beans, canned English peas, canned green beans, cooked diced carrots, diced lettuce hearts, chopped celery, chopped green pepper, diced tomatoes.

Mix and fill salad bowl. Lay sliced eggs over top - completely covering vegetables. Then pour a fairly thick layer of Roquefort Cheese dressing completely over entire salad.

PEA SALAD VARIATIONS

1. English peas - No. 10 can - drained; chopped celery, diced tomatoes.

2. English peas - No. 10 can - drained; chopped celery, diced tomatoes, asparagus tips.

3. English peas - No. 10 can - drained; whole kernel yellow corn, drained; chopped celery, chopped pimento, kidney beans, washed and drained, lima beans, washed and drained, onion - minced, to taste.

4. English peas - No. 10 can - drained; diced cooked carrots, chopped celery.

MEXICAN COTTAGE CHEESE

INGREDIENTS	LBS	OZS	METHOD
Green onions (1 med. bunch)			Chop green onions, olives &
Dill pickles (2)			pickles fine, but not too fine.
Sutffed Olives		4	
Cottage Cheese	5		Mix the above with cottage
Mayonnaise		8	cheese and mayonnaise.

Note: Amount of mayonaise may be varied according to the dryness of the cottage cheese.

Serve in display bowl garnished with slices of dill pickles.

POTATO SALAD

Ingredients	LBS	OZS	Method
Boiled, diced potatoes	10		Mix all ingredients together
Diced celery	2		varying mayonaise if necessary.
Chopped hard boiled eggs	1		
Salt		2	
Dash of white pepper			
Sweet pickle relish	2		
Chopped pimentoes		3	
Finely chopped onions	1		
Prepared mustard		4	
Mayonaise	3		

Portion weight: 4 ozs.

NOTE: For hot potato salad, mash potatoes instead of dicing.

HOT POTATO SALAD

2 Onions, chopped
2 Peppers, chopped
2 Sq. potaotes
2 Cookspoons Mustard
3 Hard boiled eggs
1/2 cup Pimento
3 Cookspoons salad dressing
3 Pickles, ground

Mix thoroughly.

August 8, 1966

HOT POTATO SALAD

(For Polish Sausage)

VERNON SCHRADER

```
9# potatoes (use R.O. hash brown and few R.O. mashed potatoes)
1  bunch green onions, top and bottom
10 tomatoes, small dice
1# chopped bacon (use grease also)
1/3 pick up pot mayonnaise
2  cookspoon mustard (prepared)
2  cups chopped dill pickles, use some pickle juice
Salt, pepper, accent
```

Mix all wet ingredients together for a better mix.

Heat up only 1/2 bean pan at a time. CAUTION: Do not overheat - mayonnaise will separate.

August 8, 1966

ITALIAN POTATO SALAD

BILL PARSONS
PORT ARTHUR

"B" size new potatoes	Salt
Tomatoes	Black pepper
Green onions	Vinegar
Lettuce	Oil
radishes	Garlic Powder

Cook potatoes evening before (with jackets on). Peel after done (but firm) and chill whole. Next morning, dice new potatoes, and add diced tomatoes, chopped green onions, medium chopped lettuce and sliced radishes. Season with salt, black pepper, vinegar, oil and garlic powder.

CALICO BEAN SALAD

1 - #10 Can Cut Green beans
3/4 - #10 can whole kernel corn   Drain. Add 1 cup chopped onion
1- #10 can cooked sliced carrots

Dressing:

2-1/2 cup brown sugar
1-2/3 c. vinegar
5 tbsp salt (1/3 c)   Shake in jar until sugar dissolve
1/4 c celery seed
1 tsp pepper   Marinate, covered overnight

SWEET PICKLES

Chop 4 gallons sour pickles and wash thoroughly in cold water. Press out liquid. Mix 12 cups sugar, 6 cups vinegar, 4 cups water. One double hand mixed spices (tied in bag). Boil well. Pour over pickles.

RELISH PLATE OR BOWL

Celery hearts, carrot sticks, pepper rings, green onions, radishes, sliced cucumbers. Arrange on garnished plate and put chipped ice over vegetables.

TOMATO SALAD VARIATIONS

1. Tomatoes diced with equal amount of diced celery, mayonnaise.

2. Tomatoes stuffed with cottage cheese, ham salad or tuna salad.

TOMATO ASPIC

(18 molds)

2 bay leaves
Few drops tobasco sauce
5 tb. finely chopped onion
1 tsp. salt
7 1/2 cups tomato juice
4 tb. gelatin
1 1/3 cups cold water
4 tb. vinegar

Combine bay leaves, tobasco sauce, onion, salt and tomato juice. Simmer 10 min. Soften gelatin in cold water. Dissolve in juice mixture. Add vinegar. Strain and jell.

TURNIP SALAD

Peel and chop raw turnips. Add equal parts chopped cabbage and carrots. Mix with mayonnaise. Sprinkle with nut meats.

MACARONI SALAD VARIATIONS

1. Macaroni, celery, onions, bell peppers, dill pickles, pimentos, mayonnaise, tomatoes, salt & pepper.

2. Macaroni, diced American cheese and green onions.

SHELLRONI SALAD WITH VEGETABLES

2 Cups cooked shellroni washed and drained.
2 No. 2 cans English peas - drained.
Diced American cheese, celery - chopped.
Chopped sweet pickle, chopped pimento.
Minced onion to taste. Mix with mayonnaise.

As a change, omit English peas, and add dill pickle.

CHICKEN OR HAM SALAD

Chicken, celery, onions, pimentos, sweet pickles, olives, apples mayonnaise.

CHICKEN SALAD

1 large chicken cut
12 boiled eggs cut
Diced celery, sliced stuffed olives, salt to taste. Mayonnaise.

MEAT SALAD

1 Pt. apples
2½ quarts cubed meat
1 3/4 quarts diced celery

1 pt. shredded carrots
1 C. green pepper
1 quart peas

Mix with mayonnaise.

FRANK SALAD

3 C. Potatoes
8 T. Celery
Salt, pepper, mayonnaise

1 1/3 C. sliced radishes
1 lb. cooked Franks (sliced)

Chapter I

August 16, 1965

CHICKEN SALAD

MRS. HULDA REID
LUBY'S BROADWAY
CAFETERIA

½ amount chicken
¼ amount celery
¼ amount grapes

Chicken torn into pieces 1 inch to 1½ inch long
Celery hearts sliced thin (no tops)
Sweet pickle cut the size of match stick and 1 inch long
Pimento chopped
Green seedless grapes whole, or Red grapes half and seeds out
Lowery salt and black pepper to taste
Toasted slivered Almonds
Mayonnaise to moisten (not wet)

To a level bean pan full use 1 cup pickle, ½ cup pimento and 1 cup almonds (toasted).

Do not use left over fried chicken. Left over broiled chicken OK when mixed with boiled chicken.

May 24, 1966

CHICKEN SALAD OR CASSEROLE

MALCOLM McKAY

4 - 10½ oz. cans Campbells Condensed Cream of Chicken Soup
2½# cut chicken or turkey
1 cup chopped onion
8 cups cooked rice
6 cups mayonnaise
3 cups shredded almonds (toasted slightly)
5 hard boiled eggs (diced)
8 cups diced celery (small)
3 cups pimento (diced and drained well)

Serve as salad on garnished plate. May also be served as a hot dish. Cook 35 minutes at 350°. Top with bread crumbs.

Chapter I   Page 15a

EGG SALAD

Slice and cut eggs, celery, pimento, sweet pickle, mayonnaise. As a change, use green onion, dill pickle, black pepper.

DEVILED EGGS

3 Doz. eggs - hard boiled and sliced in halves
1/2 cup chopped sweet pickles
1/4 cup chopped pimento
1 cup vinegar-oil dressing
Little vinegar for tart taste

Mash egg yolks. Add vinegar-oil dressing, pickles, pimento and vinegar. Stuff egg whites with above mixture. Arrange egg halves on large garnished plate. Sprinkle tops of eggs with little paprika. (Taste for tangy-tart taste).

EGG AND OLIVE SALAD

Eggs sliced and cut
Sliced stuffed olives, celery, mayonnaise.

WHOLE BOILED EGGS

Place peeled hard-boiled eggs in large garnished bowl and insert tooth picks in eggs. On exposed part of toothpicks, stick a stuffed olive or a piece of pimento. Serve in garnished bowl at counter. Boil eggs 15-20 min. Remove from stove and cover immediately with cold water and peel. This helps to prevent dark rings from forming around yolks.

FISH SALAD VARIATIONS

1. **Salmon:**
   Drain, bone and crumble salmon. Add 4 hard boiled eggs, diced, to each can of salmon used.
   Add lots of chopped celery, chopped sweet pickle. If more color is desired, sprinkle with little paprika before mixing with mayonnaise. Add salt to taste. Garnish top with grated egg yolk and little paprika.

FISH SALAD VARIATIONS (CONT'D)

2. Tuna:
   Flake tuna, add 3 hard boiled eggs, diced, to each 3 oz. can of tuna. Add chopped celery, chopped sweet pickle. Salt to taste. Mix with mayonnaise. Garnish top with grated egg yolk or olive slices. Lettuce hearts - chopped or shredded, may be added.

3. Tuna Fish - Fritos:
   3 cans Tuna, flaked
   9 hard boiled eggs, diced
   4 1/2 cups crushed Fritos
   1 cup chopped sweet pickles
   1 med. chopped green pepper
   1 med. onion, finely chopped
   3 cups chopped celery
   1/2 tsp. black pepper
   Salt to taste
   Mix with mayonnaise.

4. Shrimp Salad:
   Cook and clean shrimp. Cut in small pieces. Add chopped celery hard boiled eggs, salt to taste. Mix with mayonnaise.

5. Shrimp Cocktail:
   Half fill sherbet dishes with shredded lettuce. Stand a portion of lettuce leaf at one side of dish. Arrange shrimp on lettuce and garnish with 1/2 lemon slice.

6. Oyster Cocktail:
   Put 1 tb. cocktail sauce in vegetable bowl and lay 3 oysters in sauce. Arrange groups of these on counter.

7. Salmon, celery, pimentos, green onions, sweet relish, eggs, mayonnaise.

8. Shrimp, eggs, olives, celery, onions, pimentos, bell pepper, dill pickles, mayonnaise, salt & pepper.

9. Herring with onion rings, sour cream, black pepper.

10. Herring, potatoes, onions, sour cream, salt & pepper, beets, sour pickles.

11. Dutch salmon, sour pickles, onions, eggs, potatoes, mayonnaise, vinegar, salt & pepper.

12. Crab meat, sliced celery, sweet pickles, green onions, pimentos, apples, mayonnaise.

TUNA AND SHELLRONI

One 2 lb. can tuna
1 qt. cooked shellroni
1 cup finely chopped stuffed olives

1 cup finely chopped pineapple
Handful chopped onion to taste
Salt to taste

Mix with mayonnaise.

Chapter I   Page 17

June 21, 1966

SHRIMP SALAD

EL PASO #2
ABIGAIL (ROSA) DELGADILLO

3 boxes R. F. Skroodles (cooked)
1 #10 can cut green beans (drained)
5# shrimp pieces (cooked)
1 bunch of celery (chopped medium)
3 green onions (sliced thin)
1/2 cup of pimentos (chopped)
Salt and pepper to taste

Mix with Tartar Sauce or mayonnaise.

August 8, 1966

GREEN GODDESS DRESSING

HULDA REID

4 cups sour cream
2 cups mayonnaise
3 cups salad oil
1 cup wine vinegar
1 cup sugar
1/4 cup prepared mustard
1/2 cup lemon juice
1 1/2 teaspoon garlic powder
4 teaspoon fine grated onion
1/4 cup salt
2 tablespoon minced anchovies
2 tablespoons salad herbs (crushed)
2 or 3 drops green coloring.

Blend salad oil and sour cream till smooth. Then add mayonnaise.
Stir till well blended. Add other ingredients and blend.

Chapter I   Page 17a

COTTAGE CHEESE VARIATIONS

Mix these with mayonnaise

1. Dry cottage cheese and chopped carrots. Salt to taste. Mix well.

2. Dry cottage cheese, chopped carrots, green pepper, chopped, and chopped pimento. Salt to taste.

3. Dry cottage cheese. Add chopped celery, chopped carrots, little minced onion, chopped green pepper, chopped sweet pickles.

4. Cream cottage cheese. Little salt, few chopped cooked prunes and cover top with chopped nut meats.

5. Dry, creamed cottage cheese. Diced fresh tomatoes, chopped green pepper and minced onion (use fresh onions - white part only) to taste. Little salt. Garnish top with pimento strips and sliced olives.

6. Dry cottage cheese and drained fruit cocktail.

7. Cottage cheese, diced pineapple and chopped marshmallows. Soak marshmallows in pineapple juice until soft and mix. Garnish with chopped nuts.

8. Cottage cheese with sliced, stuffed olives and garnish with pecans.

9. Cottage cheese, chopped carrots, chopped pepper, chopped celery and little fine chopped onion.

10. Cottage cheese, chopped celery, chopped carrots, chopped pimento, sweet pickle relish.

11. Cottage cheese, chopped chives, few caraway seed, mixed together. Sprinkle few caraway seed on top.

12. 5 lb. cottage cheese, drained. 1 1/2 cups coarsely grated American cheese. 1 cup thin sliced stuffed olives. Salt cottage cheese to taste. Mix with American cheese and olives and little mayonnaise.

13. Cottage cheese, green onions, bell peppers, salt, pepper, mayonnaise.

14. Cottage cheese, onions, olives (2 kinds), mayonnaise, salt & pepper.

15. Cottage cheese, onions, sour cream, salt & pepper.

16. Cottage cheese, raisins, chopped celery, shredded carrots, salt.

17. Cottage cheese, apples and celery.

COTTAGE CHEESE VARIATIONS (CONT'D)

18. Cheese and green seedless grapes
19. Cottage cheese, chives, salt & pepper, mayonnaise.

COTTAGE CHEESE

Mix cottage cheese with mayonnaise, salt and black pepper. Add green pepper, tomato pieces and carrots - grated large on hand grater. Toss lightly. Garnish with green peppers, carrots

---

SPECIAL SALADS

TOMATO SALAD WITH CREAM CHEESE DRESSING:
Place tomato slice on lettuce leaf. Garnish with cream cheese dressing made as follows: Mix: Cream cheese and mayonnaise. Garnish with chopped chives or chopped parsley.

COTTAGE CHEESE SPECIAL

1. Cottage cheese centers. Slices of oranges and honey-dew melon balls arranged alternately around cheese. Cherry - top of cheese.

2. Cottage cheese centers. Slices of apple and cantaloupe balls arranged alternately around cheese. Garnish cheese with stuffed olives.

On Garnished Plate:

1. Pineapple ring with cottage cheese ball in center. For cottage cheese balls: cream cottage cheese with little mayonnaise and salt. Add few chopped marachino cherries and shape into small balls. Roll balls in cocoanut.

2. Pineapple ring. Spread little whipped cream over pineapple ring, then sprinkle grated cheese over this. Slice cherries on top.

3. Peach half with cottage cheese ball. (See No. 1.)

4. Pear half with cottage cheese ball. (See No. 1.)

5. Apricot half with cottage cheese ball. (See No. 1.)

6. Pear half with fruit topping. Cover with grated cheese.

SPECIAL SALADS (CONT'D)

7. Pear or peach halves or pineapple rings may be served with following dressing: Fruit topping mixed with grated American cheese, finely chopped celery, chopped pecans.

8. <u>Cranberry Salad:</u>
   1 qt. cranberry sauce, cooked and cooled (jelled)
   3 or 4 apples - diced fine
   3 cups celery hearts, diced fine
   8-10 English walnuts - coarsely borken. Mix above ingredients. Serve on garnished plate with orange slices and little whipped cream or mayonnaise.

9. <u>Tomatoes - stuffed with fish salad:</u> (Good way to use run-out) Stick fork in tomato. Hold over flame a few seconds. Skins will then slip off. Cut tomato in equal sections down to bottom but not all the way through. Spread apart and fill with fish salad. Serve on lettuce leaf and garnish with hard boiled egg slice.

10. Prune halves stuffed with cottage cheese (cream cottage cheese with very little mayonnaise, salt and little fruit juice.)

11. Pineapple ring with banana stick in center (cut banana pieces about 1 inch long). Put a dab of mayonnaise on banana tip and garnish with a cherry or chopped pecans.

Chapter I
Page 20

CAULIFLOWER SALAD
EL PASO #1

Combine: 1 cup salad oil, ½ cup Heinz tarragon vinegar, 2 tsp. sugar, 1 tsp. salt, ½ tsp. paprika in a jar. Shake well.

Combine: 1 small head cauliflower, separated in flowerlets; ½ large onion, thinly sliced and separated into rings; 1/3 cup slice olives.

Marinate in dressing 1 to 1½ hours. Immediately before serving, add 1 cup crumbled blue cheese and 1 small head lettuce, shredded fine. Then toss well.

GREEN SALAD WITH CROUTONS

2 cups croutons
Tear 2 heads Romaine lettuce into bowl. Sprinkle with
    1/4 tsp. dry mustard
    1/4 tsp. black pepper
    1/2 tsp. salt
    1/2 cup Parmesan cheese

Add 6 tablespoons olive oil and juice of 2 lemons. Break 2 eggs on the greens and toss to mix thoroughly until no trace of egg is seen. Do not bruise greens. Add croutons just before Serving. A dash of Worcestershire sauce may also be added if desired, and extra cheese may be shaken on salad after it is placed in individual bowls.

CAULIFLOWER SALAD
August 8, 1966

HELEN BLODGETT

Separate cauliflower into flowerlets, bite size.
To 1 large or 2 small heads add
2 diced tomatoes
1/2 cup green onion with tops
1/2 cup diced bell pepper
1/2 cup sliced stuffed olives
1/2 cup diced radishes
1/2 cup diced celery
1 cup diced cheddar cheese

DRESSING:

Mix 1/4 cup sugar
1/2 teaspoon white pepper
1 cup mayonnaise
1/3 cup horseradish

Pour over vegetables and toss. Garnish with radish roses or olives.

Chapter I   Page 21

FRUIT SALAD COMBINATIONS

(Served with fruit juice or whipped cream-mayonnaise topping)

1. Diced pineapple and pear. Equal parts. Sprinkle topping with grated cheese.

2. Diced pineapple, apple (peeled banana and diced cheese.)

3. Diced pineapple, peach, marshmallows and sliced bananas.

4. Fruit cocktail, drained. Add diced apples (peeled) fresh green grapes, sliced bananas. Save cherries out of fruit cocktail and slice over topping for color.

5. Diced pineapple, apple (peeled), apricot, sliced bananas. Either slice cherries over topping or sprinkle cocoanut over topping.

6. Diced pineapple, oranges, bananas and dates. Slice cherries over topping.

7. Diced pineapple and marshmallows. Slice cherries over topping.

8. Diced apple, unpeeled, diced oranges, diced pineapple. Mix with cocoanut.

9. Apple, chopped pineapple, cocoanut and chopped celery. Fold in whipped cream topping and garnish with pecans.

10. Fruit cocktail, drained, diced oranges, diced marshmallows, sliced bananas. Fruit topping garnished with cherry slices and pecans.

11. Crushed pineapple, chopped dates, chopped pecans. Mix with few drops almond extract. Top with whipped cream dressing and sprinkle colored candy pepper over top, or chopped pecans.

12. Fresh pineapple, diced, small amount of fruit cocktail. (Soak pineapple in little sugar few minutes before mixing with fruit). Cover in juice from fruit cocktail.

13. Diced peaches and pineapple and green grapes with cream cheese dressing.

FRUIT COMPOTE

Fruit cocktail, diced apples, grapes, sliced bananas and sliced cherries.

Chapter I

FRESH FRUIT COMPOTE

Make syrup of equal parts of sugar and water and cover this fresh fruit: (Blackberries may be omitted)
Fresh: Peaches, cut in medium size pieces, diced pineapple, strawberries, raspberries, blackberries, sliced bananas.

FRESH FRUIT SALAD (COMPOTE)

Green grapes
Tokay grapes
Fresh pears (in winter, fresh apples)
Fresh peaches
Fresh apricots
Fresh strawberries
Bananas
Fresh pineapple

FRUIT SALAD

(Drain all fruit well)
2 lb. 8 oz. cubed pineapple
1 lb. 8 oz. seeded Royal Anne cherries
5 lb. 8 oz. peaches, cubed
2 lb. pears, cubed

AMBROSIA

Diced oranges, pineapple in juices of pineapple and oranges. Cocoanut over top.

APPLE-CELERY VARIATIONS

1 pt. mayonnaise
1/2 cup whipped cream (opt. 8 oz. cut marshmallows added to dressing)

1. 8 lb. diced apples. Add each apple to dressing as soon as diced.
    1 lb. chopped celery
    1 oz. salt
    6 oz. sugar (may omit)

2. 3 lb. diced apples
    3 lb. cubed pineapple
    2 lb. cubed oranges

3. Same as No. 1 plus 8 oz. chopped walnuts just before serving.

Chapter I   Page 23

APPLE - VARIATIONS

1. Diced apples, cut dates, and marshmallows. Mayonnaise.

2. Diced apples, celery, carrots and mayonnaise.

3. Apples, celery, green pepper and pimento. Mayonnaise.

4. Apples, peaches and pears - plain.

    Add pineapple juice or lemon juice to prevent apples from turning dark.

5. Apples, oranges, celery. Mayonnaise.

BAKED APPLES

Make a syrup of one part sugar and two parts water. Bring to a boil in a heavy sauce pan. Core and wash apples, drop in syrup and cook from 15 to 20 minutes, or until done. If apples are not red, a few drops of coloring may be added to syrup.

WHOLE COOKED FRESH APPLES (BAKED APPLES)

Core 8 red apples and drop in following mixture and cook until they crack, or, are tender:

6 Cups sugar
5 Cups water
1/2 Cup red-hots
Apples must be continually watched and turned while cooking.

APPLE SALAD

8 medium apples, peeled and diced
2 handfuls diced celery
2 cups seeded white or pink grapes
Mix with mayonnaise

APRICOT VARIATIONS

1. Apricot halves - plain

2. Apricots, diced mixed fruit

CREAMY CRANBERRY RELISH SALAD

1 pkg. orange flavored gelatin
1/2 cup sugar
1 cup boiling water
1 cup evaporated milk
2 cups (1/2 lb.) raw cranberries
1 small or medium-size orange
1/2 cup chopped pecans

Add boiling water to gelatin and sugar in bowl. Stir until gelatin and sugar are completely dissolved. When gelatin mixture is cold, stir in milk. Wash and dry orange. Cut into quarters, leaving rind on; remove any seeds. Put orange through food chopper, using medium blade. Put washed and drained cranberries through food chopper.

When gelatin mixture is the consistency of unbeaten egg white, add ground orange and cranberries with juices together with pecans. Stir to blend well. Spoon into orange shells, or into individual one-half cup molds, or into a one quart mold. Chill in refrigerator until set, about three to four hours.
Makes eight servings.

MANDAVIN DELIGHT

JOHN A. LEE, JR.

1 No. 10 can Pineapple chunks
2 No. 2½ can Mandavin Oranges
2 Large handfulls of Cocoanut
1 Bag Miniature Marshmallows
2 lbs. Sour Cream Dressing

(Suggested price .30¢)

BANANA VARIATIONS

2 Bananas
2 C. Strawberries
2 Tbsps. Cherry Syrup
1 C. Diced Pineapple

---

1. Bananas, grapes, pineapple, marshmallow, whipped cream and mayonnaise.

2. Cubed bananas, tangerines, pineapple, whipped cream and mayonnaise. Paprika garnish.

3. Cut banana in thirds and lengthwise. Roll in thin boiled dressing (or honey thinned with pineapple juice.) Roll in chopped nuts or corn flakes. Arrange with slices of tangerine.

CANTALOUPE VARIATIONS

1. Cantaloupe, bananas and pineapple. <u>Plain</u>. May be varied with grapes, peaches, pears, strawberries.

2. Cantaloupe sliced, diced, or halves.

3. Cantaloupe and melon, diced.

BING CHERRY SALAD

1 lb. 8 oz. lemon jello
1 qt. boiling H_2O
<u>Cool</u>

Add:
3 1/2 qt. H_2O and cherry juice
2 drops red coloring
<u>Chill</u>

When mixture begins to thicken, add:

2 No. 2 1/2 cans Bing Cherries, seeded and stuffed with nuts
12 oz. nuts
3 cups olives, stuffed, sliced
Pour into 50 molds or a 12 x 20 pan

GRAPES

1. Grapes on platter.

Chapter I

GRAPEFRUIT VARIATIONS

1. Grapefruit halves.

2. 1 C. grapefruit   Mix with: 1 pkg. (3 oz.) cream
   1 C. pineapple   cheese
   1 C. orange sections   1 Tbsp. liquid honey
   1 C. sliced banana   1 Tbsp. lemon juice
   ½ C. nuts   ½ C. whipping cream

PEACH VARIATIONS

1. Peach and pear.

2. Frozen peaches, apricots, pineapple chunks, strawberries and bananas. You can also use these canned or fresh.

3. Fresh peaches. Cover with sugar water to keep from turning black.

4. Peach half stuffed with American cheese, chopped celery, pecans. Mix with cream dressing.

PEAR

Diced pears, pineapple and apricots with whipped cream dressing.

PINEAPPLES VARIATIONS

1. Mixed diced pineapple, marshmallow, white grapes, nuts. Whipped cream dressing.

2. Diced pineapple, celery, white grapes. Whipped cream dressing.

3. Sliced pineapple. Arrange strips of dates, radiating from center, on pineapple. Mayonnaise in center and nuts.

4. Roll edge of pineapple ring in paprika. Fill center with cream cheese mixed with minced green pepper.

5. Cut pineapple ring in half and place in upright position on lettuce leaf. Place 3 long pieces of Cheddar cheese through notch at bottom of pineapple.

PINEAPPLE DATE SALAD

Crushed pineapple
Chopped dates
Chopped nuts
Almond extract

Cover top with whipped cream dressing. Sprinkle cream with colored candy pepper.

PINEAPPLE GRAPEFRUIT SALAD

Pineapple ring
Grapefruit sections placed on top. Fill center with Ph. cream cheese and top with cherry slice. Serve on lettuce leaf.

PRUNE VARIATIONS

1. Plain stewed.

2. Stuffed with cream cheese and pecans
   or with cottage cheese
   or with American cheese

3. Prunes mixed with other dried fruit.

RAISINS

1. Stewed

RAISIN CHEESE SALAD

2 lbs. raisins - soaked in hot water 20 minutes
Drain and add:
Thin slices of cheese - diced
Chopped celery
Mix with mayonnaise

TANGERINES OR ORANGE VARIATIONS

1. Oranges and cocoanut

2. Oranges and grapes

3. Oranges and grapefruit (fresh or frozen)

    Fresh with or without cream cheese dressing

4. Tangerine sections, cut and seeded. Use them as you do oranges.

5. Thin sliced oranges, chopped cranberries (raw). Sugar to taste.

WALDORF SALAD

Mix with mayonnaise.

1. Diced apples (unpeeled if red and peelings are not tough and bitter) chopped celery, chopped pecans.

2. Diced apples (peeled) chopped celery, green grapes.

3. Diced apples (unpeeled, if nice), chopped celery, raisins. Be sure and soak raisins for at least 20 min. in hot water before mixing with salad.

4. Diced apple, Tokay grapes, white seedless grapes, fresh pineapple and juice, diced marshmallows and nut meats.
   No mayonnaise.

COOKED FRUITS

COOKED RHUBARB:
Wash and cut in medium small pieces. Put in sauce pan with <u>very little water</u> and sugar to sweeten. Cook until rhubarb is tender, stirring frequently. Add a few drops of red coloring. Mix evenly and chill.

COOKED DRIED APPLES:
Cook and remove all peel and core from 4 lbs. dried apples. Soak in water 1½ hrs. Cover with water and add about 2 cups sugar and 2/3 cups red-hots. Cook until tender but not mushy. Cool and serve.

COOKED DRIED PEACHES:
Soak overnight and slip skins off. Add sugar and water and cook till tender. If peaches are dark, add lemon juice while cooking.

Chapter I

COOKED FRUITS (CONT'D)

COOKED DRIED FRUITS:

Soak all dried fruits overnight.
In figs, use lemon slices only.
In prunes, use lemon and orange slices.
Do not use either on peaches and apricots.

COOKED DRIED STEWED PRUNES:

Wash and soak prunes overnight. Cook in the same water with little sugar, orange and lemon slices.

JELLO WITH FRUIT

LEMON:

1. Chopped cabbage, crushed pineapple, green pepper halves.

2. Chopped cabbage, unpeeled apples, diced, crushed pineapple, raisins. Raisins may be substituted with pimento.

3. Chopped cooked prunes, chopped pecans.

4. Diced pineapple, pimento. Unmold and cover top with mayonnaise and sprinkle with grated cheese.

STRAWBERRY:

1. Fruit cocktail, drained, sliced bananas, diced apples.

2. Diced pineapple, diced peaches and sliced bananas.

3. Strips of unpeeled apples, chopped celery and chopped pecans.

4. Diced pineapple, diced orange, sliced bananas.

5. Pear halves or peach halves and sliced red cherries.

6. Bananas - sliced lengthwise and layed on bottom of pan. Cover with sliced peaches. Pour red Jello over this. Cut in order size squares.

7. Marshmallows, chopped, fruit cocktail and pecans.

CHERRY:

1. Shredded apples and nut meats (walnuts)

JELLO WITH FRUIT (CONT'D)

LIME:

1. Avocado pieces - dipped in lemon juice before using - sliced, stuffed olives, chopped pecans.

2. Apple strips, unpeeled, chopped celery, chopped pecans.

3. Diced pears, diced pineapple, red cherry slices.

4. Crushed pineapple, chopped pimento.

5. Diced pineapple, cottage cheese.

6. Diced pears, sliced red cherries, shredded cocoanut.

7. Diced pineapple, cottage cheese, and chopped pimento.

8. Cottage cheese, sliced red cherries.

ORANGE:

1. Diced oranges, sliced bananas, diced pineapple.

2. Diced pineapple, apricots - halved.

3. Fruit cocktail.

4. Diced oranges, sliced bananas, sliced cherries.

5. Chopped celery, grated carrots, pecans.

6. Diced peaches, pineapple and pear.

7. Whipped cream, shredded American cheese. Mold in large ring mold.

OTHER:

1. Layer red Jello, plain gelatin and cottage cheese - crushed pineapple in red Jello. Cut in squares.

2. Jello whipped and whipped cream added. Serve in a bowl.

3. Tomato aspic and cottage cheese.

Chapter I   Page 31

ROYAL FRUIT GELATIN - SELF LAYERING

FRUITS THAT FLOAT:

Apricots, fresh quartered
Apples, fresh diced or sliced
Bananas, sliced
Blueberries, canned, frozen, fresh
Cantaloupe cubed
Grapefruit section, fresh frozen
Honey dew melon, cubed
Orange sections, fresh
Peaches fresh, sliced
Pears, fresh, sliced
Plumbs, fresh, sliced
Raspberries, fresh
Strawberries, fresh, halved

FRUITS THAT SINK:

Apricots, canned, frozen
Cherries, Maraschino, canned
Cherries, Royal Anne, canned
Cherries, Bing, frozen
Fruit cocktail, canned
  (check individual fruits)
Grapefruit sections, canned
Grapes, canned, fresh, frozen
Orange sections, canned
Peaches, canned, frozen
Pears, canned
Plumbs, canned, frozen
Pineapple, canned, frozen*
Prunes, dried, cooked
Raisins, dried, seedless
Raspberries, canned, frozen

*Frozen pineapple must be cooked before adding to gelatine mixture.

FRUITS THAT MAY SINK AND/OR FLOAT:

Apples, frozen, cubed
Cherries, Red Sour, Frozen

Cherries, Bing, fresh, pitted
Strawberries, frozen

FROSTED LIME CONGEAL

1 can Lemon Jello 24 oz.
1 can Lime Jello 24 oz.
1 #10 can crushed pineapple
12 cups boiling water
3 tablespoons horseradish
6 cups homogenized milk
4 lbs. wet cottage cheese
2 cups chopped pecans
3 tablespoons onion juice
6 cups mayonnaise

Mix mayonnaise, milk and Jello together. Let thicken, then add other ingredients.

Either individual molds or cut in squares.

LIME JELLO CONGEAL SALAD

8 oz. Lime Jello
8 oz. Lemon Jello
6 cups hot water
6 tablespoons horseradish (moist)
1/2 can (No. 10) crushed pineapple

3 cups homogenized milk
1/2 box (4# box) cottage cheese
1 1/2 cups chopped pecans
3 teaspoons onion juice
3 cups mayonnaise

Either mold or cut in squares.

Chapter I   Page 32

Nov. 6, 1964

STRAWBERRY CONGEAL

GLORIA LEWANDOWSKI
CORPUS CHRISTI

2 packages strawberry jello
8 cups hot water
9 cups ice
4 cups mayonnaise
6 cups milk

Drain: 8 cups fruit cocktail
       4 lbs. cottage cheese

Add few cherries for color.

Nov. 6, 1964

SPINACH CONGEAL
(In Lemon Jello)

GLORIA LEWANDOWSKI
CORPUS CHRISTI

2 packages chopped spinach (fine)
8 cups cottage cheese

Dissolve 2 cans or packages with $\underline{12}$ cups of hot water. When dissolved, add 2 gallons ice. Stir occasionally until mixture is fairly thick. Fold in 2 cups mayonnaise, chopped spinach, cottage cheese and ½ cup lemon juice.

FRUIT CONGEAL

1 can cherry Jello (1 lb. 8 oz. can)
1 qt. cherry juice
1 qt. water
Mix cherry juice and water and bring to a boil. Pour over Jello and stir until completely dissolved. Add ten bottles of Coca-Cola. Let above mixture set until it starts to congeal, then add the following:
2 cups cherries, cut fine
1 cup pecans, cut in medium size pieces
2 packages marshmallow, cut in small pieces
Pour into molds and set until firm.

PINEAPPLE - AVOCADO SOUFFLE SALAD

1 Pkg. Lime gelatin
1 Cup hot water
½ Cup pineapple syrup (drained from crushed pineapple)
1 tablespoon vinegar or lemon juice
½ cup mayonnaise
¼ tsp. salt
1 1/2 cups drained Dole "Crisp cut" crushed pineapple.
1 large ripe avocado, cut in cubes (about 1 cup).

Dissolve gelatin in hot water. Add pineapple syrup, vinegar, mayonnaise and salt, and blend well with a rotary beater. Pour into tray and freeze for about 20 minutes or until firm about 1 inch from edge but soft in center. Turn mixture into a bowl and beat until fluffy with rotary beater. Fold in drained, crushed pineapple and avocado cubes. Pour into 1 qt. mold or individual molds. Chill until firm. Unmold on salad greens.

Makes 4 to 6 servings.

GRAPEFRUIT SURPRISE

Four teaspoons plain gelatin
1 No. 2 can unsweetened grapefruit juice
1/2 cup finely shredded carrot
1/4 cup sugar
1 cup fresh cottage cheese
1/8 teaspoon paprika
1/2 teaspoon salt and dash of pepper

Soften gelatin with 1/4 cup grapefruit juice. Heat 1 cup of remianing juice and sugar to boiling. Pour over gelatin and stir until dissolved. Add remaining juice. To half of mixture add the shredded carrot. Rinse 7 or 8 inch ring mold with cold water. Pour carrot mixture into bottom of mold and place in refrigerator until firm (about 1/2 hour). Chill remaining gelatin mixture until it begins to thicken. Season cottage cheese with salt, paprika and pepper. Mash with spoon until smooth. Add slightly thickened gelatin slowly, stirring until well blended. Pour over carrot mixture. Chill until firm.

Chapter I   Page 33

JELLO WITH VEGETABLES

LEMON:

1. Chopped cabbage and apples - or grated carrots, chopped celery, chopped pecans over top.

2. Grated carrots, apples - peeled and diced - crushed pineapple.

3. Grated carrots, green grape halves, crushed pineapple.

4. Chopped cabbage, grated carrots, chopped green pepper, chopped pimento, chopped celery.

LIME:

1. Hand grate carrots, bell peppers, chopped cabbage, celery (more cabbage than any of the others)

    To 2 cans Jello, add 1 sq. pan cabbage, 2 cups grated carrots, 3 cups fine chopped celery. Pepper to color.

ORANGE:

1. 1 c. jello. Pack full of fine shaved carrots, drained crushed pineapple, little mayonnaise. Small molds.

2. Coarse chopped carrots, crushed pineapple (apples, diced, instead of pineapple when apples aren't too tart).

TOMATO ASPIC - 18 Molds

2 bay leaves	7½ cups tomato juice
Few drops tobasco sauce	4 tbsp. gelatin
5 tbsp. finely chopped onions	1 1/3 cup cold water
1 tsp. salt	4 tbsp. vinegar

Combine bay leaf, tobasco, onion and salt to tomato juice. Simmer 10 minutes. Soften gelatin in cold water. Dissolve in juice mixture. Add vinegar and strain.

COLESLAW SALAD (JELLO)

1 Pkg. Lemon Jello
1 c. hot H_2O
1/2 c. mayonnaise
1/2 c. cold H_2O
2 tbs. vinegar
1/4 tsp. salt
1 1/2 c. finely shredded cabbage
1/2 c. sliced radishes
1/2 c. diced celery
2 - 4 tb. diced green pepper
1 tb. diced onion

Dissolve Jello in hot H_2O. Blend in mayonnaise, cold H_2O, vinegar and salt. Chill till partially set. Beat till fluffy. Add other ingredients. Mold. Garnish each mold with radish slices and speck of parsley.

LIME SALAD

2 Boxes Lime Jello
1 sm. Can crushed pineapple
1 c. chopped celery
2 pkg. (3 oz.) Phil. Cheese
1 c. chopped pecans

Cream cheese - add to 1 pkg. Jello when slightly jelled - whip. Add nuts, pour in mold and jell.

Add drained pineapple and celery to other pkg. of Jello when slightly congealed. Pour on first layer when it is firm.

July 5, 1963

24 HOUR VEGETABLE SALAD

HELEN BLODGETT

½ #10 Can of cut green beans
½ #10 Can of small green peas
½ #10 Can of yellow wax beans
½ #10 Can of small diced cooked carrots
4 Stalks of celery cut long and thin like the green beans
½ #2½ Pimento stripped thin
½ #10 Can of bell pepper sliced thin strips
6 Boiler onions sliced on #12 on the slicer

All the above vegetables should be well drained, then mixed together and placed in crock.

DRESSING: Put 1½ cup vinegar, 2 cups sugar, and 3 teaspoons salt into beater bowl and mix. Then add 3 cups salad oil slowly while beating.

Pour dressing over vegetables and place under refrigeration for 24 hours. Drain before serving.

Suggested price - .20¢

ANCHOVY DRESSING

3 tbsp. minced canned anchovies or anchovy paste
3 tbsp. chopped chives or green onion tops
3 tbsp. tarragon wine vinegar
1 tbsp. lemon juice
1 clove garlic, peeled & minced fine
1/2 cup sour cream
1 cup mayonnaise
1/3 cup minced parsley
1/4 tsp. salt
1/8 tsp. coarsely ground black pepper

Mix ingredients in order, then chill well. Makes about 2 cups and will keep, if covered and in refrigerator, for several days. (Use on tossed green salads.)

ANCHOVY SAUCE

4 Tbsp. butter	1 Tbsp. anchovy paste
2 Tbsp. flour	1/8 Tsp. pepper
1 cup hot water	1/2 Tsp. lemon juice
1/3 tsp. salt	1 Tsp. Lea and Perrin Sauce

Melt half the butter, add flour, salt and pepper and mix well. Add hot water gradually, stirring constantly. Cook over hot water about a minute. Add lemon juice, Lea and Perrin sauce, anchovy paste and remaining butter in small pieces. Stir until well blended.

CARDINAL DRESSING

3 cups Mazola Salad Oil	Few grains pepper
1½ cups vinegar	4 cloves garlic
4 tsp. minced onion	1 cup catsup

Measure all ingredients into a bottle or jar. Cover tightly and shake well. Chill several hours. Shake thoroughly before serving; remove garlic if desired. Make about 6 cups.

Cream Cheese Variation: Add four 3-oz. packages cream cheese to vinegar in above recipe. Mix well. Add other ingredients and beat with rotary beater until smooth.

Good on chef and green salads.

CELERY SEED DRESSING

1¼ cups sugar
2 tsp. dry mustard
2 tsp. salt
2 tbsp. celery seed

1 tbsp. onion juice
2/3 cup vinegar
2 cups salad oil

Combine sugar, mustard, salt, onion juice and 1/2 of the vinegar. Beat well. Then gradually add the oil alternately with the remaining vinegar, and beat until a stable emulsion has been formed. Add the celery seed. Yield: about 3 cups. Use immediately. Do not keep over night.

CREOLE DRESSING

To 1 cup mayonnaise add:

2 T. chopped green peppers
2 T. catsup
2 T. chopped celery
1 T. horseradish

Serve on lettuce or vegetable salad.

FRENCH DRESSING - 1 GAL.

3 cups sugar
1/2 cup salt
1/2 cup paprika
Beat above on No. 3
1/2 gallon salad oil, add slowly to above

Mix:
4 cups vinegar
1 cup prepared mustard

Add gradually to above mixture while it is beating.

FRENCH DRESSING

2 cans Campbell Tomato Soup (No. 1)
1½ cups salad oil
1 cup vinegar
½ cup sour wine
1 cup sugar
3 teaspoons worchestershire sauce

2 teaspoons ground mustard
  (We use that mild mayonnaise mustard)
2 teaspoons salt
1 teaspoon paprika
½ teaspoon white pepper
2 cloves garlic, chop to a paste

Make a paste of mustard, paprika, pepper with a few drops of vinegar to avoid lumps. Put all ingredients in 2 quart fruit jar and shake until thoroughly mixed. (We mix on mixer, of course.)

Chapter I   Page 37

DRESSINGS

1/2 pt. sour cream
1/2 pt. mayonnaise
   Tsp. prepared mustard, salt & pepper.

---

1 Pkg. (3 oz.) cream cheese   1 tsp. mayonnaise
3 Tsp. cream   1 tbsp. orange juice
Salt   1/2 grated orange rind

Lemon-Lime

2 tbsps. lemon juice
2 tbsps. lime juice
2 tbsps. sugar
1/2 cup whipped cream
1/2 cup mayonnaise

Orange Cream Mayonnaise

1/2 Tbsps. orange rind grated
   Mayonnaise and whipped cream

Mayonnaise and mustard to make very tangy and black pepper.

---

1 Pkg. (3 oz.) cream cheese
1 Tbsp. liquid honey
1 Tbsp. lemon juice
1/2 cup whipped cream

---

1 cup French dressing
6 large chopped radishes
2 hard boiled eggs
1/4 cup chopped green pepper
2 T. chopped onion
2 T. chopped parsley

Chapter I   Page 38

FRUIT SALAD DRESSING

1/4 Cup pineapple juice
1/4 Cup lemon juice
2 eggs
1/4 Cup sugar

Beat the two eggs, add sugar, pineapple juice, and lemon juice. Cook in double boiler, stirring until thickened. Set aside to cool.

Variation: One cup whipped cream may be folded into dressing.

GARLIC OIL DRESSING

To 1 pint of salad oil add 6 buttons (whole) of garlic. Let stand at least two days before using on salads. Use only oil, leaving garlic buttons in bottom of jar.

MAYONNAISE - 4 GALLONS

(Do not thin with milk. Thin mayonnaise used on counter with a little milk, but only that on counter).

20 Eggs
 3 Gal. salad oil
 1/2 cup dry mustard
 2/3 cup salt
 2 cups sugar
 5 cups vinegar

Place eggs and dry ingredients in beater bowl. Beat to mix well. Add oil slowly. When all oil has been added, add vinegar slowly. Mix well.

PINEAPPLE DRESSING

4 cups cooked dressing or mayonnaise
1/2 cup whipping cream
1/4 cup sugar
1 - #2 can crushed pineapple, drained

Beat whipping cream until stiff. Add sugar. Fold into salad dressing. Add drained crushed pineapple to dressing and mix together.
Serve over canned pear salads.
Yield: 50 servings.

POPPY SEED DRESSING

Yield:	1½ Cups		1½ Quarts
	1/4 cup		1 cup sugar
	1 tsp.		4 tsp. salt
	1 tsp.		4 tsp. dry mustard
	1 tbsp.		4 tbsp. grated onion
	1/4 cup		1 cup vinegar
	1 cup		4 cups salad oil
	1 tbsp.		4 tbsp. poppy seeds

Mix sugar, salt and mustard; add onion and vinegar. Add oil one tablespoon at a time, beating constantly with a rotary or an electric beater. Stir in poppy seed.

Use on plain mixed fruit salad.

ROQUEFORT CHEESE DRESSING - 1 GAL.

1 heaping soupspoon roquefort cheese or blue cheese.
4 medium buttons garlic chopped fine.
Cream cheese and garlic together with a little mayonnaise till smooth. Then add 4 large dippers of mayonnaise and mix together well. Add a little French dressing for color, if desired.

SHRIMP COCKTAIL SAUCE - 1 GAL.

1 gallon catsup
4 soupspoons horseradish
2 soupspoons red hot
1½ cups chopped sweet pickles
4 soupspoons worcestershire

SOUR CREAM DRESSING

3 cups sour cream	2 tb. vinegar
1 tb. prepared mustard	White pepper
1 ts. salt	Bacon pieces

SWEET CREAM DRESSING

4 cups mayonnaise	2/3 cup sugar
1 cup vinegar	1 teaspoon black pepper
2/3 cup sweet cream	

Add ingredients in the order given above. Mix thoroughly after each addition.

Chapter I

TOPPINGS

FRUIT TOPPING

4 cups fruit juice (save all juices from canned fruit for this topping)
4 heaping tb. cornstarch
4 egg yolks, beaten

Mix enough water with cornstarch to make a smooth paste. Add beaten egg yolks. Have fruit juice hot and add cornstarch and egg mixture. Cook until smooth.

This should be stored in ice box and mixed with whipped cream only as needed.

Topping can be garnished with sliced cherries, chopped pecans or cocoanut.

TARTAR SAUCE

1 gallon mayonnaise
3 large sour pickles chopped fine
2 large onions

THOUSAND ISLAND DRESSING
(Use a gallon crock)

Approximately 1 gal. mayonnaise
3 Pimentos, chopped fine
2 Green peppers, ground
1 Large onion, ground
2 Cups catsup

Put pimento, green pepper and onion in bottom of crock. Add catsup. Fill crock with mayonnaise and mix well.

VINEGAR DRESSING

4 cups sugar
1/2 cup salt
1 cookspoon prepared mustard
2 cups salad oil added to above to mix well
Then add 6 cups vinegar, one at a time and mix well.

Chapter I   Page 41

AVOCADO DRESSING

May 31, 1963

HELEN BLODGETT

2 quarts mayonnaise
1 tablespoon dry mustard
5 Avocados (mashed)
Juice of 1 lemon
½ large onion grated
¼ cup wine vinegar
Salt & pepper to taste

Blend above ingredients together and spread over one inch thick lettuce slices and garnish with grated egg. Also use to spread ½ beef steak tomatoes.

(Run out guacamole salad may be substituted for mashed avocado)

COOKED FRUIT DRESSING

April 3, 1963

HELEN BLODGETT

Ingredients:

    16 eggs
    2 cups sugar
    2½ cups pineapple juice
    1½ cups lemon juice

Procedure:

    Beat eggs by hand till yellow and whites thoroughly mixed. Add other ingredients. Cook in double boiler (stirring constantly) until it begins to thicken (about 15 minutes). Remove from heat and let cool.

    Put over any fruit salads which have canned fruit or stewed fruit in it.

October 15, 1964

POLAR BEAR SALAD

J. W. CUNNINGHAM, JR.

1 gallon of fruit cocktail, very well drained
2 qts. cottage cheese
2 cups sour cream
2 cups whipped cream
1 - 10 oz. package large colored marshmallows

Toss together lightly. Sprinkle a little cocoanut on top.

February 26, 1965

APPLE DELIGHT

BEAUMONT

(A) Apples - Chunked (25)

(B) Cherries - Sliced (2 cups)

(C) Pineapple Chunks (2 gal.)

(D) Pecans (2 cups)

(E) 1 package Richning whipped in mixer with the following:

    1 qt. ice and fill with water
    2 tbls. vanilla
    1 cup sugar

Beat until heavy, then mix with A, B, C & D.

Chapter I   Page 43

Oct. 23, 1964

AVOCADO SALAD

HULDA REID
BROADWAY

Avocado, diced in 1 inch squares
Tomatoes, diced a little smaller than avocado
Hearts of lettuce, diced in 1 inch pieces

Combine above ingredients with Italian Wish Bone Dressing and toss together lightly. Pour the dressing over top of bowl also.

Oct. 23, 1964

ITALIAN WISH BONE DRESSING

HULDA REID
BROADWAY

Juice of 4 lemons
5 cups white vinegar
2 cups tarragon vinegar
8 cups salad oil
5 large cloves garlic, minced
1 teaspoon garlic powder
3 red cherry peppers, minced very very fine
2 Italian mild peppers, minced very very fine
1 cup sugar
Salt to bring out flavor
1½ teaspoon oregano, ground

Oct. 23, 1964

SOUR CREAM DRESSING
(For Baked Potato)

DAVIS W. SIMPSON
AUSTIN

2 lbs. margarine
2 lbs. sour cream
1 lb. mayonnaise
1 bunch parsley

Whip margarine until fluffy, about 8 or 10 min. on #3. Add sour cream, mayonnaise and parsley and mix thoroughly.

ADD:
1 tbsp. salt
1 tbsp. garlic powder or 10 medium sized pods of garlic

June 4, 1965

ROMANO TOSS SALAD

VERNON SCHRADER

INGREDIENTS:

Romaine and lettuce leaves (½ & ½)
Dry toasted Sesame seeds
Finely shredded Romano cheese
Luby's Wishbone Dressing

PROCEDURE:

(1) Mix dressing first, then
(2) Add liberal amount of Sesame seeds and Romano cheese
(3) Mix

Do not use too much dressing. Mix only one bowl at a time.
Do not "run out" over night.

August 8, 1966

HAWAIIAN SALAD

JAMES DOVE
EL PASO #2

4 #2½ cans Mandarin oranges
2 cups of cocoanut (shredded or flakes)
1 lb. package miniature marshmallows
2 qts. of sour cream
1/2 of #10 can of crushed pineapple

Mix and let chill overnight. Can be made in jello molds (either large or small)

Chapter I   Page 45

April 21, 1967

FRONTIER DRESSING

Yield - 3½ Qts.

ALICIA SANCHEZ

2 cups sour cream
2 cups prepared Bleu Cheese Dressing
2 cups Thousand Island Dressing
2 cups mayonnaise
1 bunch parsley, chopped
1 bell pepper, chopped
2 bay leaves, crushed
4 tbsp. celery seed
4 tbsp. Durkee's Dressing
1 lemon, squeezed
1 tbsp. Tarragon Vinegar
1 tsp. Wine Vinegar
2 tbsp. Ocean Spray Cranberry Juice
1 dash Louisiana Red Hot Sauce
1 dash Lea & Perrins Worcestershire Sauce
½ cup catsup
Salt and white pepper to taste

April 21, 1967

ROMANA SPECIAL DRESSING

(Run on Romaine or Sliced Lettuce)

H. O. JONES, JR.

4 cups sour cream
2 cups mayonnaise
2 cups salad oil
1 cup Wine Vinegar
1 cup sugar
Juice of one lemon
4 tbsp. Anchovy paste
½ cup catsup
1 cup Lowry's Italian Mix
1 cup parsley flakes

Blend sour cream and salad oil well. Then add mayonnaise. Add other ingredients and mix well.

CRANBERRY SAUCE

25	lbs Cranberries
25	lbs sugar
5	lemons
1	tablespoon soda
1 1/2	gallons water

Put sugar on fire and cook until it becomes syrupy. Add cranberries, soda and lemon and let cook 30 minutes, stirring constantly.

Makes 4 long steam table pans.

*****

MANHATTAN SALAD

INGREDIENTS	LBS	OZS	METHOD
Lemon Jello	1	8	Dissolve jello in hot water.
Hot Water	1	8	
Ice Water	4		Add ice water, vinegar & salt.
Vinegar		4	Chill.
Salt		1/2	
Diced apples (unpeeled)		8	When slightly thickened, fold in
Finely chopped walnuts			apples, nuts & celery. Turn into
or pecans		6	molds. Chill until firm.
Finely cut celery		8	

******

CHEESE FRUIT SALAD

	LBS	OZS	METHOD
Lemon Jello		13	Dissolve jello in hot pineapple
Hot canned crushed pineapple			and syrup. Add lemon juice.
and syrup (130)	3		Chill until slightly thickened.
Lemon juice		2	Mash the cheese, add small amts.
Cream cheese		12	of slightly thickened jello &
			blend. Fold into slightly
			thickened jello.
White grapes, halved			Fold in fruit and whipped cream.
& sliced	1	8	Turn into individual molds.
Finely cut Marachino cherries		4	Chill until firm.
Whipped cream (1 pt.)			
			Unmold on lettuce.

Portions weight: 4 ozs.

CAESAR SALAD

Cut bread cubes and fry brown and drain well for 2 hours.

Add croutons and parmeson cheese to lettuce leaf.

Add oil dressing.

Use 1 1/2 dippers (8 oz) to 165 pan of vegetable & croutons.
Use 1 handful croutons to 165 pan of lettuce.
Use 1/2 teacup of parmesion cheese to 165 pan of vegetables.
Use fresh spinach, romaine or lettuce leaves.

CAESAR SALAD DRESSING:

1 1/2 cup garlic salt
2 cups mustard
1/2 gallon + 3 cups vinegar
1 gallon oil.

Mix salt, mustard & garlic. Add 3 cups vinegar and mix together. Add 1 gallon oil and then 1/2 gallon vinegar. Mix well and store in 3 gallon crock.

GREEK SALAD

1. Make up vinegar oil as follows:

   1 qt pure olive oil
   1 oz garlic, chopped real fine
   1 oz salt (let garlic and salt sit over night adding
               olive oil next day)

2. Cut up lettuce, endives, escarole, and watercress as for tossed salad. Keep in ice-box if close to salad table, if not on work table. Make up in as small amounts as volume of business will allow.

3. Make finished salads in individual orders as needed. Fill individual salad bowl with cut up salad greens. Sprinkle with garlic olive oil. Place one tomato wedge on each side of salad.

   Garnish with:

   3 or 4 olives
   4 filets of anchovies
   2 or 3 small squares or pieces of feta cheese
   Sprinkle with capers and oregano seasoning

MOLDED MEXICAN SLAW

INGREDIENTS	LBS	OZS	METHOD
Lemon jello	1	2	Dissolve jello in hot water.
Hot water (130°)	5		Chill.
Vinegar		8	Combine vinegar, salt and cayenne.
Salt		1	
Dash of cayenne			
Finely cut green pepper		3	Mix seasoning with celery, green
Shredded cabbage	1	2	peppers, cabbage and pimentoes.
Finely cut pimento		12	Let marinate 10 to 15 minutes.
Finely cut celery		14	When jello slightly thickens, fold in vegetables. Turn into individual molds. Chill until firm.

Unmold on lettuce.

TWO PENNY SALAD

	LBS	OZS	
Lemon jello	1	2	Dissolve jello in hot water.
Hot water (130°)	5	8	Chill.
Salt		1/2	Add seasonings, vinegar and
Celery salt (3 tsps.)			catsup. Chill.
Vinegar		8	
Tomato catsup		6	
Shredded Cabbage	1	5	When slightly thickened, fold in cabbage which has been soaked in cold water for 30 min. & drained.

Turn into individual molds. Chill until firm. Unmold on lettuce, chicory or water cress. Garnish with mayonnaise and ripe or green olives.

CARROT SALAD

	LBS	OZS	
Grated carrots	3		Place grated carrots in mixing bowl.
Diced celery hearts		12	Add celery hearts, mix lightly.
Sugar		1	Add sugar and dash of salt.
Salt (dash)			
Seedless raisins		8	Add raisins. Mix.
Mayonnaise	1		Add mayonnaise and mix thoroughly.

Serve on bed of lettuce.

EMMA SALAD

INGREDIENTS	LBS	OZS	METHOD
Sliced cucumbers		1	On a bed of lettuce, place sliced, squeezed-out cucumbers, mix with a thick sour cream dressing.
Tomatoes		3	Garnish around cucumbers with 4 half-sliced tomatoes, cut 1/4" thick.
			Sprinkle with chopped chives or green onion tops.

COTTAGE SALAD

INGREDIENTS	LBS	OZS	METHOD
Tomatoes		3	On bed of lettuce, place whole tomato, split 5 times from top to stem but base left intact.
Cottage cheese (seasoned)		1	Fold back petals and with small ice cream scoop, place 1 oz. cottage cheese over center of tomato.

ANDALUSIAN SALAD

INGREDIENTS	LBS	OZS	METHOD
Onion		2	Marinate slice of onion in French dressing and place on bed of Lettuce. Place slices of cucumber in circular pattern around onion.
Cucumbers, sliced		1	
			Garnish with pepper rings.

SLICED EGG SALAD

INGREDIENTS	LBS	OZS	METHOD
Shredded lettuce		1/2	On a bed of lettuce, place shredded lettuce.
1 1/2 sliced, hard boiled eggs			Place hard boiled egg slices on lettuce in circular pattern.
			Garnish with a sprig of water cress.

AMERICAN SALAD

INGREDIENTS	LBS	OZS	METHOD
Head lettuce		1 1/2	On a bed of lettuce, place quarter head of lettuce, weighing approx. 1 1/2 oz. Cut hard boiled egg in quarters, placing 2 pieces on each side of lettuce.
1 hard boiled egg			
			Garnish top of lettuce with strip of pimento.

AVOCADO SALAD

Avocado		3	Cut avocado lengthwise, remove seed and peel. Cut lengthwise and place 3 oz. on crisp bed of lettuce.
			Garnish with strip of bacon or minced hard boiled eggs.

THE TROPICAL

Avocado		2	Halve avocado cross-wise and remove seed. Slice rings one inch thick from each half and peel. Sprinkle with lemon juice and salt. Arrange rings on bed of lettuce.
Oranges or grapefruit		2	Make a swirl in avocado rings with 3 segments of oranges or grapefruit.

THE FESTIVE

Avocado		2	Cut avocado cross-wise into half circles and peel.
Tomato		3	Quarter one medium firm tomato, cutting almost through. Open like flower. Alternate avocado half circles in arch fashion with tomato sections. Place on bed of lettuce.
			Garnish top with sprig of parsley.

CHICKEN SALAD

INGREDIENTS	LBS	OZS	METHOD
Boiled chicken (white meat)	1	8	Shred chicken meat. Place in bowl, season & toss together.
White pepper (dash)			
Salt "			
Celery (chopped med fine)	3		Add chopped celery & lettuce and toss.
Lettuce		12	
Boiled eggs (minced)		8	Add eggs.
Mayonaise (to proper consistency)			Add mayonaise and mix gently.
Bleu cheese crackers			Arrange mix in salad bowls on bed of lettuce & place three or four blue cheese crackers around side of each bowl.

Yield: 28 salads

FRESH CRABMEAT SALAD

	LBS	OZS	
Fresh crabmeat	1		Place crabmeat in mixing bowl after going through it thoroughly for bones or tendons. Add salt, pepper & french dressing and toss. Add diced peppers and celery and toss. Add mayonaise. Then arrange salads in bowl on bed of lettuce and garnish with lemon.
White pepper dash			
Salt dash			
French dressing		6	
Bell pepper (diced)		4	
Celery "	2	8	
Mayonaise (to consistency)			

Yield: 16 salads

ANTIPASTO

INGREDIENTS	AMOUNT	METHOD
Heads Lettuce	2	Cut lettuce, endives and tomatoes as for chef salad. Add antipaste, anchovies, and half of sardines with their juice. Cut cheese and bologna in small diagonals, squares or any way desired and add. Add vinegar oil and capers & toss together. Place in small bowl for counter and decorate top with remaining sardines, cheese. It is now ready to serve. A can of grated cheese may be kept on counter and sprinkled over each individual salad if customer so desires.
Bunches endive	1	
2 1/2 oz cans antipaste	2	
4 oz cans Sardines	1	
2 oz can of Anchovies	3	
Sliced Bologna	4 ozs	
Sliced Big eye Swiss	4 ozs	
Chef oil	1 qt.	
Tomatoes	1 lb	
Grated Parmesian cheese	(sprinkle)	
Capers	(good hand full)	

NOTE· Discretion and good judgement should be used in regards to the lettuce and endives. The two heads of lettuce and 1 bunch of endives go for the normal size, but if either are extra large or small, more of less of each should be used accordingly.

FRESH FRUIT AMBROSIA

INGREDIENTS	LBS	OZS	METHOD
Oranges (5 doz)			Sectionize and seed. Squeeze juice from pulp and add to sections. Slice & add cherries
Cherries (30 each)			
#2 crushed pineapple (5 cans)			Add to above.
Coconut		1	
Sugar		4	
Water, if & as needed			
Bananas	8		Slice & add right before serving

*****

CONJEAL SALADS

BANANA NUT LOAF:

Bananas	2 lbs
Pecans	1/2 lbs
Red jello	12 oz
Water	1 1/2 qts

DATE LOAF:

Lemon jello	9 oz
Gelatine	1 ts
Dates	5 oz
Diced apples	2 lb
Grapefruit (sectioned)	2
Water	1 1/2 qts

AUTUMN DELIGHT:

Orange jello	18 oz
Hot water	2 qts
Vinegar	2 qts
Diced Peaches	1 qt
Diced pears	1 qt
Cherries	9

RAISIN CARROT LOAF:

Carrots	1 lb
Pineapple	4 slices
Raisins	1/2 box
Lemon jello	12 ozs
Gelatine	1 tbsp.

VEGETABLE LOAF:

Lemon jello	1 can
Vinegar	1 cup
Cabbage	3 lb
Bell pepper	4
Pimento	1 can
Celery	1 lb

COLE SLAW DELUXE

INGREDIENTS	AMOUNT	METHOD
Shredded cabbage	3	In a mixing bowl, place 3 lbs shredded cabbage. Add 1 lb julienned tomatoes and mix lightly.
Julienned tomatoes	1	
Julienned green peppers	4	Add to cabbage and tomato mixture, 4 oz julienned green pepper, 1/4 oz salt, dash black pepper and 1 oz sugar. Mix lightly.
Salt	1/4	
Dash of black pepper		
Sugar	1	
Sweet relish	8	Add sweet relish and mix lightly.
Mayonnaise	12	Add mayonnaise and mix until thoroughly incorporated.

COLE SLAW

INGREDIENTS	AMOUNT	METHOD
Shredded cabbage	3	In a mixing bowl, place shredded cabbage and add salt, black pepper and sugar. Mix lightly.
Salt	1/4	
Sugar	1	
Dash of black pepper		
Prepared mustard	1	Add prepared mustard, sweet pickle relish and chopped pimentoes. Mix lightly.
Sweet pickle relish	8	
Pimentoes (chopped)	2	
Mayonnaise	8	Add mayonnaise and mix until mayonnaise is thoroughly incorporated.

MEXICAN HOT SLAW

INGREDIENTS	AMOUNT	METHOD
Shredded cabbage	10	Place 10 lbs shredded cabbage, diced bell pepper and diced celery in large mixing bowl. Mix lightly.
Bell pepper	12	
Diced celery	8	
Salt	1/2	Add salt, black pepper and chili powder. Mix thoroughly.
Black pepper	1/4	
Chili powder	3/4	
Diced pimentoes	4	Add chopped pimentoes. Toss lightly. Then add mayonaise, vinegar, mustard and a dash of tobasco sauce to taste. Mix thoroughly.
Mayonaise	12	
Vinegar	4	
Prepared Mustard	3	
Tobasco sauce (dash)		

CHAPTER II

MEATS, FISH AND POULTRY

MEATS	Page		Page
Beef		**Pork (Cont'd)**	
Roast	2	Ham	
Roast Sirloin of.	1	Baked	17
Barbecued	2	Croquettes.	18
Steak		Fried	17
Chicken Fried	2	Loaf.	17
Country Fried	2	Virginia Fried.	17
Salisbury	30	and Eggs, Creamed	18
Swiss	2	and Navy Beans.	18
Short Ribs		Sausage	
Barbecued	2	Canadian.	32
and Potatoes.	3	Country	16
Ground, Fresh		Fried	16
Hamburger		Balls	15
Filets.	4	Casserole of.	15
Steak	4	Chop Suey	16
Casserole	4	Meat Roll	16
en Casserole.	5	Reubenola & Rice.	16
and Spaghetti	5	**Lamb**	
and Vegetables.	5	Curried	19
Chili	8-9	Patties	19
Chili for Enchiladas. . . .	9-9a	Stew.	19
Chili Verde	14	**Veal**	
Creole Rice	12	Casserole of.	13
Italian Casserole	8	Cutlets, Breaded.	13
Italian Cutlet.	35	and Dressing.	13
Italian Meat Balls & Spagh.	7	Sauerbraten	13
Italian Spaghetti	7-8	**Meat Specialties**	
Lasagna	36	Brains	
Meat Balls and Spaghetti. .	6	Baked	11
Meat Loaf	6	and Eggs.	11
Meat Patties, Barbecued . .	4	Corned Beef	
Swedish Meat Balls & Spagh.	38	Hash.	11
Tacos	30	and Cabbage	11
Tamale Pie.	9	Creole Rice	12
Ground, Cooked		Egg Foo Young Casserole . .	23
Baked Hash.	10	Liver and Bacon	11
Beef Roll	10	Noodle Casserole.	18
Meat Pie.	9-10	Ris Ramon	14
Meat or Chicken Roll. . . .	10	**Miscellaneous**	
Stuffed Peppers	10	New England Boiled Dinner .	12
Beef Almondine.	34	Spanish Rice.	12
Beef Kon Tiki on Rice	31	Vegetable Dinner.	12
Beef Ragout	37	Vegetable Loaf.	12
Hungarian Goulash	3		
Stew.	3	**SAUCES AND GRAVIES**	
Stroganoff.	3-33	Au Jus.	1
Tenderloin Tips in Burgundy .	32	Barbecued Short Rib Sauce . .	13
Pork		Barbecued Spare Rib Sauce . .	13
Roast	15	Beef Stock.	30
Chops		Sauce for Shrimp Tempuria . .	29a-1
Breaded	15	Sour Cream Sauce.	39
Fried in Natural Gravey . .	15	Sweet and Sour Sauce.	33
O'Brien	15	Wine Sauce.	31
		Mock Hollandaise.	9b

FISH	Page	FISH (Cont'd)	Page
Baked	24	Trout or Pompano	29
Broiled	24	Tenderloin of Trout	29b
French Broiled	29	Deviled Crab	24-24a
Fried	24		
Cod Fish Balls	24-25		
Halibut, Ruth's Oven, in cream.	25	CHICKEN AND TURKEY	
Jambalaya	25-26	Chicken	
Lobster		Fried	20
Newburg	26	Luby's Special	20
Salad	27	and Dumplings	20
Thermidor	26	and Baked Dumplings	20
Salmon		Pioneer Dumplings	21a
Croquettes	27	Baked w/Noodles	21a
Loaf	27	and Rice	20
Shrimp		en Casserole	21
Creole	28	Croquettes	21
Deviled	29a	a la King	21
Fried, Fresh	28	or Meat Roll	23
E'Touffee	29a-1	Pie	21
Tempuria, Sauce for	29a-1	Tetrazzini	22
Tetrazzini	22	Turkey and Dressing	21
Tuna			
Casserole	28	EGGS	
Creamed	29	Creamed Eggs on Toast	23
Croquettes	29	Egg Foo Young Casserole	23
Loaf	27		
and Noodles	29		

LIST HERE new recipes:

Shrimp Steak	40	Sour Cream Enchiladas	43
Chicken Enchiladas	9a	Seafood Tempure	24a
Ham Imperial	18a	Soft Tacos	43
Enchilada Sauce (Green)	9b		
Sauce for Spaghetti & Meatballs	7a		
Polynesian Beef	39		
Shrimp Curry	40		
Concentrate for Charbroil	33		
Bleu Cheese Stuffed Chopt Sirloin	41		
Pancho Sauce	41		
Stuffed Shrimp	42		
Trout Almondine	42		
Cream Sauce	43		

ROAST SIRLOIN OF BEEF

YIELD: 50 4-oz. Portions

SWIFT & COMPANY
Mr. R. E. Cooper
Salesman

20 lb.	Sirloin Butt (bnls)
3 oz (1/3 cup)	Salt
1 Tbs.	Pepper
8 oz. (1½ cup)	Onions
2 clove	Garlic
4 oz.	Carrots
4 oz.	Celery

Place sirloin butt in roast pan. Rub salt and pepper into roast. Rough cut vegetables, mince garlic add to roast pan. Place roast in 325-350° oven. Roast for 1½ hrs. Add 1 qt. beefstock or water to pan, and roast additional hour for rare. Allow roast to set for 30 min. before slicing. This will allow meat to set and result in a finer cutting job.

When meat has been removed, take pan drippings, add additional pint of beef stock, season to taste, strain, and serve as hot au jus with slices of roast.

To cook to medium, add additional 30 minutes.

AU JUS

YIELD: 7½ Gal.

SWIFT & COMPANY
Mr. R. E. Cooper
Salesman

5 lb.	Bones from chine ribs
½ qt.	Water
7½ gal.	Water
1½ gal.	Beef stock
1 oz.	Salt

Use beef bones trimmed from chine of ribs. Place in roasting pan. Add 1/2 qt. of water and brown off for 45 minutes at 450 f. Discard water after bones are browned.

Place browned bones and rib bones from rib roast of previous day in large stock pot. Add water and beef stock. Cook for 12 hours. Season.

NOTE - If any au jus if left from previous day it may be added to new au jus.

Chapter II

ROAST BEEF

Sear beef well, salt and pepper, onion and a little celery. Add water and cook until done.

CHICKEN FRIED STEAK

Fry steak until browned (flour first). Place in roast pan and cover with water and all of meat fryings. Allow to cook in oven at least 45 min. Add Kitchen Boquet to color gravy. An onion added to gravy improves flavor.

COUNTRY FRIED STEAK

Flour steak well, fry until browned. Place in roast pan and make thick gravy and pour over steak. Add 2 onions for seasoning and allow to cook in oven at least 45 minutes or until steak is tender.

SWISS STEAK

Flour steak well, and fry until browned. Place in roast pan and add 1 gal. tomatoes, onions and green peppers (chopped fine) that have been fried until tender (not browned), and 1 gal. water, salt and pepper. Allow to cook in oven at least 45 min. or until tender. More tomatoes may be added as needed.

BARBECUED BEEF

Use whole naval plate or cut into short ribs. Sear beef well, cover with barbecue sauce and cook until well done.

1 gallon tomatoes	3 cooksp. red hot
1 gallon water	3 cooksp. chili powder
3/4 cup Worcestershire Sauce	2 cooksp. mustard

BARBECUED SHORT RIBS

Bone beef plate, cut in cubes, place in roast pan, sprinkle well with flour, mix well, add the following sauce to short ribs and cook in oven until done.

1 gallon can tomatoes	3 cooksp. red hot
1 gallon water	2 cooksp. chili powder
3/4 cup Worcestershire Sauce	1 cooksp. chili quick
	2 cooksp. mustard

Chapter II   Page 2

SHORT RIBS AND POTATOES

Bone beef plate and cut in cubes a little larger than for stew. Brown short ribs in hot grease. When browned sprinkle well with flour and add water to cover. Add onion to season, also salt and pepper. Peel raw new potatoes and add a little broth from short ribs and place in oven. Cook until potatoes are tender and brown.

Short ribs and dumplings are prepared the same way. Cook dumplings in some of the broth.

Short ribs and spaghetti are prepared the same way. Cook spaghetti, add tomatoes and some of the broth for seasoning.

HUNGARIAN GOULASH

Cut short ribs, brown in fat, sprinkle well with flour and mix well. Add water to cover. Salt and pepper. Add buttering onions. When done, add paprika. Cook noodles and serve in long pan, ribs in one end and noodles in the other.

BEEF STROGANOFF   Kenneth Weaver

20 lb. Meat
   (We stripped some good lean chuck in strips about 2 inches long and 1/2 to 3/4 inches thick.)
20 Medium Onions
   Chop as fine as possible in food cutter.
1 lb. Melted Oleo

Cook all this together in roast pan until meat is tender.

Then make gravy for above separately. We used about 3/4 lb. oleo and enough flour to take up oleo. Then add roast beef gravy. This should be a rich thick gravy. We used the large aluminum skillet that we fry chicken in, and it was about 2/3 full of this gravy. After gravy is ready, you add 1 qt. commercial sour cream and 1 qt. of tomato sauce alternately. A little sour cream and stir vigorously, and a little tomato sauce and stir vigorously, and continue until all is used up. Add this gravy to meat and cook slowly for about an hour. Serve with rice.

BEEF STEW

Bone beef plate and cut in cubes, cover with water, add salt and pepper and allow to cook about an hour. Add carrots, buttering onions and new potatoes. Cook until vegetables are tender. Add a little brown thick gravy.

HAMBURGER STEAK

8 lbs. hamburger
4 lbs. ground pork
12 eggs
1 pt. tomato juice
Salt and pepper.

Mix meat well, add eggs, tomato juice, and salt and pepper. Make into oblong patties and fry. When done, add water and all of meat fryings in a roast pan and allow to cook in oven about ten minutes. Add a few green peas and cooked diced carrots to add color.

HAMBURGER FILETS

15 lbs. ground beef
15 eggs
Salt and pepper

Shape into thick patties. Wrap with bacon and broil in skillet with lid on, turning often.

BARBECUED MEAT PATTIES

10 lbs. hamburger
 5 lbs. ground pork
75 slices bead (crumbled)
 1 qt. tomato juice
15 eggs
Salt and pepper

Crumble bread and moisten with tomato juice. Add meat, mix well, add eggs, salt and pepper. Make into patties and fry. Cover with barbecue sauce and cook in oven for about 30 min.

SAUCE FOR PATTIES:

1 gal. catsup
1 gal. water
2½ cups Worcestershire Sauce
10 onions (chopped fine)

2 cooksp. chili powder
2 cooksp. chili quick
2 cups sugar

HAMBURGER CASSEROLE

5 lb. hamburger
1/2 lb. bacon cut in small cubes (put in skillet and fry a little) Add hamburger and grind.

Fix spaghetti as for Spanish spaghetti. Add to meat, add one can mushrooms (chopped). Bake

Chapter II   Page 4

HAMBURGER EN CASSEROLE

Brown 3 lbs. hamburger until done. Dice carrot and potatoes and cut buttered onions in half. Put a little brown gravy over this. 2 cans tomato soup over all. Bake.

HAMBURGER AND VEGETABLES

5 lbs. hamburger cooked in salad oil
3/4 sq. pan diced carrots
3/4 sq. pan small onions
Cook onions and carrots together until done, then add hamburger meat. Add 1 can baby limas to mixture. Put in serving pan and bake in oven.

HAMBURGER AND SPAGHETTI

5 lbs. hamburger
1/2 lb. bacon cut in little cubes. Put in skillet and fry a little, then add hamburger and fry. Fix spaghetti like spanish spaghetti, then add to meat & add 1 can mushrooms, chopped, to it, and bake.

---

3 bunches celery cut like chop suey
3 medium onions, cut
1 gal. tomatoes
1 can mushrooms

1/2 can bean sprouts
1/2 can chestnuts
1 white bowl of diced meat
1 or 1 1/2 cup olive oil

Put mushrooms in pan and brown, add celery, onion and tomatoes. Put on lid and cook until celery is done. Add beansprouts, chestnuts and the meat and cook around 20 minutes. Stir often. Thicken as needed, serve with noodles like chop suey and rice.

Fry hamburger meat in salad oil, 2 medium onions and 5 cloves garlic chopped. 3 serving spoons chili powder, 1 1/3 cup corn meal to thicken 1 gallon tomatoes. Add all this to beans, cook slowly; when beans are tender, put in oven, cover with grated cheese. Let cheese melt. Use 1/2 gallon beans.

MEAT LOAF

10 lbs. hamburger
5 lbs. ground pork
15 eggs
100 crackers

3 onions (chopped fine)
6 pieces celery (chopped fine)
1 qt. tomato juice
Salt and Pepper

Mix meat well, add crackers crumbled, eggs, onion and celery and tomato juice. Mix thoroughly and make into loaves and cook in well greased roast pan for about 20 min. in the oven. Add 1 gallon can tomato catsup and little water as needed. Cook in oven about 1 1/2 hours. Slice and arrange in pan with hot broth poured over it.

MEAT BALLS AND SPAGHETTI
(Asa Hubbard)

7 qts. water
1 #10 tomato paste
1/2 cup sugar
1 tablespoon oregano
Pepper and salt to taste
Cook spaghetti in salt water

2 qts. chopped onion (chopped fine)
1/3 cup garlic (chopped fine)
Fry onion and garlic in 1 1/3 cups salad oil until cooked. Then pour in above mixture.

6 lbs. beef and 3 lbs. pork
1 bunch parsley
5 large onions
36 slices bread or 18 day old rolls ground in fine meat grinder
Moisten bread with tomato juice before grinding.

1 egg per lb. of meat
1 tablespoon oregano
1/2 teaspoon powdered garlic
Salt and pepper to taste

MEAT BALLS AND SPAGHETTI

4 lbs. Hamburger
2 lbs. ground pork
6 eggs
42 crackers

1 cup cracker meal
1 pt. tomato juice
Salt and pepper

Mix meat well, add crumbled crackers, eggs, cracker meal, tomato juice, salt and pepper. Make into balls and fry. When done, arrange on top of Spanish spaghetti.

Prepare meat balls and noodles the same way only use noodles seasoned with the meat fryings and some of the gravy.

Chapter II   Page 6

ITALIAN MEAT BALLS AND SPAGHETTI

6 lbs. hamburger
3 lbs. ground pork
45 slices bread
3 large onions (chopped fine)

3 large bunches garlic (chopped fine)
9 eggs
1 qt. tomato juice
Salt and Pepper

Crumble bread and moisten with tomato juice, add meat, onions and garlic, eggs, salt and pepper. Make into small balls and fry in salad oil.

SAUCE FOR SPAGHETTI:

4 large onions (chopped fine)
3 large bunches garlic (chopped fine)
6 cans Italian tomato paste

3 qts. water
1 cup sugar
Salt and Pepper

Fry onions and garlic in 1½ cups Italian olive oil. Drain oil into pot, tie onions and garlic into sack, put in pot. Add tomato paste and water, sugar and salt. Simmer at least 2 hrs. Pour over Italian spaghetti and place meat balls on top.

ITALIAN SPAGHETTI   (FULL BATCH). El Paso

16# Hamburger
4 #10 Tomatoes
1/2 #10 catsup
8 Bay leaves
8 tsp. thyme
8 tsp. garlic

8 whole cloves
1/2 cup Worcestershire sauce
4 tsp. Cayenne pepper
8 tbs. salt
1 cup chopped onion
2 tbs. file

Brown onions, garlic, and beef in salad or olive oil. Add remaining ingredients and cook slowly for two hours. Add file after sauce is done. Sauce can be thickened with corn starch if desired. Add sauce to cooked spaghetti.

ITALIAN SPAGHETTI   (1/2 BATCH) El Paso

8# Hamburger
2 #10 Tomatoes
¼ #10 Catsup
4 Bay leaves
4 tsp. Thyme
4 tsp. Garlic

4 whole Cloves
¼ cup Worcestershire Sauce
2 tsp. Cayenne Pepper
4 tbs. Salt
½ cup chopped Onion
1 tbs. File

Brown onions, garlic and beef in salad or olive oil. Add remaining ingredients and cook slowly for two hours. Add file after sauce is done. Sauce can be thickened with corn starch if desired. Add sauce to cooked spaghetti.

December 2, 1965

SAUCE FOR LUBY'S SPECIAL SPAGHETTI & MEATBALLS

LESLIE DANDRIDGE

2 #10 cans tomato pears
2 #10 cans tomato sauce
1 cookspoon chicken base
2 cups chopped bell peppers
2 cups chopped onions
4 cloves chopped garlic
2 cookspoons sugar
½ lb. uncooked beef tips
1 bag Italian herbs

Saute bell peppers, onions and garlic in ½ cup olive oil. Then add tomato pears and tomato sauce. Add 3 #10 cans hot water. Add salt, pepper and accent to taste. Thicken with cornstarch. Saute 1 can (50 oz.) mushrooms in butter and add to sauce. <u>Simmer 7 hours</u>. Add ½ cookspoon gumbo file last 30 minutes of cooking time.

Chapter II　　　　　　　　　　　　　　　　　　　　　　　Page 7a

ITALIAN SPAGHETTI

12 lbs. Hamburger
Fry in salad oil until done. Make sauce as you do for the Italian Meat Balls and Spaghetti.
Cook spaghetti in salted water until done, add sauce and meat to spaghetti and allow to cook 15 min. together. Serve with Italian cheese sprinkled over each order.

ITALIAN CASSEROLE

Leslie Dandridge
El Paso

Double Recipe	Single Recipe	
12	6	7 oz. boxes scroodles
8	4	pounds hamburger
16	8	cloves garlic, crushed
16	8	tablespoons salad oil
1	1/2	No. 10 can tomato puree
2	1	No. 10 can tomatoes
2	1	cup minced onions
2	1	tsp. salt
2	1	tsp. pepper
12	6	tsp. oregano
1	1/2	lb. Mozzarella cheese
1	1/2	lb. American cheese
4	2	cups Parmesan cheese

Cook scroodles and drain. Brown onions, garlic, and meat in salad oil. Add remaining ingredients and simmer 20 minutes.

Alternate layers of scroodles, cheese, and sauce in a long pan with meat sauce on top layer. Bake in oven at 350° for 25 minutes. Remove from oven and add grated egg yolk to top of casserole before serving.

Single recipe yields about 2½ bean pans.

CHILI

6 lbs. hamburger
2 lbs. ground suet
3 bunches garlic (chopped fine)
3 onions (chopped fine)

3 cooksp. chili powder
2 cooksp. chili quick
1 heaping cooksp. flour
1 gallon can tomatoes

Melt suet in pot; fry onions and garlic until tender; add meat and fry until done; add chili powder, chili quick and flour and salt. Mix well. Add tomatoes and cook until thick. Add to chili beans. (Ranch style or Spanish).

CHILI

6 lbs. meat
1 lb. suet
4 cooksp. chili powder
3 cooksp. paprika

3 cooksp. salt
1 cooksp. camino seed
2 garlic
4 large onions

CHILI FOR ENCHILADAS

2 cups grease in skillet
3 cooksp. chili powder
1 cooksp. chili quick
1/2 cooksp. salt
3 cups flour

1. Melt grease in skillet and add chili powder, chili quick and flour and make a gravy thickening.
2. Put water on in pot, when hot add chili, meat and thickening. Stir until thick and add #2½ can of tomatoes.

TAMALE PIE (Mrs. Lewis)

Suet
6 lbs. beef (cut in strips to go in grinder)
2 lbs. pork (cut in strips to go in grinder)
a few pods chili pepper, seeds removed
1 small button garlic, chopped fine
  Salt

Cook the above in pot until very tender.

Remove meat and pepper pods and grind them. Season with chili powder and Mexene and ground camino seed. Use the broth that the meat was cooked in to make mush. Make a medium thick mush with corn meal and cook thoroughly (about 20 minutes). Line pan with meat then mush. Heat in oven until thoroughly hot.

TAMALE PIE

Make chili, including beans, and put in baking pan. Cover with a thin mush, made with 4 cups boiling water and 2 cups corn meal and salt to taste. Run in oven a few minutes. Mush can be added first before chili and then a layer on top.

MEAT PIE

Cut cold roast beef in cubes and dice carrots and potatoes and onion. Cook together until it is done. Thicken a little. Put in baking pan and put dumplings on top and bake.

November 27, 1964

CHILI FOR ENCHILADAS

ANNIE MUSGROVE
BROADWAY

10 lbs. chili meat (Grind through chopped sirloin grinder)
2 cups chopped onions
½ cup shopped garlic
1 #10 can of tomatoes
1 lb. suet
¼ cup cumin
3 cups chili powder (Frank's)
1½ cups paprika
   Salt & pepper to taste

Simmer meat, onions & garlic in suet. Then add cumin, chili powder and paprika, mix well. Now add the tomatoes, mash before adding. Add 2½ gallons of beef stock. Thicken with flour water.

I use a 26 qt. heavy pot.

August 16, 1965

CHICKEN ENCHILADAS

BOYD MORROW

7 dozen Tortillas

FILLING: 3 lbs. cooked chicken
          1½ lb. grated Jack cheese
          ½ cup finely chopped onion
          Mix well

SAUCE: 8 lbs. green tomatoes, cooked and strained
                 through china cap collander
          ½ cup finely chopped chilies
              (I used about 1 cup chopped Mountain Pass Peppers)
          1 gallon slightly thickened chicken broth
          1 quart Sour Cream
          Salt to taste
          Mix well

TOP: 2½ lbs. of grated Mozzarella Cheese

Roll tortillas with filling, pour sauce over enchiladas, top with Mozzarella Cheese, heat in oven - serve.

Chapter II   Page 9a

Oct. 1, 1965

ENCHILADA SAUCE
(GREEN)
4 gals.

EL PASO

5# Onions, chopped medium fine
1# Oleo
5 Cans Green Chili Strips No. 2½ size
2 Cans tomatoes 2½ size
3½ Gals. Chicken stock

Saute onions in oleo until limp but _not_ browned.

Empty chili and tomatoes in colander
Add juice to onions with chicken stock.
Wash seeds from chili and tomatoes.
Chop medium fine and add to above.
Season with 2 tablespoons ground cuminos
1 tablespoon mexican oregano (crumbled)
Salt to taste.
Boil 20 minutes - thicken with 1# cornstarch dissolved
in cold water.
Cool. Then refrigerate. This will keep several days.
If chicken base and water is used, omit salt as most
soup bases are loaded with salt.

This sauce ideal for Chicken Enchiladas.

\# = pound (s)

MOCK HOLLANDAISE
Use on Broccoli

Mayonnaise
Enough lemon juice to taste
Sprinkle of salt

After the Broccoli is drained and placed in pan _Dribble_ the sauce over lightly & sprinkle with paprika.

Chapter II   9b

BEEF ROLL

Grind beef, chop a little onion and green pepper. Fry until brown, then add ground beef and rice. Mix with a little milk, have it pretty stiff. Make a rich biscuit dough and roll rather thin. Put meat 2 inches thick layer and then roll it in dough. Lay in pan. Slice a good 1/2 inch thick and lay in pan. Add tomato sauce with chopped onion and celery. Put over top after the meat roll sliced. Bake and serve.

MEAT PIE

Cut cold steak or roast beef or any other cold cooked meat into 1 inch cubes. Cover with boiling water or meat stock. Add 1/2 small onion chopped fine and cook slowly until tender. Make gravy of thickening (cold water and flour) 2 T for each cup of liquid in kettle. Add 1 T seasoning and few cold cooked potatoes cut in thick slices. Put all in pudding pan. Cool and cover with a crust of baking powder biscuit dough. Bake in hot oven 400° until dough is a nice crust.

CHICKEN OR MEAT ROLL

Grind cooked chicken or beef or pork, add 1/2 mashed potatoes and 1/2 ground bread crumbs to equal the amount of meat, chopped onion and celery (more celery than onion) 1 egg to lb. of meat. Mix with thickened chicken broth, roll into pastry dough, making a loaf. Slice about 1 inch thick. Place in greased baking pan and bake in oven until pastry is done. Arrange in serving pan and add thickened chicken broth to roll. Add a few green peas for color.

STUFFED PEPPERS

Grind cooked beef or pork, add 1/2 amount mashed or ground potatoes, chopped onion. 1 egg to pound of meat, a little cracker meal and milk to mix well. Stuff into peppers, place in baking pan and add tomatoes and some water and bake in oven until peppers are tender.

BAKED HASH

Baked hash is prepared in the same way as corned beef, using ground beef or pork (cooked) instead.

Chapter II

CORNED BEEF HASH

1 Can corned beef
1 Can diced potatoes (cooked)
2 large onions (chopped fine)
Milk to mix well (must be quite moist)
Salt and pepper, 6 eggs also. Mix well, pour into baking pan that has some hot grease melted and bake in oven until browned.

CORNED BEEF AND CABBAGE

Place corned beef in pot and cover with water and allow to boil at least 3 hours. (If corned beef is not spiced add pickling spice and a few pods of garlic.) Cook cabbage, arrange cabbage down one side of pan and slice corned beef and put it down the other side.

BRAINS AND EGGS

Soak 5 lbs. brains in salt water at least 15 minutes. Clean and wash. Put in beater and whip. Melt 1/2 lb. butter in roast pan, pour in whipped brains and cook in oven, stirring often, until half done. Add 3 dozen eggs, beaten and finish cooking. Do not let them cook too dry.

BAKED BRAINS

1/2 gallon tomatoes
1/4 lb. cooking butter
Small amount compound

Melt, and place brains in pan. Salt and pepper and bake in not too hot oven for 20 or 30 min. until done.

LIVER AND BACON

Slice liver in order size, flour well and fry until liver is done and browned. Served dry or place in roast pan and add gravy made from fryings, flour (browned in fryings, flour and water). Add 2 onions to season gravy and liver. Allow to cook in oven 45 min.

SPANISH RICE

3/4 cup raw rice
1½ cup sliced onions, browned
2 tblsp. fat
3½ cups canned or fresh tomatoes
1½ tsp. salt
Pinch of pepper

1 cup diced celery
¼ cup diced green pepper
1 Bay leaf
1 tsp. sugar
1 tsp. Worcestershire Sauce
2 cups water

CREOLE RICE

12 lbs. hamburger (fry in salad oil until done)
3 large onions (chopped fine)
4 large green peppers (chopped fine)
1 large bunch celery (cut like chop suey)
1 gallon can tomatoes
Salt and pepper

Fry onions and peppers in salad oil until tender but not browned, add tomatoes, and cook together about 30 minutes. Add meat and allow to simmer for at least 15 minutes. Serve with rice balls arranged on top of creole.

NEW ENGLAND BOILED DINNER

1 Tray carrots (cut like stew)
1 Tray onions (buttering onions)
1/2 Tray turnips
1 1/2 Tray new potatoes

6 heads cabbage
Green Beans
Beets

Cook and season all vegetables separately. When done arrange in long pan as follows: Green beans, new potatoes, carrots, onions, beets, turnips and cabbage.

VEGETABLE LOAF

4 qts. grated cabbage
4 qts. grated raw carrots
2 qts. whole wheat bread crumbs
1 qt. roasted ground peanuts
3 small bunches celery, chopped fine

4 bell peppers, chopped fine
5 medium onions, chopped fine
2 cups parsley
1 2/3 cups salad oil
8 eggs

Beat eggs and mix with all ingredients. Mold and bake as meat loaf. I just used 1/2 recipe and it made plenty. Use tomato sauce.

VEGETABLE DINNER

Cook green beans, season with ham. When half done add carrots, new potatoes, buttering onions and whole kernel corn. Cook until all are tender.

VEAL AND DRESSING

Loosen bones from naval end of beef plate. Sear well in hot grease, flour well, add salt and pepper and water for broth. When well done, remove bones and slice in thin slices and arrange on squares of dressing. Pour broth over each pan as you serve.

BREADED VEAL CUTLETS

Make batter, using 2 eggs and 1 qt. milk, salt. Dip cutlets in batter and then in cracker meal. Fry until browned.

CASSEROLE OF VEAL

Bone beef plate, cut in cubes the size of stew. Brown short ribs slightly in hot grease, add water to cover, salt and pepper and cook in oven an hour. Add carrots, buttering onions, new potatoes and celery. When vegetables are tender, add 2 t. curry powder to broth and add a little cream for richness.

SAUCE FOR BARBECUED SPARE RIBS

1 gallon tomatoes
1/2 cup Worcestershire Sauce
2 serving spoons red hot
2 serving spoons chili powder

BARBECUED SHORT RIB SAUCE   (1/2 amount)

1/4 cup Worcestershire Sauce
1 cooksp. hot sauce
1/2 gal. tomatoes
1 cooksp. chili
1 good pt. water
Salt

SAUERBRATEN

25¢ - 30¢ Veal butts
1 gal. vinegar
2 qts. water
1 handful salt
1 handful whole pickling spice

Turn bottom pieces to top on second day.

Chapter II   Page 13

JOSEPH OWEN LUBY SR.'S ORIGINAL COOKBOOK

<u>RIS RAMON</u>　　　　　　　　HILL- BEAUMONT

Green Onions
Cooked Chicken Liver or Beef Liver
Cooked Rice

Cut up 1/2 dozen green onions (tops and all) in approximate 1/2 inch pieces. Saute in 1/4 lb. oleo. Add approximately 2 square counter pans of cooked rice. Add 1/2 pickup pot of diced cooked liver. Stir together and salt and pepper to taste. This is relatively highly seasoned with salt and pepper.
Steam until hot.

The above quantities of rice or liver may be altered to suit the clientele in the various locations.

<u>CHILI VERDE</u>　　　　　　　　(Dub Evans)

1 #10 can of Jalapenos (drain and save juice)
2 quarts of chopped onions
1 #10 can of tomatoes
2 tablespoons of salt
2 tablespoons of sugar
2 cups of vinegar

Take drained Jalapenos and grind through the meat grinder along with the chopped onions. Add mashed up tomatoes, salt, sugar, Jalapeno juice and vinegar. Place in a heavy duty cook pot and bring to a boil and boil for at least five minutes. This recipe is a great improvement over the one we have been using in the past. It has a finished taste and I think that all who try it will be very much pleased.

Chapter II　　　　　　　　　　　　　　　　　　　　Page 14

ROAST PORK

Bone pork loin, flour well and salt and pepper to taste. Allow to brown in a little grease. Add water for broth.

BREADED PORK CHOPS

Prepare pork chops in the same way as cutlets.

FRIED PORK CHOPS IN NATURAL GRAVY

Flour pork chops well, fry until browned. Make a gravy using fryings and water and pour over pork chops. You can use Kitchen Boquet for color if needed.

O'BRIEN PORK CHOPS

Prepare pork chops as for fried pork chops. Add onions and green pepper (chopped fine) to gravy and allow to cook in oven for 45 min. to season gravy and chops.

PORK BALLS

6 lbs. Ground Pork
3 cups uncooked rice
6 green peppers (chopped fine)
4 onions (chopped fine)

2 cups tomato juice
8 eggs
Salt and pepper

Mix well. Make into balls. Place in roast pan, add tomato juice and bake until done.

CASSEROLE OF PORK

Chop 1 onion
2 medium peppers
3 stalks celery, chopped fine

Fry a little, add ground pork and can tomato soup, and let cook. Cook 1 pkg. noodles and add together and sprinkle bread crumbs and cheese and brown in oven.

Chapter II   Page 15

PORK SAUSAGE

8 lbs. pork butts
3 lbs. pork trimmings
4 cooksp. rubbed sage
10 chili potiens (little hot red peppers)
   Salt and pepper

Mix meat well, add sage, red peppers (crushed) salt and pepper and mix well.

COUNTRY SAUSAGE MEAT   (In America's Cook Book)

5 lb. ground pork   1 T. black pepper
3-1/2 T. salt   2 T. sage

CHOP SUEY

3 large bunches celery (cut large)   1/2 can water chestnuts (chopped)
3 large onions (cut rather large)   1 cup chop suey sauce
1/2 can bean sprouts   4 lbs. pork loin (cubed)
1/2 can mushrooms (chopped)   1 cup salad oil

Cook celery, onions, bean sprouts, water chestnuts and mushrooms in water to half cover vegetables, until barely tender. Fry pork in salad oil until browned, add to the above when done. Thicken a bit and serve with rice. Use chicken broth when available.

REUBENOLA & RICE

4 T. butter   1 gallon can tomatoes
1 can mushrooms   1/2 can bean sprouts
3 bunches celery (cut like chop suey) 1/2 can water chestnuts
3 large onions (cut like chop suey)
   Use chicken, cooked beef or pork

Melt butter in frying pan, brown mushrooms lightly. Add celery, onions, and tomatoes and cover. Let simmer until onions and celery are almost tender. Add sprouts, water chestnuts and meat. Cook 10 min., stirring frequently. Serve with rice and dry noodles. Garnish rice balls with green pepper rings.

MEAT ROLL

See Chicken or Meat Roll under BEEF.

Chapter II   Page 16

BAKED HAM

Bone ham, trim skin from ham, place in roast pan and cover with the following sauce:
 1 Pkg. brown sugar
 3 Cooksp. mustard (spread on ham)
 Add pineapple juice and water for broth

VIRGINIA FRIED HAM

Slice ham in order size, and dip in following sauce. Then fry until ham is done and add a little water to make gravy. Pour over ham.

SAUCE:
 1 Pkg. brown sugar
 3 Cooksp. mustard (mix well)

FRIED HAM STEAK

Slice ham in order size, flour well and fry until ham is done. Add water to fryings and when boiling, pour over ham.

HAM LOAF

Grind cooked ham, add 1/2 mashed potatoes and 1/2 cooked rice to equal the amount of ham. Chopped onion, green pepper and celery to season. Enough cracker meal to allow loaf to hold together. Use catsup to mix. Add 1 egg to the lb. Make into loaf, bake in oven until set, add enough water to keep loaf from burning on bottom. Serve with cream sauce that is seasoned with horseradish.

HAM LOAF

2 lb. ground ham
2 T. horseradish
2 small onions, minced fine
4 T. green pepper, minced

2 cups cracker crumbs
2 well beaten eggs
1 t. mustard
3/4 cup catsup

Mix all together well and place in baking dish. Bake one hour in medium oven.

Chapter II   Page 17

HAM CROQUETTES

Grind cooked ham, add equal amounts potatoes and 1/2 amount of cracker meal. 1 onion chopped fine, also green pepper if desired. 1 egg to lb. of meat and milk to mix well. Make into croquettes and fry in deep fat until browned.

HAM PATTIES are prepared in the same way, making patties and frying in skillet.

MEAT PATTIES are prepared in the same way only using cooked beef or pork instead. Serve with peas.

HAM AND NAVY BEANS

Dice raw or cooked ham in small pieces. Add to navy beans and cook until beans are tender.

CREAMED HAM AND EGGS

Dice ham in small pieces, put in bottom of pan. Take 8 to 12 hard boiled eggs and slice each one in five slices. Put over ham. Make a cream sauce and put over this mixture. Serve on toast for 15 cents.

NOODLE CASSEROLE

Enough noodles for one pan
3 large onions chopped fine
8 franks sliced fine - fry in oil until brown
1½ cup water

3 cans tomato soup
3/4 lb. grated cheese
6 t. Worcestershire Sauce
1½ t. salt
Pepper

Let cook until cheese is melted, then add to noodles and bake 20 min.

August 16, 1965

HAM IMPERIAL

JAY LEE SMITH, JR.

6 lbs. lean ham
6 lbs. lean pork (raw)
6 eggs
3 cups bread crumbs
3 cups milk
  Salt and pepper to taste

Trim excess fat off meat and grind (use small hole plate). Grease pans. Press into loaf, flat on top - in bean pan. Refrigerate 3 to 4 hours. Before baking cover by patting loaf lightly with a mixture of brown sugar and a little dry mustard. Bake at 325° for 1½ hours.

CURRIED LAMB

1 lb. lamb (shoulder) cubed. Stew in water and salt until well done.
2 T. butter (melt in skillet)
1 Large onion (chopped fine)
Stir until onions begin to turn color. Add 2 T. flour, 1 t. curry powder and pepper to taste. Pour broth from meat and add meat (no bone) and mix with gravy. Serve with steamed rice.

LAMB STEW

Soak in salt water a while and then drain and wash off salt water. Put in oven and brown the meat. Chop large onion fine and sprinkle over the top of meat. Cover the meat with water and cook until done. Cook 6 qts. of carrots cut smaller than for stew, on top of stove. Mix a little flour, salt and pepper in meat. Cook carrots on top of stove until done and add to stew just before sending out. Add 2 cans of green peas just before sending out and thickening and Kitchen Bouquet.

LAMB PATTIES

10 lbs. ground uncooked lamb
10 eggs
Salt and pepper
1 pt. tomato juice

Make into patties and fry in very little grease, turning often. Serve on sauted pineapple rings.

FRIED CHICKEN

Cut fryers in quarters, dip in batter using 2 eggs, beaten and 1 qt. milk, then dip in flour and fry in shortening and butter mixed. Cook in oven. Be sure and use plenty of grease to fry in.

LUBY'S SPECIAL CHICKEN

About 3 gallons chicken broth
2 large bunches celery (cut like chop suey)
3 large onions (cut like chop suey)
Cook until tender in broth. Thicken broth (like chicken pie broth) and add 1 qt. cream, 2 t. curry powder dissolved in some of the broth. Add cooked new potatoes and place a layer of chicken in pan and cover with the above broth. Add real green peas for color.

CHICKEN AND BAKED DUMPLINGS

Dice chicken in small pieces, cover with thickened broth and drop the dumplings from teaspoon to cover all. Bake in oven until done.

BAKED DUMPLINGS:

10 Cups flour
 7 eggs (beaten a little)
10 soup spoons baking powder (not too full)
 3 soup spoons salt
10 soup spoons melted oleo
 8 cups milk

Beat well and drop by spoonfull on top of chicken.

CHICKEN AND DUMPLINGS

Dice chicken in small pieces. Make dumplings and cook in chicken broth. Place a layer of chicken in serving pan and add a layer of dumplings, pour thickened chicken broth over the above.

CHICKEN AND RICE

Place a layer of diced chicken in pan, cover with thickened chicken broth, and place rice balls over top.

CHICKEN A LA KING

5 green peppers
5 pimentos (chopped fine)
3 gallons chicken broth
1 large onion

Cook peppers and pimentos in chicken broth with onion until tender. Thicken (like chicken pie). Add 1 qt. cream and 1 can mushrooms. Place diced chicken in pan and pour broth over it. Serve with patty shells or toast.

CHICKEN EN CASSEROLE

Place a layer of asparagus in serving pan. Add a layer of diced chicken, and a few mushrooms. Cover with thickened chicken broth, and sprinkle buttered bread crumbs over top and sprinkle well with grated cheese. Place in oven to brown.

CHICKEN PIE

Dice chicken in small pieces
Dice potatoes in small pieces
Place layer of chicken in baking pan and add layer of potatoes. Pour thickened chicken broth to cover. Cover over with pastry dough or biscuit dough cut with doughnut center and place on top. Place in oven to brown. Cut into 24 orders.

CHICKEN CROQUETTES

1 Salad pan of chicken (cut)
1/2 Salad pan cooked potatoes

Grind each of these separately

1 small onion, chopped fine
1 medium green onion, chopped fine
1 t. black pepper
3 eggs
12 Saltine crackers (mashed)

Mix all ingredients together well and shape as salmon croquettes. Fry in hot grease. Serve with cream peas.

TURKEY AND DRESSING

Bake turkey, slice and arrange over squares of dressing, using dark meat that has been cut in small pieces, and cover with the sliced white meat. Pour the thickened turkey broth over all.

Chapter II   Page 21

May 8, 1964

BAKED CHICKEN 'N NOODLES

M. H. LANGFORD

12 oz. uncooked egg noodles
7 oz. celery, diagonally sliced
½ cup chopped onions
2 tbsp. oleo
1½ qts. chicken broth
2 cups milk
2 lbs. diced, cooked chicken
¼ cup diced pimento
½ cup buttered bread crumbs

METHOD

Cook noodles in unsalted water until done but firm; drain. Cook celery and onion in butter until vegetables are transparent. Blend soup and milk with celery and onion. Add chicken and pimento. Fold in cooked noodles and pour into bean pan. Sprinkle buttered crumbs on top. Bake in moderate oven (350°F.) for 45 minutes or until sauce is bubbling and crumbs are brown.

YIELD: 1 Bean Pan

May 20, 1964

PIONEER DUMPLINGS

LOTTIE CHAPPEL

2½ cups Pioneer Biscuit Mix
4 tsp. melted shortening
2 eggs
3 serving spoons of whole milk

Combine in order given.

Drop by teaspoon or cut into approximately 1½' by 4" rectangular or parallelogram shaped strips into boiling chicken or beef broth. Cover tightly and simmer without removing cover for five (5) minutes. Serve on top of cut chicken or with Beef Short Ribs. Also may be served with ¼ or ½ Broiled Chicken.

CHICKEN TETRAZZINI

BANDERA ROAD

1 lb. Uncooked Spaghetti
1/2 cup Chopped Onion
1 Clove of Minced Garlic
2 tablespoons Margarine
50 oz. can Cream of Mushroom Soup
2 cups Water
1 lb. Sharp Cheddar Cheese
1 1/2 lb. Diced Cooked Chicken
1/4 cup Chopped Pimiento
1/4 cup Chopped Parsley

Cook spaghetti in boiling, salted water until tender but not soft. Drain and mix thoroughly with a little butter. Saute onion and garlic in butter till tender. Blend in soup and water, stir until smooth. Add one-half of the cheese - save remaining cheese. Cook over low heat until cheese is melted, stirring occasionally. Fold in chicken, pimiento and parsley. Mix with spaghetti. Sprinkle remaining cheese on the top. Add dash of paprika. Bake in 450 degree oven for 10 minutes or until sauce bubbles and surface browns. This makes a bean pan full. We charge .52¢. (Left over chicken may be used in this recipe). Taken from Campbells Soup Recipe Booklet.

August 1, 1963

SHRIMP TETRAZZINI

3 lbs. Uncooked Shrimp
1 1/2 cups Chopped Onion
3 Cloves of Minced Garlic
6 tablespoons Margarine
2 50 oz. cans Cream of Mushroom Soup
2 50 oz. cans of Milk
3 lbs. Sharp Cheddar Cheese
4 1/2 lbs. Cooked and cleaned Shrimp pieces
3/4 cup Chopped Pimento
3/4 cup Chopped Parsley

Cook spaghetti in boiling, salted water until tender but not soft. Drain and mix thoroughly with a little butter. Saute onion and garlic in butter till tender. Blend in soup and water, stir until smooth. Add one-half of the cheese - save remaining cheese. Cook over low heat until cheese is melted, stirring occasionally. Fold in shrimp, pimento and parsley. Mix with spaghetti. Sprinkle remaining cheese on the top. Add dash of paprika. Bake in 450 degree oven for 10 minutes or until sauce bubbles and surface browns. This makes a bean pan full. We charge .59¢.

Chapter II   Page 22

CHICKEN OR MEAT ROLL

Grind cooked chicken or beef or pork, add 1/2 mashed potatoes and 1/2 ground bread crumbs to equal the amount of meat, chopped onion and celery (more celery than onion) 1 egg to lb. of meat. Mix with thickened chicken broth, roll into pastry dough, making a loaf. Slice about 1 inch thick. Place in greased baking pan and bake in oven until pastry is done. Arrange in serving pan and add thickened chicken broth to roll. Add a few green peas for color.

CREAMED EGGS ON TOAST

3 doz. eggs (hard boiled)

Make medium thick cream sauce, using butter, flour and milk. Slice eggs longwise, getting about 3 slices to the 1/2 egg. Put in serving pan. Pour sauce over eggs and sprinkle with a little paprika. Serve on toast.

EGG FOO YOUNG CASSEROLE

1 lb. ground beef)	
8 stalks celery, chopped)	Brown in oil or shortening
4 onions, chopped)	
12 eggs well beaten)	
Salt and pepper)	Beat together
2 tablespoons soy sauce)	

2 cans bean sprouts, drained
2 cans mushroom soup (whip in beater)

In bottom of greased pan, put the bean sprouts. Pour egg mixture over this. Then add meat mixture. Then pour soup over top of this. Bake at 350° for 45 minutes to 1 hour.

FRIED FISH

Cut fish in order size, dip in following batter and then in cracker meal. Fry in deep fat in skillet until browned and tender.

1 qt. milk
2 eggs (beaten)
2 cups corn meal (mix well)
You can omit the eggs.

BAKED FISH

Cut fish in order size, arrange in baking pan and cover with tomatoes, a few slices of onion and lemon. Add some butter for seasoning. Bake in oven until tender.

BROILED FISH

Cut fish in order size, arrange in baking pan and add a little water, butter and lemon. Bake in oven until tender and browned.

DEVILED CRAB

3 large cans crab
4 green onions
5 stalks celery (chopped fine)
3 green peppers
3 eggs

1/2 cup cracker meal
1 serving bowl mashed potatoes
1 cooksp. Worcestershire Sauce
2 cooksp. red hot sauce

Fry onions, celery and peppers in butter until tender. Mix with above ingredients and stuff into crabshells. Sprinkle with cracker crumbs. Pour melted butter over top and bake in hot oven until golden brown. Use a medium sized potato to each pound of meat.

COD FISH BALLS

1 box codfish (dried salt codfish). Soak 1 hour or longer. Drain. Put on to cook in fresh water and cook until tender. Drain all water off well. Shred codfish and mix with equal amount of mashed potatoes, 1 egg and 1 teaspoon baking powder. Beat on electric beater until light and fluffy. Make into balls and fry in deep fat. Serve hot.

Chapter II   Page 24

DEVILED CRAB

Oct. 23, 1964

ROMANA PLAZA
CAFETERIA

5 lbs. crab
7½ lbs. potatoes

1 onion   )
1 bell pepper   )   Saute
1 stalk celery   )

1 egg per lb.

hot sauce   )
salt   )
pepper   )   To Taste
accent   )

Mayonnaise and crackers on top.

YIELD: Approximately 11 crabs per pound.

SEAFOOD TEMPURE

1 - 4 oz piece of fish cut in 6 pcs.
1 - small pc shrimp
2 - small pcs. scallops
1 lg. qtr. pc. onion

Alternate onion: fish, onion, scallop, onion, fish, onion, shrimp, onion, fish, onion, scallop, onion, fish, onion.

Roll kabob in flour then buttermilk then cracker meal
Sweet sour sauce after Tempure is cooked (deep fat fried)
Serve on rice.

Chapter II   Page 24a

COD FISH BALLS

1 box or package codfish, cook 30 min. or longer in water. Drain off the water and then boil until tender in saucepan of fresh water.

Drain the water again and be sure it is all drained off. Shred the fish carefully and add an equal amount of cold mashed potatoes. Beat 1 egg, add 1 t. of baking powder. Combine with the codfish and mashed potatoes. Make into balls or cakes and fry in very hot deep fat until browned.

RUTH'S OVEN HALIBUT IN CREAM

Take desired amount of halibut steaks, place in greased pan. Season to taste. Sprinkle lightly with flour. Cover with cream. Bake in 350° oven for about 30 minutes.

JAMBALAYA

Melt in stock pot:

2 T lard
2 T flour - cook one minute

Add:

2 lb. chopped ham
2 cups shrimp (cooked & cleaned)
3 cups tomatoes

Cook a few minutes, then add:

2 onions, chopped
2 buds garlic, chopped
2 green peppers, chopped
  parsley, salt and pepper, dash of thyme, tobasco, red pepper,
  2 T Worcestershire, 8 cups water. Let simmer for about 10 minutes.

Add:

2 cups raw rice and boil until rice is done - about 20 minutes. Care must be taken not to stir the mixture or rice will be gummy. However, it is necessary to lift mixture with a fork from the bottom of the pot occasionally to keep rice from burning. Keep pot covered while cooking.
Takes about one hour to prepare. Yield: 12 servings.

Chapter II   Page 25

JAMBALAYA

Cook in kettle:	4 T lard, 2 large onions, finely chopped, until it just begins to take on color, stirring often.
Add:	4 crushed bay leaves, 1/2 teaspoon thyme, 2 T. chopped parsley, teaspoon black pepper and a few grains cayenne.
Add:	2 T. flour and stir well. When well blended add 2 cloves of garlic, chopped and salt to taste. Cook for 2 or 3 minutes, stirring constantly.
Add:	3 cups tomatoes, 1 teaspoon chili powder and 3 quarts water. Bring to a boil and stir in gradually 2 cups raw rice and 3# cleaned shelled raw shrimp. Cover and simmer very gently for 35 or 40 min. or until rice is tender, stirring occasionally very carefully.

You may substitute diced ham for part of the shrimp.

LOBSTER NEWBURG

1 1/2 lbs. cooked lobster meat
3 tablespoons butter
1 1/2 cups Madeira or Sherry wine
1 1/2 cups cream
3 egg yolks, beaten
1/4 teaspoon salt
    Dash cayenne pepper

Cut lobster meat into large pieces and heat slowly in butter about 5 minutes. Add wine and simmer slowly until the wine is almost all reduced. Beat cream into egg yolks. Add lobster and season. Cook, stirring constantly until thickened. Serve on hot toast.

LOBSTER THERMIDOR

1 boiled lobster	1 tablespoon minced parsley
3 mushrooms, sliced	1/2 cup sherry
1/4 cup butter	1 1/2 cups cream sauce
Dash paprika	2 tablespoons grated Parmesan Cheese
1/8 teaspoon mustard	

Cut lobster lengthwise into halves. Remove meat and cut into pieces. Cook mushrooms 5 minutes in butter, add paprika, mustard, parsley, sherry and 1 cup cream sauce. Mix well, fill lobster shell with mixture, cover with remaining sauce and sprinkle with cheese. Bake 10 minutes in hot oven - 450 degrees.

LOBSTER SALAD

2 1/2 cups flaked lobster meat
1/3 cup diced celery
2 tablespoons French dressing
  Mayonnaise

Combine lobster and celery and marinate in French dressing. Add mayonnaise. Garnish with pimento strips.

SALMON CROQUETTES

1 can salmon
1 can mashed or ground potatoes
1 small onion (chopped fine)
1 egg
1/2 can cracker meal

Milk if needed to mix well. Make into croquettes and fry in deep fat. Salmon patties are prepared in the same way. Make into patties and fry in skillet. Serve with peas.

SALMON LOAF

3 cans salmon
3 cans mashed potatoes
2 cans cracker meal
5 eggs
1 onion (chopped fine)
2 green peppers (chopped)

Milk to mix well. Make into loaf and bake in oven until done.

SALMON OR TUNA LOAF

1 T lemon juice
2 cups flaked salmon or tuna
1 cup medium white sauce
1/2 cup top milk
1/2 t. salt
1 beaten egg
1/2 cup chopped celery
1 cup dry bread crumbs

Add lemon juice to salmon; add remaining ingredients; mix well. Bake in greased baking dish in moderate oven 350 degrees until brown and set, about 30 min. Serves 6.

SALMON LOAF

4 cans salmon
4 pans potatoes
2 cups cooked rice
4 eggs
Handful cracker meal

Chapter II   Page 27

FRIED FRESH SHRIMP

Peel and clean raw shrimp. Cut open (pocket book) and dip in following batter and roll in cracker meal.

Batter for fried shrimp:

5 egg yolks (beaten)
3 1/2 cups milk
3 1/2 cups flour
  Salt

SHRIMP CREOLE

3# shrimp
3 cups chopped onions
3 cups chopped green pepper
3 stalks chopped celery
1/2 teaspoon paprika
1 pod garlic cut fine
2 #2½ cans of tomatoes
Salt and pepper to taste

TUNA CASSEROLE

2 - 3 oz. Pkgs. potato chips
1 large can tuna
1/2 cup mushrooms, sliced (these may be omitted)
1 large can cream of mushroom soup

Place tuna in sieve and pour boiling water over it to remove oil. Crush potato chips, flake tuna. Combine everything except a few potato chips. Pour into a buttered casserole and scatter remaining crushed potato chips over top. Bake 350 degrees for about 1/2 hour.

CREAMED TUNA

6 T of butter, melted
6 T flour blended with melted butter
1/2 t. paprika
2 cans cream mushroom soup
2 cans white tuna fish
4 hard boiled eggs

Combine butter, flour, mushroom soup and paprika and cook until it thickens. Add the tuna and hard boiled eggs cut into small pieces. Serve in patty shells or on toast. (Serves 16) (1 pint of oysters cooked in their own liquid until their edges curl of shrivel, or canned salmon may be added to the creamed sauce instead or tuna, if preferred.)

Chapter II

TUNA AND NOODLES

1/2 lb. pkg. of noodles	1 - 8 oz. can mushrooms
1 - 7 oz. can of tuna	1 - 8 oz. can mushroom soup
2 T butter	2 T flour
3/4 cup buttered bread crumbs	

Arrange the cooked noodles in the bottom of a buttered casserole. Make a sauce of the butter, flour and liquid from mushrooms and peas, add the can of soup to this. Arrange tuna and mushrooms over noodles. Next a layer of peas and sliced olives. Pour the hot sauce and soup over all this. Cover with buttered crumbs. Bake in a slow oven until crumbs are brown and mixture thoroughly heated. About 1 hour.

TUNA FISH CROQUETTES

#1 can tuna (shredded)
1 dozen hard boiled eggs (chopped fine)
1 1/2 cups cracker meal
2 cups cream sauce

Mix well, make into croquettes. Roll potato chips fine and roll croquettes in chips, dip in egg and roll again. Fry.

TROUT OR POMPANO   Boyd's Method

1/4 lb. butter
2 lemons (juice)

Let butter get soft but not melted. Add lemon juice and salt and beat slightly until the butter and lemon juice go together. Rub fish well, inside and out, with the above.

Pepper
Put in foil and seal airtight
Bake 2½ hours in 240 degree oven
This amount will cover 6 pompano

FRENCH BROILED FISH
May 15, 1963
BROADWAY
JERRY ELDREDGE

This method of French broiling may be used on any broiling fish.

Place fish in broiling pan, season with salt and accent. Then spoon French dressing liberally over entire top surface of fish. Sprinkle fine ground bread crumbs over the French dressing. Broil with chicken broth in bottom of pan. (With oleo and lemon juice added to chicken broth optional)

Works good on 10 lb. chicken - Halibut - split in half - quartered long way. Thaw and debone after splitting and quartering on powersaw.

DEVILED SHRIMP
HARLINGEN

3 lb. fish (R.O. or fresh)
1 cup chopped onions
1 cup chopped celery
½ lb. chopped cooked shrimp
3 lbs. mashed potatoes
4 eggs
¼ cup Worcestershire sauce
Salt, pepper and tobasco to taste
Cracker meal to take up moisture
25 large raw shrimp (billfold)

Saute vegetables and mix all ingredients as you would a salmon pattie. Roll into 5 oz. balls and pack on leg side of shrimp. Fold shrimp tail over back of shrimp ball and cover entire shrimp with crushed crackers (deviled crab). Bake in moderate oven until shrimp on bottom is done.

SHRIMP E'-TOUFFEE

May 8, 1964

SAM RICE
BEAUMONT

```
15# shrimp (peeled and divided pieces)
12  medium onions (chopped small with knife)
 6  bell peppers (chopped small with knife)
 6  pieces celery (diced small)
12  buttons garlic (chopped fine)
½   #10 can tomato sauce, salt, pepper
    cayenne pepper
```

Make Roux (as for cream gravy) with shortening and flour - brown but do not burn. Then add chopped vegetables and garlic, salt, pepper and cayenne pepper (this should be slightly on the hot side) and cook until vegetables are tender and add raw shrimp and cook on low heat until shrimp turn pink. Then add tomato sauce and a little water (2 cups) if needed. Simmer on low heat until tender.

SAUCE FOR SHRIMP TEMPURIA

May 20, 1964

BOYD MORROW

```
  1 qt. chicken broth
 12 tsp. chicken base
  2 cups vinegar
  4 cups sugar
  1 cup pineapple juice
3/4 cup corn starch
  6 tbsp. water (enough to dissolve corn starch)
  2 tbsp. La Choy Bead Molasses
1/8 tsp. salt
```

Use 1 - 46 oz. can pineapple juice and boil down to very thick. (About 1 cup) Then add chicken broth, salt, vinegar, chicken base and sugar. Bring to a boil and thicken with corn starch. Dissolve in water. Add Bead Molasses and let cook for about five (5) minutes.

BATTER

```
2 cups flour
2 eggs
1 tbsp. baking powder
1/2 tbsp. soda
1 1/2 tsp. salt
2 cups butter milk
2 cups water
```

Chapter II

Page 29a-1

TENDERLOIN OF TROUT   May 21, 1963

LUBY'S ROMANA PLAZA CAFETERIA

Step No. 1. Buy 1 lb. Iceland Haddock. (Grocery store pack) (Don't buy domestic!) (We use Fresh and Samband)
Split in 4 equal parts, 4 oz. pieces on power saw. (Cut both ways on saw.)
Batter frozen and fry frozen if possible. (We batter for each meal)

Step No. 2. Batter: 1 Qt. Buttermilk
                       12 Eggs
                          Salt
                          Pepper (Lightly)

Beat eggs thoroughly and very thin, then add Buttermilk. (We make fresh batter every meal because it will thicken up.)

Step No. 3. Crackers: Chop crackers on vegetable chopping machine to exact cut. (Do not over chop, should be very coarse, but much finer than shrimp crackers). Also chop crackers twice daily.

Step No. 4. Sprinkle salt and accent on fish. Roll fish in flour and shake off all surplus. Dip in batter then roll and pat in chopped crackers.

This fish will float when done. Fry at 300 degrees.
Looks larger than other type of Haddock.
Does not break up on counter.
Does not get tough. (Will run out the next day. We run it close each meal)
Has exceptional customer acceptance.

Step No. 5. Notes: We have been running this fish every day, every meal lately. Does not refreeze well with batter on it.
75 lbs. of old type Haddock 10/5 -
180 orders @ .59¢ = $106.20
75 lbs. of this type Haddock 12/1 -
300 orders @ .59¢ = $177.00

This 1 lb. Haddock is .42¢ per lb. in San Antonio, but be sure and procure from your regular source of supply.

Fry cook cannot batter this fish. We batter on Vegetable table.

This figures 20% food cost. (Batter and fish)
Fish cost 10½¢ an order. Batter approximately 1½¢ per order. Cost .12¢ each to lay on counter, sells for .59¢.

If you are now selling 75 lbs. a day of Haddock and can hold this poundage, (which is much increased sales on fish) you will increase your present net over $60.00 per day, or your total net profit per day on fish will be in excess of $140.00.

Chapter II   Page 29b

SALISBURY STEAK (10 lb. batch)

JOHN LEE, JR.

10 lbs. Lean Chuck ground through coarse chili blade then through chopped sirloin blade.
10 Eggs (1 egg per lb.)
3 3/4 lbs. Diced Fresh Tomatoes (6 oz. per lb.)
1 1/4 lbs. Diced Onions (2 oz. per lb.)
Salt and Pepper to taste.

Mix well and make into 8 oz. pattie. Grill on 3.5 and cover with pan. Takes about 11 minutes to cook. When done, brush on Durkee (Famous) Meat Sauce lightly.

We charge .65¢

BEEF STOCK

R. M. LUBY

23 lbs. Bones - Chuck and Round
4 Large Onions
1 Stalk Celery plus extra leaves
6 Large Carrots
3 Tablespoons Salt

Bake bones dry in 350 degree oven for one hour. Place bones and remainder of the above ingredients into 40 qt. stock pot and fill the stock pot with water. Slow boil for 12 hours and then strain broth through cloth. Then boil broth down for about four hours. Let cool and place in refrigeration to conjeal. After the stock has conjealed, take the fat layer off of the top and it is ready to use in all beef gravies and soup (onion) bases.

BEEF TACOS

SAM RICE
BEAUMONT

6 lb. Chili meat
2 Large Onions (chopped)
4 Large Buttons Garlic (chopped)
Camino to taste
Salt and Pepper

(A) Cook onions, garlic, meat, salt and pepper in skillet. (leave tomatoes out)
(B) Drain off grease.
(C) Put one soupspoon meat on fried tortilla.
(D) Add chopped (with knife) lettuce and tomatoes on top of meat.
(E) Sprinkle with american cheese and place in oven until cheese melts, then serve.

Chapter II Page 30

February 18, 1963

BEEF KON TIKI ON RICE

BILLIE LOWE

30 lb. Lean Strips of Chuck (like Beef Tips)
2 - #303 cans of bamboo shoots (thin strips)
1 - Tray of bell pepper strips (thin long strips)
Chicken Broth (unsalted)

Brown off meat in stew pan just like short ribs, then drain any grease and add chicken broth. Season and color with Soy Sauce. Thicken with corn starch about like Chop Suey. Add bamboo shoots and peppers about 15 minutes before pulling - so the peppers wilt. Serve on Rice.   Price .68¢

March 5, 1963

WINE SAUCE

EL PASO #1

3 cups white wine
2 #6/10 tomatoes
1 tray chopped green onions
1 pt. chopped bell peppers
1 cookspoon dry mustard
½ cookspoon sugar
½ cookspoon salt
¼ cookspoon black pepper
1 cookspoon oleo

Cook onions and peppers in butter until tender. Add all above ingredients and simmer 20 minutes. Remove from heat and add 6 cookspoons of sweet pickle relish. Serve over all baked fish.

October 18, 1963

TENDERLOIN TIPS IN BURGUNDY WINE SAUCE

EL PASO #1

One Half Recipe	Whole Recipe	
1	1	pound oleo
10	20	pounds beef, cut thin in 2"-3" strips
1	2	cups chopped onions
4	8	medium sliced bell peppers
1¼	2½	cups beef gravy
1½	3	cups Red Burgundy Wine
4	8	oz. sliced mushrooms

Add salt, oleo and beef together in pan. Brown beef tips, then add water and beef gravy. Let cook until almost done, then add onion and bell peppers and thicken. Fry mushrooms in skillet. When beef and vegetables are done, add mushrooms and burgundy wine. Season to taste (salt and pepper).

CANADIAN SAUSAGE

BROADWAY
GEORGE WENGLEIN

10# pork (ground)
3 tablespoons salt
1 tablespoon black pepper
1 tablespoon red pepper
1 tablespoon sugar
1 tablespoon accent
4 tablespoons sage

To this amount of sausage add equal amounts of cooked ham by volume. We use picnic ham and ham scraps left after boiling green beans for this and it is a very popular item. Sausage is best cooked on grill.

This can be served 4½ portion with scrambled eggs. Suggested price .55¢
With hominy .45¢

Chapter II

October 23, 1963

BEEF STROGANOFF

RENA & AL BENNIE
PORT ARTHUR

20 lb. meat (lean) cut in strips.
Cook meat in 1/3 lb. of oleo until brown
Add beef broth and cook until meat is tender
Then add 2 cans (20 2¢) of mushrooms
Add salt, pepper and accent to taste
Add ½ qt. sour cream and ½ can of tomato puree
Allow to thicken, then add 1 square pan of dill pickle sticks cut in half.

Serve on rice. Suggested selling price .65¢

October 23, 1963

SWEET AND SOUR SAUCE

HULDA REID

1 cup water
8 tbsp. cornstarch
2 tsp. salt
1 cup brown sugar
1 - 1½ cups vinegar
4 cups pineapple juice
4 tbsp. soy sauce

Cook above items until slightly thick. Stir constantly - then add:

4 cups pineapple chunks
3 cups green peppers - sliced thin
1 cup boiler onions - sliced thin

Let cook three minutes only and remove.

May 24, 1966

CONCENTRATE FOR CHARBROIL

DAVIS SIMPSON
AUSTIN

10 cups catsup
2 cups Worcestershire
1 cookspoon chili powder
1 tablespoon garlic powder
6 shakes Louisiana hot sauce
¼ cup Jalapeno juice
¼ cup liquid smoke

Add 1 coffee cup to each 15# meat.

Chapter II   Page 33

BEEF ALMONDINE

Nov. 20, 1963

HELEN BLODGETT

INGREDIENTS:
- 16 pound lean beef chuck (cut slightly larger than Chop Suey pork)
- 2 heaping trays of celery (cut as for Chop Suey)
- 1 tray of chopped onions
- 1 tray of stripped bell peppers (cut long) wedged
- 1 tray of sliced carrots (thin)
- 3 gal. of rich beef stock (not greasy)
- 2 pounds of fresh snow peas
- 1½ pounds whole almonds (lightly toasted)
- 4 cups Soy Sauce
- 2 cups oleo
  - Accent
  - Salt
  - Cornstarch (dissolve in cold water)

PROCEDURE:

Saute beef in large stock pot. Add beef stock, soy sauce, salt and accent. Simmer till done and thicken.

Saute half of all vegetables in 1 cup of oleo, accent and salt till just barely tender - 6 to 8 minutes. Do not overcook. Combine with beef and broth as you carry out to the counter. Serve on bed of white or fried rice with almonds sprinkled on top.

Yield approximately 65 orders. We get .61¢ for this. Very popular item.

Chapter II

                            January 6, 1964
            ITALIAN CUTLET
                            AUGUST PROLL, JR.

Veal Cutlet - 4 to 4½ oz. veal cutlet. We sometimes use the frozen
           cutlets we make out of the bit pieces left from making
           our chicken fried steak. Small pieces of meat run
           through the tendorizer and then frozen will hold together
           fine if cooked from a frozen state.

Flour and Salt - Add salt to season cutlet in your flour.
Egg and Milk batter - 3 eggs to 1 qt. of milk and beat.
Bread Crumbs - finely chopped dry bread crumbs.
Mozzarella Cheese - slices of cheese sliced on #12.
Tomato Sauce - 1 qt. of onions cut in 3/4 inch squares
           1 qt. of bell peppers cut in 3/4 inch squares
           1 #10 can tomatoes with tomatoes hand mashed
           2 qts. of beef stock
           Salt to taste
           Dash of oregano
           Combine all above ingredients and cook till onions and
           peppers are soft.

    Batter the cutlet in flour first, then in egg and milk batter, and then into bread crumbs. Place about six on greased sheet pan and broil until done. Put a slice of cheese on each cutlet and run back into the oven until cheese wilts. Put tomato sauce in bottom of a flat bean pan and place the cutlets on top of the sauce. The brown cutlet, white cheese, and red sauce make a very attractive setup.

Chapter II   Page 35

LASAGNA

January 30, 1964

AUGUST PROLL, JR.

2   No. 10 cans tomatoes (break up tomatoes by hand)
1   No. 10 can tomato sauce
3   tablespoons salt
3   tablespoons oregano
1   teaspoon black pepper
3   tablespoons onion salt
8   cups minced onion
8   cloves garlic minced
1 1/3 cups salad oil
8   lbs. lean ground meat ground through fine grind (some use 10 lbs.)
8   teaspoons accent
4   packages of Lasagna noodles (total of 4 lbs.)
Parmesan cheese (shredded)
Mozzarella cheese sliced on #10
American cheese slices to garnish top

Combine first six items in pot and simmer for about 30 minutes.

Saute garlic and onions in salad oil in large aluminum skillet and then add meat and accent and cook till meat is done. Then add meat to tomato mixture and let it simmer for about 30 minutes.

Cook Lasagna noodles till done and rinse noodles in cold water.

PROCEDURE - Broadway

Combine the above items in pan as follows:

Place a thin layer of meat sauce in bottom of pan. Then place a layer of Lasagna noodles over the meat sauce. Next put a layer of sliced Mozzarella cheese on top of the Lasagna noodles. Then sprinkle a thin layer of Parmesan cheese. Repeat the same sequence until pan is almost full. Top with a meat sauce layer and then sprinkle a light layer of Parmesan cheese and garnish with American cheese strips as desired for eye appeal. Heat in oven and serve. .45¢ per order. Offer more Parmesan cheese to customers if desired at counter.

PROCEDURE - Romana Plaza

Same procedure as above except they alternate pan this way:

> Layer meat sauce
> "   Mozzarella cheese
> "   Lasagna noodles
> "   Parmesan cheese

Repeat until the pan is full. End up with Parmesan cheese on top with American cheese strips as desired for eye appeal.

Yield: 4 - 165 pans

BEEF RAGOUT-BURGUNDY

M. H. LANGFORD

20 lbs. beef (chuck) cut in 1 inch cubes
4 cups flour
4 cups shortening
4-51 oz. cans tomato soup
1 soup can water
4 cups Burgundy wine
8 tbsp. salt
8 tbsp. Worcestershire
8 bay leaves
4 tsp. thyme, powdered
8 lbs. carrots, peeled and cut in 1 inch chunks, then quartered
8 lbs. boiler onions
8 lbs. Idaho potatoes, chunked
1 pack peas, frozen

METHOD

Dust meat with flour; brown in shortening. Combine browned meat, soup, water, wine, salt, Worcestershire, bay and thyme. Cover and cook one hour. Add carrots and onions, cover and cook another hour. About ½ hour before serving time, add potatoes. Cover and cook until vegetables are done. Use cooked peas for garnish.

Portions: 132 - 8 oz. servings

Oct. 15, 1964

SWEDISH MEAT BALLS AND SPAGHETTI

HENRY O. JONES, JR.

  9 lbs. Veal
  4 lbs. Pork
26 Rolls
13 Eggs
  6 large Onions
  1 bunch Parsley
Salt
Pepper
Accent
  3 Tablespoons Celery Salt
  3 Tablespoons Nutmeg

Grind all above ingredients together

SAUCE:

1 batch Canadian Cream Soup
   (double vegetables in soup and thicken more than usual)

PROCEDURE:

Bake or fry off meat balls. Marinate in sauce in the oven. Serve meat balls on top of spaghetti, that is in sauce also. Sprinkle finely chipped bacon over each setup.

YIELD: 90 orders of 1 3/4 oz. meat balls.

PRICE: .47¢

Oct. 30, 1964

SOUR CREAM SAUCE
(For New Potatoes and Corned Beef)

H. O. JONES, JR.

1/3 cream sauce
2/3 sour cream

Heat the cream sauce and add a small amount of sour cream at a time, stirring constantly.

New potatoes with Sour Cream Sauce goes well with Knackwurst, or may be run as a potato on vegetable counter.

Dec. 2, 1965

POLYNESIAN BEEF

CORPUS CHRISTI

25# lean chuck, (cut in strips)
 5 tbsp. garlic salt
 1 cookspoon paprika
 1½ cups salad oil

Mix above together and let brown, before adding beef stock. Add enough beef stock to completely cover meat. Then add below:

1# brown sugar
2½ cups soy sauce
1½ cups Gallo Sherry Wine; and 1½ cups Wine Vinegar

Let above cook as normal for Beef Tips.

VEGETABLES

½ tray sliced celery (cut as for Chow Mein)
½ tray sliced bell pepper rings)
1 tray sliced onion rings   ) Slice on #30 on slicing machine
20 tomato wedges

Add celery and onions about 25 minutes before pulling from oven; add bell peppers 5 minutes before pulling from oven. Just before thickening with cornstarch, add 1 #10 can of pineapple chunks with juice (or tidbits with juice). Add tomato wedges after above is thickened and pulled from oven.

(Use ice to absorb grease off of fat roast beef such as chuck, prime rib, etc..)

Chapter II   Page 39

June 4, 1965

SHRIMP STEAK

MORT LANGFORD
BANDERA ROAD

Using peeled and deveined shrimp, let it thaw and then weigh out into 4 oz. portions, then run thru your Steakmaster machine. The first or second time thru it will come out in several small pieces. If you will keep working it with your hand, forming a ball each time, and continue to run thru the machine, on the fifth or sixth time it will begin to knit into a pattie about 4" long and 2" wide. Then place it on freezer paper on a tray. Using a pan of ice water and working with your hand, gently pat the shrimp into a pattie about 6" long and 4" wide and ¼" thick. Then we give it a hard freeze.

After the hard freeze, we procede to prepare them as we would our fried fish. We fry them from the freezer and the cooking time is about six minutes in a 350 d/e fryer Served on a platter with a little garnish of lemon and parsley. We sell them for .69¢ and run a 25% food cost.

This also makes an excellent broiling item, with a sprinkle of Lowry's seasoned salt and cooked in lemon butter.

December 29, 1965

SHRIMP CURRY

BOYD MORROW

¼ lb. oleo
6 lbs. raw peeled and drained shrimp (whole or cut in large pieces)
5 cups chopped onions
2½ cups thin sliced celery
3 fresh red ripe tomatoes, peeled and diced
1 cup sliced green onions
1 package curry mix (3 small squares)
2 tbsp. salt
1 qt. water
Thicken with cornstarch if necessary.

PROCEDURE:

Use small aluminum **heavy** stock pot. Melt oleo, add chopped onions and celery. Cook until clear or tender but not soft. Add shrimp and water - cover tightly. Cook until shrimp are just tender (do not overcook shrimp). Add 1 package of curry mix and 2 tablespoons of salt. Thicken with cornstarch if necessary.

Serve over rice on platter.

Suggested price - .85¢

June 21, 1966

BLEU CHEESE STUFFED CHOPPED SIRLOIN

LES DANDRIDGE
EL PASO #1

```
6       cups chopped onion
1 1/2   cups salad oil
8       cloves garlic, minced
16      lbs. ground beef chuck
16      eggs
  1/2   cup chopped parsley
2 2/3   tbsp. salt
2       tsp. pepper
```

FILLING:

```
2       cups crumbled Roquefort Cheese
1       cup soft butter
1       cup Brandy
```

Saute onion in oil until transparent. Add garlic; cook about 1 minute. Add to beef with eggs, parsley, salt and pepper. Mix well. Shape in 7 oz. giant, oval hamburger patties.

For filling, blend remaining ingredients until creamy.

Make a deep hole on one side of each ball. Fill with cheese mix and mold the meat over opening. Repeat on other side. Brush with oil; sprinkle with salt and pepper. Broil. Serve with Pancho Sauce.

June 21, 1966

PANCHO SAUCE

LES DANDRIDGE
EL PASO #1

```
  1/2   gal. tomato catsup
1       qt. mayonnaise
1       qt. chili sauce
  1/2   cup dry mustard
2 2/3   tbsp. prepared horseradish
1 1/3   tbsp. ground ginger
  2/3   tbsp. Accent
1       cup pineapple juice
  1/2   cup wine vinegar
5 1/3   tbsp. Worcestershire sauce
3       tsp. bottled hot pepper sauce
```

Combine ingredients thoroughly. Serve at room temperature or hot. Makes approximately 1 gallon sauce.

Chapter II   Page 41

STUFFED SHRIMP

June 21, 1966

ROMANA CAFETERIA
HOUSTON, TEXAS
H. O. JONES, JR.

Use 21 to 25 count shrimp

12 to 13 pieces of fried fish
1 double handful of potatoes
2 lbs. of frozen crab, cut in cubes as you would for Deviled Crab
   (approximately 1/4 inch thick) (add crab last)
2 pieces celery   )
2 green peppers   ) Chopped fine and saute as for Deviled Crab
1 large onion   )
10 to 12 eggs

Season with 1 3/4 bottles of Durkees Steak Sauce, salt, pepper, Accent, garlic powder and 1 pinch of nutmeg. Mix well. Then use cracker crumbs to tighten mixture firm enough to hold. Fan cut shrimp, stuff with approximately 2 oz. of crab stuffing.

Batter like fish. Fry in Frialator.

FOR CRAB CAKE:

Same as Stuffed Shrimp except add one extra pound of crab meat. Form into 4½ oz. patties. Batter same as fish. Fry in Frialator.

August 8, 1966

TROUT ALMONDINE

LUTHER HUNT

1. Season trout with salt and Accent.
2. Roll in flour.
3. Dip in batter.

   BATTER:
   6 eggs
   6 cups flour
   7 cups milk
   Salt and pepper

4. Sprinkle sliced almonds on <u>flesh</u> side of fish.
5. "<u>Pat</u>" fish with cracker crumbs as you would shrimp, leaving almond side up.
6. When serving, spoon some Butter Sauce on it.

   BUTTER SAUCE:
   3# oleo
   Juice from 2 lemons
   1/2 cup pineapple juice

Chapter II
Page 42

January 27, 1967

CREAM SAUCE

McCRELESS

7½ lb. grated American cheese
1½ scoops flour
1½ scoops powdered milk
2 gallons boiling water
1½ lb. melted oleo - warm

Mix cheese, flour, oleo and powdered milk in beater bowl at low speed w/heavy whip (like you mash potatoes with).

After well mixed, add boiling water and mix until smooth.

January 27, 1967

SOUR CREAM ENCHILADAS

EL PASO #3

2 #10 cans crushed tomatoes
1½ gallons chicken broth
1 can M. Pass peppers (chopped not too fine)
1 cup chopped onions (saute)
1 cup Chili Verde or chopped jalapenos
1 qt. sour cream

Saute onions. Combine all of above and thicken with enough cornstarch to give body.

SOFT TACOS

Chop R.O. Meat in food chopper. Cook in heavy pot with onion, garlic, salt and pepper and comino seed & slight part of grated cheese. Dip Tortillias in warm grease. Roll meat in tortillo & flatten.

      Sauce:

1 no. 1 can tomatoes
1 # 2-1/2 can chilli strips
1 # 10 can water

1 onion   )
3 bell peppers) chop and saute in Oleo

1 Tablespoon Comino
1 Tablespoon Oregano

Simmer 15 minutes & thicken with cornstarch.
Cook like enchiladas with white or yellow cheese and garnish with shredded lettuce, diced tomatoes & chopped onion.

Chapter II   Page 43

SOUTHERN BEEF HASH

INGREDIENTS	LBS	OZS	METHOD
Cooked Clod	15		Dice cooked clod in pieces about the size of your thumb nail. Place in roasting pan with diced onions, beef broth and seasoning. Cook for approx. 1 hour. Add diced potatoes and more water as needed. Cook till potatoes are done. Tighten as desired with flour water and using kitchen bouquet get a rich brown gravy.
Raw diced potatoes	10	15	
Onions--chopped	7		
Beef stock (1 1/2 gallons)			
Salt & pepper	to taste		
Kitchen Bouquet	as desired		

*****

VEAL POT PIE

INGREDIENTS	LBS	OZS	METHOD
Veal tips cut small	20		Salt & pepper veal tips, roll in flour and glaze in oven. Pour off excess grease.
Water	10		
Potatoes	10		Add water, potatoes, carrots, onions, peas & mushrooms. Cook.
Carrots	6		
Onions--chopped	2		
Peas (English)	3		After ingredients are done, place in bay-marie and use as needed.
Mushrooms (1 can)			
Salt & pepper	to taste		

Top with pastry and serve.

NOTE: Kitchen bouquet may be used for color.

*****

VEAL POT PIE

INGREDIENTS	LBS	OZS	METHOD
Chuck meat (cubed)	20		Place all ingredients in pot and bring to a boil.
Onions	2		
Water 4 gallons			
Salt, pepper & Accent	to taste		
Carrots--diced	5		Add carrots. Cook 15 minutes.
Potatoes--diced	10		Add potatoes. Cook till all ingredients are done. Tighten as desired with flour water. Add gravy color.
#10 Peas--drained	1/2 can		Add.
Mushrooms	8 oz. can		

Place in pan to bake with either plain or cheese pastry, brown well.

BEEF TIPS

INGREDIENTS	LBS	OZS	METHOD
Stew meat	20		Place stew meat in heavy roasting pan. Add chopped onions and seasoning. Rub into meat. Add water. Braize.
Onions	2		
57 Sauce 1 bottle			
Water 1/2 gallon			
Salt, pepper & Accent		to taste	
Water (to cover)			Add water to cover and cook till done. Tighten with flour and water mix, as desired.

Serve with noodles, potatoes & carrots, potatoes, dumplings, etc.

*****

BEEF TIPS AND VEGETABLES

Cook equal amount of Beef Tips]   Thicken beef tips with W-13
                             Carrots   ]
                             New Potatoes]

Keep beef tips, carrots and potatoes separated in pan on counter, use beef tip broth to keep vegetables moistened on counter.

Serve equal amounts of each on service plate.

*****

BEEF TIPS AND NOODLES

Cook separately---------Serve 1/3 part Beef Tips
                                         2/3   Noodles

*****

BEEF TIPS AND DUMPLINGS

Same as Beef tips and Noodles.   Using thickened beef tip broth on both noodles and dumplings.

CURRIED BEEF TIPS

INGREDIENTS	LBS	OZS	METHOD
Veal tips	10		
Garlic salt		4	
White pepper		3	Bake in oven all ingredients
Salt		6	until done and: Add water,
Chopped onions -- 5 large			tomato puree.
Paprika		2	
Chopped celery	2		Thicken with flour to proper
Tomatoe puree -- 2 cups			consistency.
Bay leaves -- 3 leaves			

*****

CURRIED BEEF TIPS

	LBS	OZS	
Veal tips	10		
Garlic salt		4	
White pepper		3	Add water. Bake in oven
Salt		6	Add flour to thicken.
Chopped onions -- 3 cups			
Tomato puree -- 2 cups			
Bay leaves -- 3			

*****

BEEF STEW

Beef tips	15	Cook separately. Mix together
New potatoes	15	and add broth from beef tips.
Carrots	15	
Salt & pepper	to taste	Thicken with W-13

*****

IRISH STEW

Same as Beef Stew, only add:

Onions and Cabbage

BEEF STEW

INGREDIENTS	LBS	OZS	METHOD
Stew meat	15		Place meat in roaster, rub in flour,
Onions	3		and add salt, pepper, onions &
Flour	1		Accent. Add water and braise
Salt, pepper & Accent	to taste		for 1 hour.
Water 1/2 gallon			
#10 Tomatoes	1 1/2 gallons		Mash tomatoes good and add. Add
Carrots	8		2 gal. water and then carrots.
#10 Potatoes 3 cans			When carrots are just about done
#10 Whole Onions 1 can			add potatoes, onions, stringbeans
Cooked & drained Stringbeans 1 gal.			and peas. Tighten with flour
Cooked & drained peas 1/2 gallon			to the consistency desired.

NOTE: For brown beef stew, omit tomatoes.

* * * * *

SHORT RIBS OF BEEF

	LBS	OZS	
Short Ribs (uncut)	25		Flour rib strips well, place in
Onions	2	8	roasting pan. Add seasoning,
Chopped Garlic to taste			onions and water. Braise well.
Salt, pepper & Accent to taste			Drain off all grease. Cover
Flour	1	8	with water and cook till tender.
Water (to cover bottom of pan)			

Remove short ribs when done and strain gravy. Tighten as desired with flour and water. Serve with brown potatoes with some chopped green onions added.

* * * * *

IRISH STEW

	LBS		
Veal tips	10		Glaze veal tips in oven, after
New potatoes	10		they have been salted and rolled
Diced carrots	10		in flour.
Water	20		
Chopped onions	5		After glazing, add water, chopped
Cabbage	10		onions and carrots. Cook until
Paprika to color			done.
Salt and pepper to taste			

Add new potatoes and cook for 10 minutes or until potatoes are hot.

Steam cabbage and add to above as needed.

SPANISH STEW

INGREDIENTS	LBS	OZS	METHOD
Veal tips	20		Salt & pepper veal tips, roll in
Carrots	10		flour and glaze in oven.
New potatoes	10		
Chopped onions	5		Add carrots, onions, water and
Tomatoes	6		tomatoes.
Paprika to color			
Salt, pepper & Accent to taste			20 minutes before done, add new potatoes.
			Paprika to color.

*****

STUFFED PEPPERS

	LBS	OZS	
Veal or beef chuck	16		Grind through sausage plate.
Onions	3		Season and mix.
Bell peppers	2	8	
Fresh ripe tomatoes	6		Mash tomatoes good and add with
Cooked Macaroni or Rice	6		the rest of the ingredients to
Hot sauce		8	above. Mix well. Tighten with
Egg whites	2		crackermeal as needed.

Prepare pepper shells in uniform size. Fill with 4 ozs of mix and bake in raw shell in desired sauce.

NOTE: If macaroni is used it is advisable to cut it, but not too small.

*****

SPANISH RICE

	LBS	OZS	
Rice	5		Brown rice golden brown in bacon
Bacon drippings	2		drippings. Brown on slow fire as it may scorch or burn.
Onions	2		Saute onions and peppers in bacon.
Bell peppers	2		
Slab bacon		8	
#10 Tomatoes (3 cans)			Add all these ingredients to
Chili powder		1	sauteed onions and peppers. Cook
Salt		4	ten min., add browned rice. Let
Pepper (1 tsp.)			all of this cook 20 min. or until
Beef stock (1 gallon)			rice is done. Then simmer
Water (2 gallons)			

NOTE: Ham or shrimp Jambalaya may be made by substituting ham or shrimp in place of rice.

CREOLE RICE

INGREDIENTS	LBS	OZS	METHOD
Chuck	5		Grind meat through sausage plate add water and braise. After braising, tilt roasting pan and pour off grease.
Water (1 pt.)		1	
Celery	5		Add all ingredients and cook till' tender, stirring occasionally.
Bell peppers	4		
Onions	5		
Chili powder 2 cookspoons			
#10 Catsup 1 can			
Water 2 gallons			
Salt, pepper & Accent to taste			

*****

CHILI SUPREME

	LBS	OZS	METHOD
Kidney suet	7		Grind suet through sausage plate. Rinder in one pint of water.
Water	1		
Lean bull or beef chuck	40		Grind chuck through sausage plate and add to rindered suet. Also add the water, salt, and chopped garlic. Cook over low fire till tender.
Water	2		
Salt to taste			
Button garlic (chopped fine)		4	
Flour	1		Add flour and blend in. Continue cooking approx. 10 minutes.
Camino seed		8	Add to above, stir in and remove from fire.
Paprika		8	
Chili Powder	1		

Allow to cool, then place in ice box.

For chili or chili and beans, add 1/2 gallon water to every 5 lbs. of chili. Tighten if necessary.

For Enchiladas with chili gravy, add 1 1/2 gallons water to every 5 lbs. of chili. Tighten.

CHILIBURGERS

Beef	12 lbs)	Grind beef & pork through fine
Pork	8 lbs)	plate.
Garlic	3 buttons)	Chop fine

Salt, pepper, chili powder and paprika to taste.

Soak 60 slices bread in beef broth. Add to above and grind.

Add 2 lbs. Whole eggs   Mix thoroughly.

Fry patties 2/3 done.

Bake in oven with sauce.

SAUCE:

Tomato paste or puree	2 qts.	
Catsup	2 qts.	
Water	2 qts.	
Garlic	4 buttons	
Onions	6 large)	Chopped fine
Bell Peppers	2)	Chopped fine.

Salt, pepper & chilli powder to taste.

Fry onions, pepper & garlic in salad oil before adding to tomato sauce. Simmer at least 30 min. after blending.

Take patties from oven when fully baked. Sprinkle lightly with grated cheese.

Place in oven for 30 seconds before serving.

Serving: 3 1/4 ozs.

ITALIAN SPAGHETTI

INGREDIENTS	LBS	OZS	METHOD
Trimmed Chuck Water 1/2 gallon	15		Grind chuck through sausage plate. Place in roasting pan, add water and braise. Pour off grease after braising
Onions Peppers Garlic pods (3) Tomato paste (2 #10 cans) Water (3 gallons) Salt, pepper & Accent to taste	3 2	 8	After draining add all ingredients bring to a boil, then simmer. Tighten slightly.

Boil and drain spaghetti and add to above.

*****

ITALIAN MEAT BALLS

Ground beef Peeled garlic Onions (5 large) Parsley (1 bunch) Tomato juice (1 qt.) Whole eggs Salt & Pepper	15	 8 12	Grind through fine plate. Chop onions, garlic pepper & parsley fine before mixing with meat. Add eggs & mix thoroughly. To taste.

Tighten with cracker meal if needed.

SAUCE FOR MEAT BALLS & SPAGHETTI

4 Large onions chopped fine
3 Large cloves garlic chopped fine
6 Cans Italian tomato puree
3 Qts. water
   Salt & pepper to taste

Fry onions & garlic in 1/2 cup olive oil. Add tomato paste and water.

1 Soupspoon Rose Marie and simmer 2 hours.

ITALIAN SPAGHETTI

12 lbs.	Ground beef	Grind through fine plate.
3	Large onions	Grind onions & garlic together
2 cloves	Garlic, chopped fine	through fine plate. Mix together with meat.

Fry in salad oil until done, make sauce as you do for Italian Meat Balls & Spaghetti. Cook spaghetti in salted water until done, add sauce and meat to spaghetti and allow to cook 16 min. together. Serve with Italian cheese sprinkled over each order.

*****

ITALIAN MEAT BALLS

INGREDIENTS	LBS	OZS	METHOD
Beef chuck	15		Grind chuck through hmb. plate.
Parsley (3 bunches)			Grind parsley, onions, celery
Cleaned garlic (1/2 8 oz. glass)			& garlic through the same plate
Celery (1 large bunch)			and mix thoroughly.
Onions (4 large)			
Egg Whites		3	Add egg whites and blend.

NOTE: Portions to be made in 1 oz. round balls, and fried in deep fat. Simmer in sauce one hour before serving over spaghetti.

SAUCE:

Onions	4 large	Grind onions & garlic in food
Garlic	3 large cloves]	chopper and saute in 1/2 cup
Tomato paste	1 #10 can	salad oil. Add tomato paste
Water	2 #10 cans	and water and simmer for 2
Salt & pepper	to taste	hours.

Add: 1 soup spoon Rose Marie

MEAT BALLS AND SPAGHETTI

INGREDIENTS	LBS	OZS	METHOD
Boneless Chuck	20		Wet bread in roast beef broth. Put damp bread and other ingredients in large dishpan, season, and mix together. Grind through chili plate and mix together. Regrind through hamburger plate and mix.
Cleaned Garlic 2 pods			
Loaves Bread 2			
Onions		2	
Bell peppers		1	
Parsley 1 bunch			
Egg whites		2	Add eggwhites, mix, and tighten with crackermeal to the right consistency.

Roll into 1 1/2 oz. balls

SAUCE:	AMT.	
#10 Tomatoes	2 cans	Put all ingredients into large cooking pot being sure to mash tomato pulps real well. Bring to a bristling boil then turn fire to simmer. Tighten as desired with starch.
#10 Catsup	1 can	
Garlic pods	2	
Water	5 gals.	
Celery	3 lbs.	
Onions	3 lbs.	
Mustard	6 ozs.	
Lea & Perrins	10 ozs.	

*****

HAMBURGER & NOODLES

INGREDIENTS	LBS	OZS	METHOD
Noodles	4		Cook noodles separately, in salted water.
Ground Beef	10		Cook ground beef in roasting pan in oven.
Onions, chopped	8		Saute chopped vegetables in 1/2 cup salad oil.
Bell Peppers, chopped	3		
Tomatoes (2 #10 cans)			Add tomatoes, vegetables and cooked ground beef together, cook for 1 hr. and add drained noodles.
Paprika for color			
Salt, pepper & Accent to taste			

Hamburger Casserole may be made by adding grated cheese to above.

VEAL CHOP SUEY

INGREDIENTS	AMOUNT
Diced Veal	18 lb.
Celery, cut lengthwise,	12 lb.
Onions	12 lb.
Soy Sauce	2
#10 Chop Suey Veg.	2
#2 Bean Sprouts	6
Bead Molasses	2
Oleo	1/2 lb.
Cornstarch	1 box
Mushrooms	4 cans

Saute veal in chicken fat or oleo. Add about 1 1/2 gallons stock, chicken or beef. Put in celery and let cook about one hour.

Add onions and cook until done. Strain sprouts and vegetables, then make a mixture of sprouts, vegetables, soy sauce, bead molasses and mushrooms. Thicken with cornstarch. Add to above.

YIELD: 180 orders.

*****

BOILED SPARE RIBS

INGREDIENTS	LBS	OZS	METHOD
Fresh Spare Ribs	25		Blanch off ribs in fryer till half done. Put in pot with onions and seasoning, cover with water and cook till done.
Onions	2		
Bay leaves (a few)			
Salt, pepper & Accent	to taste		
Water, to cover			

*****

COOKED MEAT PATTY

Cooked meat	6	Pick through meat carefully. Grind meat, potatoes & onions through hamburger plate. Add broth and mix. Season.
Roast beef broth (1/2 pt)		
Cooked potatoes	4	
Onions	1	
Salt, pepper & Accent to taste		

Egg White	6	Add mustard and eggwhites and mix. Add crackermeal as needed.
Yellow mustard (2 cookspoons)		
Crackermeal		

Scale into 4 oz. portions and round into patties. Cook as needed.

Variation: Leave mix moist and roll in biscuit dough. Brown in oven and serve with cream gravy.

RAW MEAT PATTIES

INGREDIENTS	LBS	OZS	METHOD

For hamburger steaks, cheeseburgers, salisbury steaks, barbecued meat patties, etc.:

Beef chuck	15		Dampen bread with roast beef
Onions	1	8	broth. Place in pan with chuck,
Bread	3	8	onions, salt & pepper & Accent.
Roast beef broth--to dampen bread			Mix together & grind all through
Salt, pepper & Accent-to taste			chili plate. Mix together and regrind through hamburger plate.

Scale into 4 oz. balls and pat out as desired. Grill on one side and finish cooking in the oven uncovered with sauce accordingly.

*****

ROAST BEEF CLODS.

Use six to seven pound veal clods. Trim well.

Place in roasting pan fat side up. Season well with chopped onions, salt, pepper & Accent and with bay leaves or garlic, or both as desired. Add 1/2 gallon of water.

Braise well in 550° oven using preheat.

After braising well, cover with water, turn off preheat and cook till tender in hot oven approximately 500°.

Test when they are done by putting roast beef fork in larger portion of roast. It it comes out easily the roast is done.

Remove roast from pan and strain gravy. Add enough gravy color to make it dark.

Portion serving 3 1/4 ozs.

CHICKEN FRIED STEAK

1. Buy U. S. Good trimmed cutlet meat.
2. Cut into 2 3/4 oz steaks and run through cubing machine till well tenderized.
3. Make batter of 1 gallon milk and 12 ozs voltex.
4. Dip into flour then into egg-milk batter and then back into flour.
5. Cook in fryer or deep fat till done. Keep flour well sifted.

SMOTHERED STEAKS

1. Cut trimmed cutlet meat into 3 oz steaks. Cube well.
2. Make gravy by using two gallons beef broth, 4 gallons water & 3 lbs of chopped onions. Bring to a good boil and tighten with flour water. Darken to medium brown with gravy color.
3. Flour steaks, place on greased grill and cook half done. Place in pan, cover with gravy, place lid on pan and smother till done in oven.

PAN FRIED STEAKS

1. Cut trimmed cutlet meat into 2 3/4 oz steaks. Cube well.
2. Make gravy by using 2 gallons beef broth, 4 gallons of water & 2 lbs whole onions. Bring to a good boil and tighten with cornstarch dissolved in water. Strain.
3. Flour steaks & cook till done on medium greased grill. Cover with gravy and serve.

SWISS STEAKS

Same as smothered steaks only instead of brown gravy use Creole sauce. Consult recipe under sauces.

BARBECUED MEAT PATTY

INGREDIENTS	LBS	OZS	METHOD
Hamburger meat (chuck)	10		Soak bread in tomato juice. Put chuck & pork in pan and season with salt & pepper. Grind through sausage plate. Add bread soaked in tomato juice. Mix and grind again through hamburger plate.
Boneless Pork	5		
Bread (30 slices)			
Tomato juice (1 qt.)			
Salt & pepper to taste			
Eggs (15)			Add eggs and mix.

Scale 4 ozs each and mold into patties. Just cook on one side. Place in pan brown side down, cover with chopped onions, add barbecue sauce and cook uncovered 30 minutes.

*****

MEAT LOAF

	LBS	OZS	METHOD
Boneless beef chuck	20		Grind all ingredients through chili plate. Season good with salt & pepper and mix together. Then grind again through hamburger plate. Mix good.
Boneless pork butts	5		
Onions	2		
Celery	2		
Bell peppers	1	8	
Tomatoes (1 gallon)			Mash tomatoes good and add.
Egg whites	2	8	Add egg whites and mix.
Crackers	6		Crush crackers and add to above. Mix, mix, mix, and mix some more. Tighten with whatever crackermeal is necessary.

Mold into desired loaves and bake at 375°. Preheat dry then add creole or tomato sauce.

Portion: 4 ozs.

PORK SAUSAGE

INGREDIENTS	AMOUNT	METHOD
Fresh Pork	8 lbs	Grind ingredients together
Hot Mexican Peppers	1 cup	
Sage, salt & pepper	2 cookspoons	Mix meat well, add sage, salt & pepper. Mix well.
Chili Quick	1 cookspoon	

*****

HAM CASSEROLE

Chopped Ham	1/2 pan	Chop pepper & onion together
Cooked Macaroni	1 pan	Add all ingredients together and bake in pan topped with grated cheese. Add enough cream sauce (as needed) to keep from being dry.
#2 can Tomatoes	1	
Green Pepper	1	
Chopped Onion	1 large	

*****

O'BRIEN PORK CHOPS

Left-over Pork Chops	1 pan	Chop celery, onions & pepper fine.
Celery	10 sticks	
Onion	1 large	
Green Pepper	1	
Water	1 gallon	Add onions, pepper & celery to gravy and allow to cook in oven with pork chops & tomatoes added.
Tomatoes	1/2 gal.	

*****

PORK CHOP SUEY

Lean Pork	2 lb.
Celery	2 large
Onions	4 large
#2 Cans Bean Sprouts	2
Chinese Mixed Vegetables	2 #2 Cans
Soy Sauce	12 oz.

CHICKEN CHOPSUEY

INGREDIENTS	LBS	OZS	METHOD
Chicken meat	6		Cut celery diagonally and saute in oleo with onions, for about 40 minutes
Celery	6		
Onions	6		
Oleo	1		
Chop suey veg. (1 #10 can)			Drain, adding vegetables to above and stir well. Keep stock for later use.
Soy sauce		2	
Bean sprouts (1 #10 can)			Add all ingredients to above and stir well. Put back on stove and let simmer.
Mushrooms		1	
Chicken stock	(2 gal)		
W-13		12	Thicken juice from vegetables with W-13 and add to above
Juice from vegetables			

Add chopped chicken to above and stir well.

Serve with chow mein noodles or rice.

CHICKEN AND DUMPLINGS

	LBS	OZS	METHOD
Flour	7	8	Place all ingredients in mixing bowl. Add water slowly and mix on #3 speed for 20 min. using dough arm.
Oleo		12	
Whole eggs (12)			
Salt		2	
Ice water	1		

Pinch dough into 1 lb balls and run through pie machine.

Stack on top of each other evenly, flouring well. Using french knife cut diagonally one way and then the other. Marinate pieces well with flour then place in sifter and sift all excess flour before cooking.

INDIVIDUAL CHICKEN POT PIE

INGREDIENTS	LBS	OZS	METHOD
Potatoes	3		Dice and cook each vegetable
Onions	2		separately in sufficient amount
Green peas	1		of chicken stock. Drain then
Mushrooms	1		mix together.
Carrots	1		
Chicken fat	1	8	Melt chicken fat in sauce pan
Flour		12	blend with flour and cook well.
Chicken stock	12		Add chicken stock and seasoning.
Salt		1	
Pepper (1/2 tsp)			
Chicken meat	2	8	

Divide Vegetables into casseroles.

Place layer diced chicken meat in each casserole.

Pour cream sauce over meat and vegetables.

Cover with pastry dough.

Brush pies and let dry for 10 min. before putting in oven

Make wash of one lb of oleo and 1 egg whipped together.

BROILED CHICKEN

Cut chicken in order size. Rub each order with salt & pepper, pleace in pan to be served in. Fill pan 1/2 to 3/4 inch with water. Season with margarine, placing one cut onion on top.

Cook 40 to 45 minutes at 425° in open pan, basting each 10 minutes.

CREAMED CHICKEN AU GRATIN

INGREDIENTS	LBS	OZS	METHOD
Milk	2		Make into cream sauce adding coloring and cooking to the consistency- of medium thick sauce.
Chicken stock	2		
Oleo		12	
Flour		8	
Yellow color (as needed)			
Potatoes (diced)	3		Cook separately in chicken stock, strain, mix together.
Onions (chopped fine)	2		
Carrots (diced)	1		
Mushrooms	1		
Peas	1		
Cheese	2		

Method of make up:

Line up casserole, cover the bottom with cream sauce, add mixed vegetables, then layer of chicken meat o oz to casserole, pour cream sauce over this and cover top with grated cheese. Display on steam table as is, and as you sell them brown them off in broiler.

CHICKEN A LA KING

INGREDIENTS	LBS	OZS	METHOD
Diced chicken meat	6		Make rue of chicken fat, oleo, and flour.
Chicken fat		8	
Oleo		8	
Flour		12	
Chicken stock (2 gal)			Add to above.
Hot milk (2 gal)			
Celery	3		Boil off diced celery, onions, and peppers and add to the above.
Onions	2		
Peppers	1		
Hot milk	4		
Olio		8	
Eggs (boiled - 6 only)			Add diced eggs, pimentoes and mushrooms to above and stir well.
Mushrooms		8	
Pimentos		8	

Serve on toast.

SMOTHERED CHICKEN

Fry chicken in batter. Place in pan to be served in, with approximately 1/2 inch of water. Season with margarine, salt and pepper, cut one onion and place in pan, remove margarine when done. Make standard chicken stock gravy and pour over chicken and serve.

TURKEY & CHICKEN CROQUETTES

Chicken	1		Ground through small plate.
Potatoes	1	8	" " " "

Use 1 egg to each 1b meat.
Use 1 onion to each 2 1b meat.
Salt and pepper to taste

Tighten with cracker meal.   Make into 4 oz croquettes.

CRABMEAT AU GRATIN

INGREDIENTS	LBS	OZS	METHOD

CREAM SAUCE:

Oleo		8	Melt oleo in sauce pan. Add
Flour		8	flour and cook well over slow
Hot Milk (1/2 lb powdered milk)			fire. Add hot milk and stir
Salt & pepper to taste			into smooth sauce. Add salt
Cooking Sherry		4	and pepper to taste, and Wine.

Grated parmesian cheese or tobasco sauce or both may be added to the sauce to bring out sharp taste.

1. Line 24 casserole dishes with layer of toasted bread cubes.
2. Pour over bread cubes one good spoon of cream sauce.
3. Take 3 cans of crabmeat and divide equally into casserole. This will give each augratin a full layer of crabmeat. A 1 lb. can of crabmeat will make 8 good augratins.
4. Pour cream sauce over layer of crabmeat, then top well with grated cheese.
5. Brown to order.

*****

STUFFED LOBSTER AU GRATIN

CREAM SAUCE:

Butter		8	Melt butter in sauce pan. Add
Flour		8	flour and cook well over slow
Milk powder (2 qts)			fire. Add hot milk slowly and
Salt & pepper to taste			stir into smooth sauce. Add salt & pepper to taste.
Cooking sherry		4	Stir into above.
Onions	1		Drain mushrooms and saute with
Mushrooms		8	onions. Add to above.
Oleo		4	
Lobsters (2 lb average) Cooked	24		Halve lobsters & clean. Hull out. Flake meat, saute in a little oleo and add to sauce.

Now stuff lobster shells with Thermidor mixture and cover with grated cheese.

Brown to order.

TUNA FISH CROQUETTES

INGREDIENTS	LBS	OZS	METHOD
Codfish (cooked)	4		Grind codfish, potatoes and onions through hamburger plate. Add flaked tuna and diced hard boiled eggs. Season. Add eggwhite. Mix. Add crackermeal as needed.
Tunafish	2		
Cooked potatoes	3		
Boiled eggs (12)			
Salt, pepper & Accent (to taste)			
Egg whites		8	
Crackermeal to tighten as needed			
Onions		1	

SALMON CROQUETTES

INGREDIENTS	LBS	OZS	METHOD
Cooked codfish	4		Grind salmon, codfish, onions & potatoes through hamburger plate. Add seasoning and mix
Pink salmon (drained)	2		
Onions	1		
Cooked potatoes	3		
Salt, pepper & Accent to taste			
Paprika to color			
Hot sauce		4	Add hot sauce and eggwhites and mix. Add crackermeal as needed and mix.
Egg whites		8	
Crackermeal as needed			

Scale at 3 ozs and roll into oblong croquettes. Cook as needed

SHRIMP CHOP SUEY

INGREDIENTS	LBS OZS	METHOD
Raw shrimp	10	Split shrimp, saute in oleo till they turn pink.
Oleo	1	
Celery (cut diagonally)	8	Put on vegetables to boil in chicken broth and water. When just about done add shrimp.
Onions (chopped)	6	
Bell Peppers (chopped)	2	
Chicken broth	2 gals.	
Water	1 1/2 gals.	
Diced mushrooms 1 - 8 oz. can		Add mushrooms and bean sprouts. Allow to simmer 15 minutes & tighten with starch. Add color or soy sauce. Serve with rice or noodles.
#1 can Bean sprouts 3 cans		
Starch as desired		
Soy sauce as desired to color		

SHRIMP CHOP SUEY

		Make fish stock by boiling off fresh fish heads in 4 gal. of water.
Onions	3 lbs	Cut celery and onions diagonally. Saute all vegetables well in oleo.
Bell peppers	2 "	
Celery	4 "	
Oleo	1/2 "	
Fish stock	2 gals.	Strain and add to above
#10 tomatoes	1 can	Strain chop suey vegetables and bean sprouts saving juice for later use. Add tomatoes, bean sprouts, vegetables, soy sauce and bead molasses to herbs and fish stock. Simmer down. Mix into juice from chop suey veg. & sprouts & tighten mixture. Add Mae Joon. Peel, wash, back & rewash shrimp. Saute in butter as needed to go on top of chop suey.
#10 bean sprouts	2 cans	
#10 Chop suey veg.	1 can	
Soy sauce	2	
Bead molasses	1/2 jar	
Cornstarch	1/2 lb	
Mae Joon powder	2 tsp.	
Shrimp (raw)	20 lbs	
Yellow rice	5 lbs.	Color rice water with yellow coloring, cook and serve behind chop suey.

Yield: Approximately 60 orders.

BROILED SPANISH MACKEREL A LA TOWN HOUSE

Size of Mackerel:	1 1/4 lb average Trim well and strive to have uniform pieces.
Preparation:	Marinate meat-side in pan of french dressing. Place mackerel meat-side up in pan the bottom of which is covered with water. Season well. Place under broiler and cook till done. Broil under medium flame. Serve in pan with butter sauce.
Butter Sauce:	1 lb Melted Oleo 1 gal. Hot water 12 Lemons (juice of) Whip together with wire whip.

If Maitre D'Hotel Sauce is desired, leave off the water and add to the oleo and juice a little chopped parsley and grated nutmeg.

*****

FRIED FLOUNDER OR TROUT

Size of fish:	3/4 lb to 1 lb average

Trim well & wash, score if unusually large. However scored fish does not have the appearance after frying that it should have so do not score unless necessary due to size of fish.

Fry at heat of 350° to 375° using golden dip as batter. Fish must be moistened first either in pan of water or milk.

*****

FRENCH FRIED SHRIMP

Initial Preparation:	Using 15/20 count shrimp, peel shrimp leaving on tail. Split down back well and wash.
2nd Step:	Make batter of 1 gallon milk and 12 ozs eggs. Dip shrimp into flour, then into batter and finally into broken crackers. Press so as to butterfly. Place in ice-box and cook as needed.

BARBECUE SAUCE

INGREDIENTS	AMOUNT	METHOD
Catsup	1 gallon	Place all ingredients on
Water	1 1/4 gal.	to boil and after boiling
Chili Powder	2 level cookspn.	let simmer for 2 hours.
Sugar	2 cups	
Onions, chopped fine	10 medium	
Hot sauce	2 cookspoons	
L & P Sauce	2 "	
Smoke sauce	1 cup	

*****

BARBECUE SAUCE

Catsup	1 gallon
Water	2 gallons
Liquid Smoke	3 cookspoons
Garlic salt	1 soup spoon
Mustard	1 cookspoon
Salt	1 "
Black pepper	1/2 "
Vinegar	1 1/2 cup
Worcestershire	1 1/2 cups
Brown sugar	1 lb.
Hot sauce	1 dash
Onions, chopped	2 small
Flour	1 cookspoon

*****

SAUCE FOR MEAT LOAF

	LBS	OZS	
Tomatoe catsup (2 gal)			Put all ingredients in pot and
Onions	1	8	let come to a rolling boil.
Celery	1	8	Cut down fire and let simmer
Bell Peppers	1		for two hours if possible.
Salt & pepper to taste			Tighten as desired with starch
Sugar pinch			and water.
Ham hock	2		
Water (3 gallons)			

Thin with tomato juice when necessary.

<u>CREOLE SAUCE:</u> Same procedure only use tomatoes in place of catsup.

<u>SPANISH SAUCE:</u> Same as creole sauce only grind herbs instead of chopping.

BAR B Q SAUCE

1 1/2 cup worchester sauce
2 1/2 Cookspoon hot sauce
2 cups figaro
1 cup vinegar
1/2 cup mustard
Salt and pepper to taste.

4 Chopped onions

2 Cookspoon chile powder
2 cookspoon paperika

1 Gal beef broth

Yield: 3 gal

CHILE SAUCE

12 Ripe tomatoes
6 Green peppers
6 Large onions
3 Cups sugar
1 tbs ginger
1 tbs cloves
1 tbs cinnamon
3 tbs salt
6 cups vinegar
1 hot pepper

Cook until thick over low flame.

CHILE

12 lb suet   Add 1/2 gal water and render
40 lb lean ground beef   Grind through chile plate and add
                                    to rendered suet.
3 oz peeled garlic   Chop fine & add to above
1 lb paprika   Add to above

                                    Cook above ingredients until tender.
12 oz ground comino
2 1/2 lb chile powder   Mix comino, chile powder, Flour
3 lb flour   & salt together and add to above.
1/2 lb salt
                                    Simmer 3 hours.

BAR B Q SAUCE # 2

1 1/2 gallons water
6 oz mujstard
14 oz catsup
1 lb flour
1 lemon
1 cup winegar
2 # celery
2 lb onions
2 1/2 oz L & P sauce

Best preparation: Cook with meat in roasting pan instead of cooking separately, as it gives a full flavor to the meat

Yield: 2 gallon.

CHEF OIL

INGREDIENTS	LBS	OZS.	METHOD
Garlic		2 1/2	Salt garlic well and allow to set over night, so salt will draw flavor out of garlic
Salt		4	
Salad oil (2 qts)			Next day add sugar, oil, and vinegar, shake well and do not use till following day.
Vinegar (1 qt)			
Sugar		8	

FRENCH DRESSING

Salad oil (1 gal)		Add 1 cup oil to the gum and mix.
Vinegar (1 qt 1 cup)		
Water (1 pt)		Put in bowl of mixer and add all water slowly, mixing thoroughly to avoid lumps. A smooth paste should be obtained which is the base of the emulsion.
Sugar	9 1/2	
Salt	4	
Gum tragacanth	1	
Paprika	1 1/4	

Add salt, sugar and paprika which has been seived to the above.

At high speed, alternately add the vinegar and the oil in small amounts.

NOTE" Additional spices and seasonings may be added if desired, such as L & P sauce, tobasco sauce, mustard, pepper, etc. The thickness of the dressing may be changed by changing the amount of the tragacantn.

BAR B Q SAUCE # 3

INGREDIENTS	LBS	OZS	METHOD
Onions (chopped)	3		Saute celery, onions, and peppers till done.
Celery (diced)	2		
Oil	1	8	
Green pepper (chopped)	1	8	
Flour	2		Add flour stirring in well. cook for 5 minutes.
L & P sauce		10	
Prepared mustard		12	
Black pepper (2 tsp)			
Cayenne pepper (tsp 1)			Add all ingredients and cook for 45 minutes on low heat.
Whole cloves (1 tbsp)			
Chile powder (4 tbsp)			
Sugar	1		
Paprika		2	
Garlic (chopped) 6 cloves			
Chicken or beef stock		32	
Ketsup		2	
Vinegar		2	

BUFFET SAUCE

2 Sections Garlic --- chopped fine
1 Cup Mayonnaise
1/2 cup Chili Sauce
1 teaspoon Yellow Mustard
1/2 cup Wesson oil
1 teaspoon Worcestershire sauce
1 teaspoon black pepper
Dash of tobasco sauce
Dash of paprika
Juice of large grated onion
2 teaspoons water

Shake well. Excellent as salad dressing.

*****

CREOLE SAUCE

INGREDIENTS	LBS	OZS	METHOD
Onions	3		Blanch off ham hocks. Add
Celery	3		chopped celery, onions,
Peppers	1		peppers and garlic.
Oil	1/2		
Garlic (1 pod)			
Ham Hock (smoked)			
#10 Tomato Puree or			After herbs are well cooked
Tomatoes (2 cans)			add tomatoes or puree and
Water (2 gals)			water.
Cornstarch		8	Dissolve cornstarch in little
Salt, pepper & Accent to taste			water. Add.

May use W-13 in place of cornstarch. Gives shiny appearance.

One gallon of sauce for every 10 lbs of raw shrimp.

Makes 2 gallons.

HORSE RADISH SAUCE

INGREDIENTS	AMOUNT	METHOD
Clear beef stock	3 gals.	Bring beef stock to a boil and tighten as desired with flour. e.g. to the consistency of pork gravy.
Flour	as needed	
Horseradish	4 cups	Add horseradish, catsup, mustard, L & P Sauce, A-1 sauce, chopped pimentoes. Simmer.
Catsup	2 bottles	
German mustard	4 ozs	
L & P Sauce	1/2 bottle	
A-1 Sauce	1/2 "	
Sugar	3 tbspns	
Chopped parsley	1 bunch	
Chopped pimentoes	1/2 #303 can	

Serve over sliced boiled brisket or pot roast.

*****

FRENCH DRESSING

Wesson oil	(1 gal)	
Vinegar	(1 1/4 qt.)	
Water	(1 pt.)	
Sugar		9 1/2
Salt		4
Gum Tragacanth		1
Paprika		1 1/4

1. Add 1 cup of wesson oil to the gum tragacanth and mix thoroughly.

2. Place gum mixture in mixing bowl and add all the water slowly, mixing thoroughly to avoid lumpiness. A smooth paste should be obtained which is the base of the emulsion.

3. Add salt, sugar and paprika to the above.

4. On high speed, alternately add the vinegar and oil in small amounts.

NOTE: Additional spices and seasonings may be added if desired, such as L & P sauce, tabasco sauce, mustard, pepper, etc. The thickness of the dressing may be changed by varying the amount of the gum tragacanth.

TARTARE SAUCE

INGREDIENTS	AMOUNT
Cabbage	5 lbs
Onions	5 lbs
Bell Peppers (ground)	1 1/2 lbs
Dill pickles	1 gal

After putting the above through the chopping machine be sure all the juice is drained before adding mayonaise. 2 lbs. mayonaise to 1 lb. of tartar.

ANCHOVY SAUCE

Chili sauce	2 1/2 lbs
Mayonaise	5 lbs
L & P sauce	3 ozs
Anchovy sauce	2 1/2 ozs
Lemon juice	3 ozs

WALDORF SAUCE

Whipping cream	1 pt
Mayonaise	1 lb
Lemons	3
Salt	1 tablespoon
Sugar	1 cup

BANANA SAUCE

Whipping cream	1 pt
Sugar	1 cup
Mayonaise	1/2 lb
Salt	1 tablespoon

SAUCES FOR SALAD ROOM

COCKTAIL SAUCE:

1	#10 can chili sauce
5	ozs horseradish
1	oz L & P sauce
2	ozs lemon juice

1000 ISLAND DRESSING:

5	lbs Mayonaise
1	lb sweet relish
2	hard boiled eggs (grated)
1	oz L & P sauce
2	lbs chili sauce

ROQUEFORT CHEESE DRESSING:

1/2	gal French dressing
1/2	lb Roquefort or bleu cheese
2	lbs mayonaise

MAYONAISE:

7	whole eggs
5	egg yolks
3	cookspoons sugar
2	" salt
2	" mustard
2	cups vinegar
1 1/2	gallons oil

Beat eggs till fluffy, add sugar, salt & mustard. Add oil slowly. When getting thick, add vinegar. Use up both at same time.

CHEF OIL:

2 1/2	ozs garlic (peeled, washed & chopped fine)
4	ozs salt (take a clean gallon jar and put in chopped garlic and salt. Shake jar around until salt and garlic are well mixed. Let sit over nite thus allowing salt to draw flavour from the garlic.)
4	lbs Wesson oil
2	lbs vinegar
8	ozs sugar (Next day, add sugar, oil and vinegar. Shake well and strain.)

BATTER FOR ONION RINGS

INGREDIENTS		LBS	OZS	METHOD
Flour		2		Mix together flour, salt, baking powder and paprika
Baking Powder			2	
Paprika			3	
Salt & pepper				
Eggs	(4)			Add milk and eggs and stir together to right consistency.
Milk	(3 1/2 qts)			

Batter sliced onion rings and drop into deep fat one at a time.

*****

CREAM GRAVY

Ingredients		LBS	OZS	Method
Shortening		1	8	Melt shortening and add flour. Brown well, stirring to avoid lumping or burning.
Flour		1	8	
Carnation Milk	(1 1/2 qts)			Add milk and water and bring to a boil, stirring as needed.
Water	(8 qts)			
Salt to taste				

Strain into 3 gallon crock.

*****

CREAM SAUCE

Ingredients		LBS	OZS	Method
Oleo		1	8	Melt oleo. Whip in flour and starch.
Flour		1		
Corn Starch	(2 tblsp)			
Milk	(2 3/4 gal)			Heat milk well in double boiler and add to above. Add salt and color and mix well.
Salt to taste				
Egg color as needed				

CHAPTER III

VEGETABLES AND SOUPS

VEGETABLES	Page		Page
Asparagus		Mustard Greens	5
Baked	1	Okra	
Buttered	1	Baked	5
Creamed	1	Baked and Rice	6
Green, Creamed on Toast	1	Buttered	6
Beans		French Fried	6
Baked	16	Fried in Bacon w/Tomatoes	6
Green	1	and Tomatoes	5
Green (Casserole)	17	Onions	
Green Lima, Creamed	2	Baked in Cream	6
Lima	1	Buttered	6
Navy	1	Creamed	6
Navy, Baked	2	French Fried	6
Ranch Style	2	Glazed	6
Spanish	1	Peas	
Black Eyed Peas	1	Blackeyed	1
Broccoli Souffle	17	Buttered	7
Carrots		Creamed	7
and Celery	2	Carrots, Celery & Onions	7
Fried in Butter	2	and Carrots, Creamed	7
French Fried	2	and Carrots, Buttered	7
Scalloped	11a	and Lima Beans, Corn & Carrots	7
Cauliflower		Potatoes	
Au Gratin	3	Au Gratin	7
Buttered	2	Baked	8
and Carrots	3	Boston Baked	8
Corn		Escalloped	7
Escalloped	3	French Fried	7
Fried	3	Fried with Onions	7
Fritters	3	German Fried	8
O'Brien	3	Hash Brown	8
Egg Plant		Luby	8a
Mashed	3	Mashed	8
with Bacon and Tomatoes	4	New, Buttered	8
Baked	4	New, Creamed	8
Baked, and Rice	4	O'Brien	7
Escalloped	4	Ruth's Potato Puffs	8
Fried	4	Potatoes, Sweet	
Parmigiana	4a	Baked	8
Stuffed	4	Candied, Sweet	8
Greens		Rice	
Spinach	5	Boiled, Creamed	9
Spinach, Italian	5	Chinese	9
Mustard Greens and Collards	5	Croquettes	9
Turnip	5	and Okra	9
Macaroni		Spanish (Asa's)	9
and Cheese	5	Spanish	9
and Tomatoes	5	Escalloped	10
Mixed Vegetables		Rutabagas	12
Creamed	9b	Spaghetti, Spanish	5

VEGETABLES (Con't)	Page		Page
Spinach		Turnips	
Cooked	5	Buttered	12
Italian	5	Greens	5
Pudding	9a		
Souffle	9a	Hollandaise Sauce	12
Baked	9b		
Salads, Hot		SOUPS	
Hot Slaw	12	Canadian Cream Soup	15
Hot Vegetable Salad	12	Chicken	
Wilted Lettuce	12	Gumbo	15
Squash		Noodle	15
Baked	10-11	Rice	15
Baked, White	10	Bean	
Baked, Banana	11	Lima	14
with Bacon	10	Navy	14
French	11b	Potato	13
Fried, White	10	Pea, Split	13
Frito	10	Sea Food	
Italian	11	Clam Chowder, Ruth's Oven	14
Italian, with Bacon	11	Clam Chowder	14
Italian, with Onions	11	Oyster	13
Scalloped	11a	Gumbo	13
White Au Gratin	10	Spinach, Cream of	15
Tomatoes		Tomato, Cream of	13
Breaded	11	Vegetable	13
Escalloped	11		
Stewed	11		

LIST HERE new recipes:

Augratin Potatoes	8a
Baked Corn	8a
Baked Eggplant Dressing	4a
Creole Gumbo Soup	15a
Spanish Style Potatoes	8b
Fried Rice	8b
Chicken and Vegetable Soup	18
Creole Green Beans	18
Italian Eggplant	4b

JOSEPH OWEN LUBY SR.'S ORIGINAL COOKBOOK

ASPARAGUS

Baked Asparagus:

#10 Can asparagus
Cover with cream sauce, place cubes of bread over top, add grated cheese and bake in oven until browned.

Buttered or Creamed Asparagus:

Heat 1 gallon can soup cut asparagus, season with butter or drain off broth and add cream sauce. Serve creamed asparagus on 1/2 piece of toast.

Baked Asparagus:

Drain broth from 1 can soup cut asparagus, pour into baking pan, cover with cream sauce and sprinkle well with grated cheese and cut 4 pieces bread in small cubes and place over top of pan. Place in oven to brown.

Creamed Green Asparagus on Toast:

Toast bread, place 6 or 7 asparagus on top of toast and cover with cream sauce.

BEANS

Navy Beans:

Pick and wash beans. Cover with water and add ham bone and skin for seasoning, also salt. Cook until beans are tender (3 hrs.).

Lima Beans:

Pick and wash beans. Cover with water and add only butter and salt for seasoning. Cook until beans are tender (about 3 hours).

Green Beans:

Wash beans, cover with water and add ham bone and skin for seasoning, also salt. Put 1 onion in for seasoning. Cook at least 3 hours or until beans are tender. If canned beans are used, put in pot and season as you do fresh beans, and cook at least an hour or until well seasoned.

Spanish Beans:

Pick and wash beans. Cover with water and add ham for seasoning. Cook about 1 hour and add chopped onion and celery cut fairly small and 1 gallon can tomatoes. Cook until beans are tender (about 3 hours.)

Black-eyed Peas:

Pick and wash peas. Cover with water and add ham bone and skin for seasoning, also salt. Cook until peas are tender - 2 hours.

Chapter III   Page 1

BEANS (Continued)

Baked Navies:

If cooked navies are used, drain off most of broth, put in baking pan, add about 3 cups catsup, 2 cups brown sugar and 3 strips bacon cut in cubes and spread over top. Place in oven and bake at least 30 minutes. Pork and beans are prepared in the same way, omitting catsup. An onion should be added (cut in fourths) and then removed before serving. Prepare baked limas the same way.

Ranch Style Beans:

Open beans and add a very little water and heat.

Creamed Green Lima Beans:

If fresh limas are used, cook in salted boiling water until tender. Either season with butter or drain off broth and add cream sauce. If canned limas are used, heat and add butter for seasoning or drain off broth and add cream sauce.

CARROTS

Carrots Fried in Butter:

Peel and cut carrots in short strips and cook in salted water until tender, drain well. Melt butter in skillet and fry until a bit browned and seasoned. A little sugar may be added.

Carrots & Celery:

Peel and cut carrots in short strips and cook in salted water until done. Add equal amount of celery cut in wide strips. When both are tender, season with butter, a little sugar, or drain well and add cream sauce.

French Fried Carrots:

Peel and cut in short strips. Cook in salted water until tender. Drain well and dip in batter and roll in cracker meal. Fry in deep fat.

CAULIFLOWER

Buttered Cauliflower:

Separate cauliflower. Soak in salt water at least 20 min. Add water and cook until tender. Drain off most of water and season with butter. Prepare creamed cauliflower the same way only drain off all the water and add cream sauce and butter.

Chapter III   Page 2

CAULIFLOWER (Continued)

Au Gratin Cauliflower:

Prepare as for buttered. Drain well and place in baking pan. Cover with cream sauce and sprinkle 1 pimento chopped over the top and place in oven until browned.

Cauliflower and Carrots (Creamed or Buttered):

Peel and dice carrots small, cook until tender in salted water. Prepare cauliflower as for buttered. When both are done, mix and season with butter or pour cream sauce over them.

CORN

Fried Corn:

Melt butter in skillet and add corn, a little sugar, salt and pepper. Cook until corn is heated, stirring constantly.
For whole kernel corn, use 1 cooksp. flour to 1 can corn, a little water may be added and seasoning. Cook until corn is heated through and a little thick.

Escalloped Corn:

2 cans corn, 3 eggs, 1 cooksp. flour, a little sugar and salt, 1 qt. milk. Mix well and crumble creakers over top and dot with butter. Place in oven until corn is set and browned.

O'Brien Corn:

3 cans corn, 3 eggs, 2 cooksp. flour, sugar, salt and 1 green pepper, 1 pimento, chopped fine, 1 qt. milk. Mix well and place in oven and cook until set and browned on top. Prepare baked corn the same way, omitting green papper and pimento.

Corn Fritters:

1 can corn, 1 egg, 1 t. baking powder, 4 cooksp. flour and 1 cooksp.

EGG PLANT

Egg Plant:

5 medium egg plants, cooked and mashed
6 cups dried bread crumbs
1-1/2 cup chopped pecans
4 well beaten eggs

parsley
salt and pepper
4 T. chopped onion

Add some water and butter and place in oven.

Chapter III   Page 3

EGGPLANT (Continued)

Escalloped Eggplant:

Peel and dice eggplant. Add a little water and cook until tender. Drain well, add cream sauce and crumble crackers over top and dot with butter. Place in oven and cook until brown.

Baked Eggplant and Rice:

Peel and dice eggplant. Fry onion (chopped fine) in salad oil until tender. Add tomatoes and pour into baking pan, mixing in a little rice with egg plant. Place in oven until set and browned.

Fried Eggplant:

Peel egg plant and slice in rather thick slices. Soak in salt water for at least ten minutes. Dip in batter, roll in cracker meal and fry in deep fat in skillet until tender and brown.

Baked Eggplant:

Peel and dice 3 large eggplants and cook until tender, then mash. Cook 3 strips bacon, cut fine, 1 onion (chopped fine). Fry until onion is tender and bacon browned, add to egg plant. Add 7 slices bread, crumbled, 1/2 cup pecans (chopped) 3 eggs. Mix well and pour into baking pan and place in oven until brown. Squash can be used instead of eggplant.

Eggplant with Bacon and Tomatoes:

Peel and dice eggplant. Fry about 6 strips bacon (cut fine) until browned. Add eggplant and fry until tender, then add tomatoes and cook together until eggplant is done and seasoned well.

Stuffed Eggplant (Kenneth Weaver)

Take an eggplant of medium size. Wash well and slice medium thickness. Eggplant may be left unpeeled or it may be peeled at your own discretion. Save the ends and irregular pieces and dice small and boil. Next make a light bread dressing, like usual, and add cooked eggplant to the dressing. You need a fairly dry dressing for this. Add just a touch of garlic powder to your dressing. Next saute about three or four garlic buds in about a fourth of an inch of salad oil in a No. 14 skillet. After garlic has sauteed enough to get the flavor, remove from oil and add a gallon of tomatoes and season with salt and pepper to taste. Next, take two slices of eggplant and put a small amount of dressing between, sandwich style, and arrange several of these in your counter pan. We put six to a half two hundred. Put a little water in your pan and cook, covered, in a medium oven. When nearly done, remove from oven and put about a cookspoon of the tomato sauce over each order and run back in oven until done.

EGGPLANT PARMIGIANA

SAM RICE
BEAUMONT

YIELD: 20 Servings

20 slices (approx. 3 oz. ea.) eggplant, peeled, ½ inch slices
flour
eggwash
  2 cups (7 oz.) cereal (bite-size shredded rice or corn biscuits)
                crushed, or bread crumbs
  ½ cup butter or margarine
  1 can (3 lbs. 3 oz.) Campbell's Tomato Soup
  1 cup water
  1 tsp. chili powder
  1 tsp. leaf oregano, crushed
  ½ tsp. garlic, instant granulated
  20 slices (½ oz. ea.) Mozzarella cheese, thinly sliced
  ½ cup Parmesan cheese, grated

METHOD

Dip eggplant in flour, eggwash, and then cereal crumbs. Melt butter and brush baking pans. Place 10 eggplant slices in each pan; dribble remaining butter on top. Bake in preheated 425°F. oven for 20 to 30 minutes. Meanwhile simmer soup, water, chili powder, oregano, and garlic together for about 5 minutes. Place ½ ounce slice of cheese over each piece of eggplant and cover each pan with 3 cups sauce. Sprinkle ¼ cup Parmesan cheese over top of each pan. Return to oven; bake 15 minutes or until eggplant is done, depending on thickness.

Dec. 2, 1965

BAKED EGGPLANT DRESSING

MALCOLM McKAY

  10# eggplant, peeled and cubed
  3½# white bread, ground fine
   ½ gallon milk
  2   cans Carnation Evaporated milk (or 26 oz.)
(1½# chopped bell peppers
(1½# chopped onions
(1½# chopped celery
   ½ cup pimentos (chopped)
   ½# oleo or butter
  3   oz. salt
  2   tsp. black pepper
  12 eggs
  12 tsp. sage

Cook and drain eggplant in 3 oz. of salt, saute vegetables in butter or oleo. Mix all ingredients in dish pan and run in oven for 25 minutes. Pull and top with American cheese. Put back in oven long enough to melt cheese.

April 21, 1967

ITALIAN EGGPLANT

Yield - 4 Pans

VERNON SCHRADER

```
20 medium eggplant, cut in French Fry cutter ) Cook eggplant and onion
 3 large onions, chopped                      ) together.  Drain well.
15 tomatoes, diced
 1 lb. bacon, chopped and cooked crisp
Cream Sauce - to be used as liquid
½ pkg. Italian Dressing Mix (Lowery's)
Salt
White pepper
Accent
Bacon grease
Green onion tops, chopped fine
```

PROCEDURE:

Mix Cream Sauce (3 qts.) and ½ package of Lowery's Italian seasoning. Add tomatoes and onions. Then heat and sprinkle a few fresh tomatoes and moistened bread crumbs over top.

GREENS

Spinach: Wash spinach thoroughly, add 1 cup salad oil and salt. Cook in as little water as possible to keep from burning. Cook about 45 minutes.

Turnip Greens: Wash greens thoroughly, add ham bone and skin for seasoning and salt. Add water to half cover greens and cook at least 2 hours.

Mustard Greens and Collards: Prepared in the same way as above.

Italian Spinach: Prepared as regular spinach.

MACARONI & SPAGHETTI

Macaroni & Cheese: Cook macaroni in salted boiling water until done. Add cream sauce and cheese and place in oven to brown.

Macaroni and Tomatoes: Cook macaroni in salted boiling water until done. Put in baking pan and add tomatoes and sprinkle well with cheese.

Spanish Spaghetti: Cook spaghetti in salted boiling water until done. Chop onions and green peppers fine, fry in salad oil until tender. Add to spaghetti and add tomatoes. Mix well and place in baking pan and cook about 20 minutes in oven.

Prepare spaghetti and cheese as you do macaroni and cheese.

OKRA

Baked Okra: Slice okra and cook. Fry chopped onions and green pepper, 3 strips bacon, chopped. Add an equal amount of tomato and rice. Put grated cheese over top and bake.

Okra and Tomatoes: Cut stem from okra, cook in salted water until tender. Pour in baking pan and add chopped onion and tomatoes. Mix well and place in oven. Cook until onions are tender (about 20 minutes).

Chapter III   Page 5

OKRA

Buttered Okra:

Cut stem from okra and cook in salted water until okra is tender. Season with butter.

French Fried Okra:

Prepare as for buttered okra. Drain well and wash off. Dip in batter and roll in cracker meal and fry in deep fat.

Okra Fried in Bacon with Tomatoes:

Prepare as for buttered okra, only slice in rather thin slices. When tender, drain off liquid. Fry about 12 slices bacon, cut small, until brown, add cooked okra and tomatoes and cook until okra is seasoned well.

Baked Okra and Rice:

Prepare okra as for buttered okra. When tender, pour into baking pan and add rice. Fry chopped onion in bacon grease until tender and add tomatoes. Mix with okra and rice and place in oven for about 20 minutes.

ONIONS

Glazed Onions:

3 lb. onions (buttering)
Put cooking butter in skillet, add onions and a mixture of 1 cup boiling water, 2 T sugar, and salt, pepper. Simmer until tender. Make a paste of 2 T flour, 4 T water and add to onion mixture. Put in baking pan and bake 20 minutes.

Buttered or Creamed:

Peel buttering onions, cook in salted water until tender. Season with butter or drain well and add cream sauce.

French Fried Onions:

Prepare as for buttered onions. When tender, drain well and dip in batter and roll in cracker meal. Fry in deep fat until browned.

Onions Baked in Cream:

Cut onions in rather thick slices, arrange in baking pan, add salt and enough cream to cover. Bake until tender.

PEAS

Buttered Peas:

Heat peas and season with butter, a little sugar, and salt to taste.

Creamed Peas:

Heat peas. Drain off broth, add cream sauce, butter, sugar and salt.

Peas, Carrots, Celery and Onions:

Peel and dice carrots small. Cook in salted water until half done. Add buttering onions and celery (cut a bit large) and cook until all are tender. Add peas and season with butter, or drain off broth and cover with cream sauce.

Peas and Carrots: (Creamed or Buttered)

Peel and dice carrots small and cook in salted water until tender. Add peas and season with butter, a little sugar and salt, or pour off broth and add cream sauce.

Peas, Lima Beans, Corn and Carrots:

Peel and dice carrots small, cook in salted water until tender, drain and add 3 cans peas, 2 cans lima beans, 1 can whole kernel corn. Season with butter, a little sugar and salt, or drain broth and add cream sauce.

POTATOES

Escalloped Potatoes:

Peel and slice potatoes thin in baking pan, salt and cover with milk and add butter. Place in oven until tender and browned (about 45 min.)

Au Gratin Potatoes:

Dice cooked potatoes or slice, salt and add cream sauce to cover. Sprinkle well with cheese and place in oven to brown.

French Fried Potatoes:

Cut raw potatoes in long strips and fry in keep fat until tender and browned:

Fried Potatoes and Onions:

Slice raw potatoes thin with 1 onion cut small and fry in skillet until tender and browned. Salt.

O'Brien Potatoes:

Dice raw potatoes in baking pan, add salt and chopped green pepper. Add a little water and butter and cook until tender and browned.

POTATOES (Continued)

Hash Brown Potatoes:

Dice cooked potatoes, fry in small amount grease until browned well. Salt.

Boston Baked Potatoes:

Peel and slice raw potatoes rather thick, add butter, salt and a little water. Place in oven and cook until tender and browned.

German Fried Potatoes:

Use equal amount of sliced potatoes and onions. Do not mash when turning.

Baked Potatoes:

Wash and grease potatoes. Place in roast pan with a small can water in center of pan. Bake until tender (1 hr.). Serve with melted butter on each order.

Candied Sweet Potatoes:

Cook sweet potatoes until tender, peel and slice medium thickness in baking pan. Add 3 cups sugar over them, butter and add a little water. Place in oven until candied (20 min.).

Baked Sweet Potatoes:

Bake as you do Irish potatoes.

Mashed Potatoes:

Peel and cook potatoes until tender, drain well. Place in beater and mash. Add butter, salt and milk. Whip until light and fluffy.

New Potatoes (Creamed or Buttered):

Cook new potatoes, peel. Melt 1 lb. cooking butter in top of double boiler and add new potatoes. Heat until potatoes are hot through and sprinkle with chopped parsley.

For creamed new potatoes just add cream sauce and heat in top of double boiler and season with butter. Peas may be added.

RUTH'S POTATO PUFFS:

1 cup cold mashed potatoes 1 cup flour
1 cup cold cooked rice 1 tablespoon grated onion
2 eggs well beaten

Drop from teaspoon and fry like doughnuts in hot fat. We modified this recipe by adding another egg, reducing flour to 1/4 cup and adding additional tablespoon of onion.

JOSEPH OWEN LUBY SR.'S ORIGINAL COOKBOOK

LUBY POTATOES

August 1, 1963

HARLEN TINKER

Sliced large new potatoes with peelings. #35 on slicer
Oleo to cover one set-up of potatoes
Accent, salt and white pepper to taste

Slice large new potatoes (Big Reds) into square pan. Sprinkle with salt, accent, and a little white pepper. Cover potatoes with liquid oleo. Cover the pan with foil and bake in hot oven till potatoes are tender. (About 35 to 40 minutes.) Drain the oleo off of the potatoes and serve. Recommended selling price is .16¢ per order. Save the drained oleo from the first pan for reuse on the following pans.

AUGRATIN POTATOES

August 16, 1965

LUBY'S ROMANA
PLAZA CAFETERIA

French Fry Cut (long diced)
Cook and drain

SAUCE
   9 tablespoons flour
  18 cups of whole milk
  18 tablespoons of chicken base
   4 tablespoons of Season All
   9 cups of grated cheese

Cook and mix with potatoes and top with bread crumbs.

BAKED CORN

August 16, 1965

LORIDA ANDRES
McALLEN, TEXAS

1 #10 can of Cream Style Corn
½ scoop of flour or (3 cups)
½ scoop of sugar or (3 cups)
4 cups whole milk
9 eggs (whole)
1 cup of oleo

Pour in mixer and beat slow until well mixed. Makes 3 square pans.

Chapter III

Page 8a

May 24, 1966

SPANISH STYLE POTATOES

HULDA REID

4 cups fine chopped bacon
2 cups fine chopped onion
1 cup fine chopped bell pepper
1½ tsp. garlic powder
Salt
Pepper
1 gal. bright red canned tomatoes
2 serving spoons cornstarch
3 cups Cheese Whiz

Fry 4 cups fine chopped bacon until crisp. Drain off most of grease. Saute 2 cups fine chopped onion and 1 cup fine chopped bell pepper in bacon drippings until just done. Add 1½ teaspoon garlic powder, salt and pepper to taste. Mash and add one gallon of bright red canned tomatoes, juice and all. Let come to a boil. Thicken with 2 serving spoons of cornstarch. Add 3 cups of Cheese Whiz and heat till cheese is melted. Just before serving, pour over cooked diced and drained potatoes. Cook potatoes like Luby's new potatoes. Do not use new potatoes.

May 24, 1966

FRIED RICE

DAISY LEWIS
BEAUMONT

1 pickup pot raw rice
1 cookspoon grease

Heat grease in heavy aluminum pot. Fry rice in grease until it pops open.

ADD: 1 pickup pot chicken broth
4 large white onions) Chopped (not fine)
4 bell peppers   )
Salt and black pepper to taste
Dash of hot sauce

RICE

Rice Croquettes:

Round bowl of cooked rice
2 pimentos
5 beaten eggs
Enough cracker meal to mix. Fry in deep fat. Make cream sauce, add cheese and serve.

Boiled, Creamed Rice:

Cook rice in salted boiling water until tender (20 min.). Drain well, wash and serve plain or with cream, butter and raisins in it.

Spanish Rice: (Asa's)

3/4 cup raw rice
1½ cups sliced onions, browned
2 tbsp. fat
3½ cups canned or fresh tomatoes
1½ tsp. salt
Pinch pepper
1 cup diced celery
¼ cup diced green pepper
1 bay leaf
1 tsp. sugar
1 tsp. Worcestershire sauce
2 cups water

Spanish Rice:

2 cups rice (wash 6 times)
4 green peppers (chopped fine)
2 onions (chopped fine)
1 gallon can tomatoes
2 tbsp. shortening

Heat shortening in skillet; pour in uncooked rice and stir until brown Pour in other ingredients, and cook without stirring, but loosen with spoon and add a little water from time to time if needed. Cook 20 min

Rice and Okra:

Fix okra whole and cook until tender. Fry onions and add ½ can tomatoes and cook 1½ cups of rice. Put a little rice in bottom of baking pan and layer okra and a thin layer of rice and okra. Pour onion-tomato mixture over it and add the other ½ gallon tomatoes. Put in oven and bake.

Chinese Rice:

½ lb. pork
2 cups rice
Fry 1 chopped onion with cubed pork, add rice to this and steam.

April 3, 1963

SPINACH PUDDING

BROADWAY
PETE ERBEN

Yield - 1 square pan - 30% cost @ .18¢ order
3 cups cooked and well drained spinach (1 box)
1 medium bell pepper
½ medium onion
1 toe garlic
3 cups fine ground bread crumbs
3 whole eggs
2 cups cream sauce
Salt to taste
Dash of nutmeg
Oleo to moisten 1½ cups bread crumbs

Grind first four ingredients through small grind in meat grinder. Add to this 1½ cups bread crumbs, 3 eggs, 2 cups cream sauce, salt and nutmeg and mix. Moisten the remaining 1½ cups bread crumbs with oleo to line the square pan and top the spinach pudding. Original recipe said to steam until set, so we place the square pan into a 200 pan with water and cover it with another inverted 200 pan and bake in oven till it is set. About 45 minutes at 400 degrees.

August 1, 1963

SPINACH SOUFFLE

HULDA REID

4 Boxes cooked and well drained spinach
16 Egg yolks beaten
2 cups grated Cheddar Cheese
6 tablespoons grated onions (real fine)
16 Egg whites beaten stiff
6 cups cream sauce
Salt to taste

Add cream sauce to spinach, then add the beaten egg yolks, cheese, salt and onions. Fold in egg whites and bake in greased pan set in shallow water for 45 minutes at 350° F. This should yield about 4 pans and we sell it at .18¢ an order.

Chapter III

BAKED SPINACH

July 5, 1963

HULDA REID

3 - 3# boxes of cooked and well drained spinach
2 - 50 oz. cans of cream of celery soup
1 pint of milk
½ cup of finely grated onions
12 oz. cream cheese
Salt to taste

Heat the 2 - 50 oz. cans of celery soup, 1 pint of milk, ½ cup onions and 8 oz. of cream cheese in thick metal pot till thoroughly blended together. Add drained spinach to mixture and salt to taste. Place in three square pans and sprinkle or crumble the remaining 4 oz. cream cheese over the top of the spinach. Heat in moderate oven till hot and serve.

Suggested price - .18¢

CREAMED MIXED VEGETABLES

October 18, 1963

AUGUST PROLL

3# lima beans - frozen
3# English peas - frozen
2 qts. diced carrots - fresh
3 qts. cream sauce

Add 3 cookspoons of minced onions or onion juice, ½ teaspoon nutmeg, and ¼ teaspoon red pepper. Serve as any other creamed vegetable.

RICE (Continued)

Escalloped Rice:

2 cups rice, not cooked
2 minced pimentos
1 cup diced cheese
1½ t. salt
Small onion chopped fine
2 cups tomato juice
1 cooksp. butter
3 cups water

Fry onion in butter, add rice, salt and boiling water. Cook until rice is nearly done. Add tomato juice, add pimento and cheese and place in oven.

SQUASH

Baked White Squash:

Peel and dice squash, add a little water, salt. When squash is tender, either mash or leave diced and season with butter.

Au Gratin White Squash:

Peel and dice squash, cook in a little water, salt. When squash is tender, drain well, mash and add butter and lots of grated cheese. Place in oven and cook until well browned.

White Squash with Bacon:

Peel and dice squash, add a little water and cook until tender. Drain water. Fry about 6 strips bacon (cut fine). When brown, pour in squash and cook together for a few minutes.

Fried White Squash:

Peel squash, slice rather thick. Dip in batter and roll in cracker meal. Fry in deep fat until tender and browned.

Baked Squash:

1 sq. pan squash, mashed
3 large onions, chopped fine
3 slices bacon, chopped and fried
2 hard boiled eggs, chopped

Mix all above ingredients together. Cover top with ¼ cup cracker meal, a little butter and paprika. Bake.

Fritos Squash:

Boil and drain squash and mash. To each square pan of squash, add 2 hard boiled eggs, 1½ cup cream sauce, and ½ (29¢) pkg. Fritos. Top with oleo and bake in oven until it set.

Chapter III   Page 10

SQUASH (Continued)

Baked Banana Squash:

Do not peel squash, wash well, cut in order size, place in baking pan, add butter to each order and sprinkle each order with nutmeg and sugar. Add a little water and place in oven. Cook until tender.

Squash:

3 eggs separated
2 cups white sauce

Beat yolk till thick into cream sauce, put in squash. Fold in egg whites. Turn in greased pan and bake.

Italian Squash with Onions:

Wash squash well (do not peel) slice medium thickness. Add a little water and salt and cook until tender. Fry onion (chopped fine) until tender. Add tomatoes and squash and cook together a few minutes so as to season.

Italian Squash with Bacon:

Wash squash well (do not peel) slice medium thickness. Add a little water and salt and cook until tender. Fry 6 slices bacon (cut fine). When brown, add squash and cook together for a few minutes.

Italian Squash:

Wash squash well (do not peel) slice medium thickness. Add a little water and salt and cook until tender. Season with butter.

TOMATOES

Escalloped Tomatoes:

Pour 1 gal. can tomatoes in baking pan, season with salt and butter (a little sugar may be added). Crumble crackers over top and place in oven until browned.

Breaded Tomatoes:

Pour 1 gal. can tomatoes in pot and add 8 slices bread, cubed, salt, sugar, and butter. Allow to cook at least 20 min.

Stewed Tomatoes:

Pour 1 gal. can tomatoes in pot. Season with butter, salt and sugar. When hot, thicken a bit.

February 18, 1963

SCALLOPED SQUASH   BROADWAY #2

HULDA REID

10 lb. grated zucchini squash
10 lb. grated yellow or banana squash
 2 cups salad oil
18 whole eggs
 3 cups onions chopped fine
1½ cup chopped parsley
Small amount of oregano to give just a slight taste
  and salt and pepper to taste.

Saute onions in salad oil till tender. Then place
  all above ingredients into large pan and mix well.

When mixed, place mixture in square pan to ½ full.
  Then put a thin layer of crackers. Top the crackers
  with a thin layer of grated American cheese. Then
  top again with your squash mixture and bake in slow
  oven till squash is set.

Yields about 5 sq. pans.

February 18, 1963

SCALLOPED CARROTS   BROADWAY #2

HULDA REID

6 qts. diced carrots (french fry cutter size)
1 50 oz. can of Cream of Celery soup
1½ cup milk
½ lb. grated American cheese
Ritz crackers to garnish

Boil diced carrots in salted water until done and drain
  well. Take 1 - 50 oz. Celery soup and add 1½ cup milk
  and heat over low flame. When hot, add cheese. When
  cheese has melted, add diced cooked carrots. We garnish
  the dish by placing Ritz crackers on top of the carrots
  with just a small piece of cheese on each cracker and
  running it into the oven letting the cheese on the cracker
  melt down just a bit.

Chapter III   Page 11a

January 6, 1964

FRENCH SQUASH

HELEN BLODGETT
OPAL SPAULDING

INGREDIENTS:
- 1 - 200 pan sliced yellow squash
- 1 - 200 pan sliced zuchinni squash
- 2 quarts sliced thin red onions (or white)
- 2 - 51 oz. cans of Cream of Celery soup
- 1 pound shredded parmesan cheese
- 1 cup chopped pimentos
    - Salt
    - Pepper
    - Accent

PROCEDURE:

Boil each squash separately and drain well. Saute onions in chopped bacon. Combine in dish pan both cooked squashes, sauted onions and bacon, 2 cans celery soup and 1 cup of chopped pimentos and 3/4 jar of parmesan cheese. Salt, pepper and accent to taste.

Sprinkle remaining parmesan cheese on top of pans. Run in oven long enough to set. Yield 4 square pans.

We get .20¢ for this item. Very popular.

TURNIPS

Rutabagas:

Peel and slice rutabagas, cook in salted water with a bit of sugar added. When tender, drain and mash. Season with butter.

Buttered Turnips:

Peel and dice turnips, cook in salted water until tender. Leave diced or mash and season with butter.

HOT SALADS

Hot Slaw:

Shred cabbage, cook until tender in salted water. Pour the following sauce over slaw:

½ cup salad oil
½ cup sugar
2 cups vinegar
When boiling, pour over slaw.

Hot Slaw:

Shred cabbage fine, cook in salted water until tender (20 minutes). Drain and place in baking pan. Heat to boiling: ½ cup salad oil, 2 cups sugar and 2 cups vinegar. Pour over cabbage and sprinkle diced fresh tomatoes over top for color. Chopped green pepper added makes it better also.

Hot Vegetable Salad:

Chop lettuce and ½ the amount of chopped raw spinach or raw mustard greens, 5 green onions (chopped) 6 strips bacon (cut fine) and salt. Fry bacon crisp and ½ cup salad oil and add 2 cups vinegar. Pour over lettuce mixture. About 3 heads lettuce makes a pan.

Wilted Lettuce:

Prepare as for Hot Vegetable Salad omitting spinach or mustard greens.

HOLLANDAISE SAUCE

1 scoop (large) flour   3 lbs. butter
1 tray cheese   1 red pepper (small amount)
1 gal. milk

Heat milk, add cheese. Mix flour and butter until smooth. Add to milk and cheese and mix until smooth. Add red pepper and remove from heat. Mix on beater.

Chapter III   Page 12

OYSTER SOUP

Heat milk in double boiler. Heat oysters (do not boil) and add to hot milk. Season with butter and salt. Never allow milk to boil.

POTATO SOUP

Dice raw potatoes small, cook until tender with a little chopped onion. Drain and add to hot milk that has been heated in double boiler. Salt and add butter. Allow to cook together for at least 10 minutes to season well.

SPLIT PEA SOUP

1 gallon can split peas, wash and cover with water. Add ham for seasoning and salt. Allow to cook at least 2 hours or until thick. Never add thickening.

SEA FOOD GUMBO

12 tablspoons butter
1 cup chopped green pepper
2½ cups fresh cut okra
1 cup chopped onion
1 gal. rich chicken broth
10 cups canned tomatoes (4 #2 cans)???
4 small bay leaves
3½ cups diced raw fish   and   ½ cup diced shrimp
4 tablespoons ground parsley
1 teaspoon gumbo file

CREAM OF TOMATO SOUP

Heat milk in top of double boiler. Heat tomato to boiling point and add 1 tbsp. soda to 1 gallon tomatoes. Mix well and add to hot milk. Season with salt and butter. Strain in soup bowl.

VEGETABLE SOUP

Put plenty of bones in pot and cover well with water. Add diced carrots, chopped onion, diced potatoes, chopped celery and allow to cook at least 1 hour. Add 1 gallon can tomato or more and cook at least 1 hour longer. Salt.

CLAM CHOWDER

1 pt. tomato juice
1 qt. canned or cut up fresh tomatoes
1 cup cubed raw potatoes
½ cups each chopped celery, onion, green peppers
1 qt. cream - half and half (thin)
3 cans Snows clam
Salt and pepper to taste
1 tablespoon cornstarch dissolved in water
   with ½ teaspoon of soda

Add juice of clams to tomatoes.
Add chopped vegetables and seasoning.
Simmer over slow fire 1 hour. Add dissolved soda and cornstarch.
Garlic salt if desired.
Add clams.
Heat cream to hot, not boiling - combine with above mixture and serve.

DO NOT BOIL.

RUTH'S OVEN CLAM CHOWDER

3 pts. tomato juice
3 qts. canned or cut up fresh tomatoes
6 cups cubed raw potatoes (shredded may be used)
½ cups each of chopped celery, green pepper, onion
3 qts. coffee cream
2 cans 46 oz. minced clams and juice
Salt and pepper to taste
3 tablespoons cornstarch dissolved in water with 1½ teaspoon soda

Add juice to tomatoes. Add chopped vegetables and seasoning. Simmer over slow fire one hour. Add dissolved soda and cornstarch. Garlic salt, if desired. Add clams and heat cream to hot but not boiling. Combine with above mixture. Do not boil.

We add one pound of finely diced haddock simmered in 2 quarts chicken broth to this recipe.

LIMA BEAN SOUP

Pick and wash beans and cover well with water. Add butter for seasoning and chopped onion. When beans are about tender, add a few canned tomatoes, chopped fine (no juice) and finish cooking. Have plenty broth.

NAVY BEAN SOUP

Pick and wash two-thirds gallon can navy beans. Cover with water well, season with ham and chopped onion. Cook until beans are tender (3 hrs.). Be sure and have plenty broth.

CANADIAN CREAM SOUP

2 quarts chicken stock
1 cup finely diced carrots
  (RO chopped carrots from
  salad dept. may be used)
1 cup finely diced celery
2 quarts whole milk
1/2 cup butter
1/2 cup minced onion
1/3 teaspoon paprika
4 tablespoons chopped parsley
2 cups Kraft Cheese Whiz
1/2 cup flour
3 tablespoons cornstarch
1/4 teaspoon soda
Salt to taste

Saute carrots, celery and onion in butter till done but not brown. Add to stock. Make paste of flour, cornstarch and paprika. Add to hot mixture. Add soda, salt, cheese and parsley.

CHICKEN GUMBO

Chicken broth
Salad oil
Onion chopped fine
3 cups okra
5 cups canned tomatoes

Cook onions until tender in salad oil. Put in chicken broth. Drain okra and add tomatoes to it and add to chicken broth. 2 spoons rice.

CHICKEN NOODLE SOUP

Heat chicken broth to boiling point, thicken a little and add cooked noodles, salt and 1/2 tsp. curry powder dissolved in some of the hot soup.

CHICKEN RICE SOUP

Heat chicken broth to boiling and thicken a little and add cooked ric and 2 fresh tomatoes, diced.

CREAM OF SPINACH SOUP

Heat milk in top of double boiler. When warm, add chopped spinach, salt and butter and heat until hot and the spinach is tender.

Chapter III   Page 15

December 2, 1965

CREOLE GUMBO SOUP

THELMA FRANKLIN

Use 26 quart pot
2 cups cooking oil   )
4 cups flour   )
Brown flour in oil until golden brown.

Add:
1 3/4 lb. chopped celery
1 3/4 lb. chopped onions
3   tbsp. garlic (chopped fine)
Saute about 5 minutes.

Add:
1 tsp. red pepper (Cayenne)
1½ tbsp. thyme
1 tbsp. oregano
Stir until mixed real well with vegetables and flour mixture.

Add 3 gals. of water, stir until smmoth and cook 45 minutes.

Add:
1 cup chopped parsley
6 cups green onions, chopped (tops & bottoms)
1¼ lbs. chopped okra or cut okra
2½ lbs. shrimp pieces
½ lb. crab meat
2 cups tomato sauce
Cook until okra is done - about 20 minutes.

Season with accent and salt to taste.

Chapter III

Page 15a

Oct. 15, 1964

GREEN BEAN CASSEROLE

M. H. LANGFORD

Yield: 2 Square Pans

1 - #10 can green beans
1 - 51 oz. can cream of mushroom soup
½ - fry basket french fried onion rings

Add 2 cups of water to mushroom soup. Stir well. Add green beans, onion rings and place in medium oven until mixture gets hot. Add grated very sharp aged cheese (we use Kraft Mayflower- 6 mos. age) over entire top of square. Place back in oven until cheese melts. Then it is ready for the counter.

(NOTE: Mix onion rings in with green beans.)

Oct. 30, 1964

BROCCOLI SOUFFLE

DAVIS SIMPSON
AUSTIN

4-316 packages of chopped broccoli
4 cups frozen egg whites
4 dippers cream sauce
2 handfuls American cheese
Salt to taste

Cook broccoli with dash of soda until very tender. Drain well. Then add cream sauce, cheese, salt and mix well. Beat egg whites until stiff and fold in. Pour into lightly greased bean pan and cook in 200 pan of water in 400 degree oven for about 45 minutes. Cover bean pan with foil.

May 24, 1966

<u>CHICKEN AND VEGETABLE SOUP</u>

DAVIS SIMPSON

Make regular Chicken Soup and add celery, onions, bell peppers and carrots cut like Almondine vegetables.

May 24, 1966

<u>CREOLE GREEN BEANS</u>

NEWT SMITH
BROADWAY

4 #10 cans cut green beans
2 #10 cans tomato sauce
2 #10 cans of water
½ tray of diced onions
1½ pickup pot of chopped bacon (about ½" square)
Salt and pepper to taste. (Very little salt)

Cook on low heat for a couple of hours.

DRY PINTO BEANS

INGREDIENTS	LBS	OZS	METHOD
Dry Pintos	10		Wash excess salt off jowls. Put on beans with jowls, onions & water. Bring to a rolling boil then turn down fire to medium heat. Season to taste with salt and pepper. Just before removing from fire, add Accent.
Salt jowls	2	8	
Onions	1		
Water (6 gals)			
Salt, pepper & Accent			

Paprika may be added for color.
Chili powder may be added if desired.

*****

FRESH GREEN BEANS

INGREDIENTS	LBS	OZS	METHOD
Fresh green beans (cleaned)	25 lbs		Bring all ingredients to a rolling boil then turn down fire to medium. Cook till done.
Dry salt jowls	5		
Onions	1	8	
Water (5 gallons)			
Salt, pepper & Accent			

*****

FRESH STRING BEANS

INGREDIENTS	LBS	OZS	METHOD
Water (1 1/2 gals)	6		Put water on stove and bring to boil. Wash salt meat to get off excessive salt and put meat in water. Let boil to good stock, approximately 1 hr. This can be prepared the day before using.
Salt meat	2		
String beans	10		Have beans snapped and washed. Add to stock, bring to brisk boil and then cut flame down.

Salt & Pepper (Add salt & pinch of pepper towards end of cooking so as to be able to better judge amts. necessary.

Cooking time varies according to the tenderness of the beans-- from 45 minutes to 1 1/2 hours.

AUGRATIN POTATOES

INGREDIENTS	LBS	OZS	METHOD
Flour		8	Melt oleo in sauce pan. Add flour and cook well over slow fire. Add hot milk slowly and stir into smooth sauce. This should make a clear medium thick cream sauce.
Milk powder dissolved in 2 qts water		8	
Oleo		8	
Sherry wine		2	Blend all these ingredients into cream sauce. Stirring in well.
Grated parmesian cheese		1	
Tabasco sauce (15 drops)			
Salt to taste			
1/2 tsp. black pepper			
1/2 jar yellow mustard			
Grated New York State Cheese	1	8	
Idaho potatoes	8		Boil, peel, allow to cool and then shred on grater.
Cheese	2	8	Grated

1) Select casserole or augratin dishes to be used. Cover bottom with spoon of cream sauce.
2) Fill well with shredded potatoes.
3) Cover potatoes well with more cream sauce.
4) Top generously with grated cheese.
5) Place in ice-box till ready for use.
6) Bake in medium oven for 5 min. or till cheese is melted and casserole is heated through.
7) A display may be put on steam table and dished, cooked to order.

*****

HASHED BROWNED POTATOES WITH CHEESE

Idaho potatoes	20		Boil potatoes in jacket preferably dry before and let get cold. Peel them then grate. Season with salt & pepper. Brown one side in skillet or on grill and just before turning over sprinkle with grated cheese. Turn over and brown well on the other side. When just about browned sprinkle top with more grated cheese. Turn into steam table pan.
Oil	1		
Salt		2	
Pepper 1 tsp.			
Cheese (grated)	1		

Individual orders may be served by grating a little on greased grill and browning.

ESCALLOPED POTATOES

INGREDIENTS	LBS	OZS	METHOD
Flour		8	Melt oleo in sauce pan. Add flour and cook well over slow fire. Add hot milk slowly and stir into smooth sauce.
Powdered milk (2 qts water)		8	
Oleo		8	
Sherry wine		2	Blend all these ingredients into cream sauce. Stir in well.
Grated Parmesian cheese.		1	
Tabasco sauce (15 drops)			
Salt to taste			
1/2 tsp. black pepper			
1/2 jar yellow mustard			
Peeled potatoes	12		Parboil till half or two thirds done. Drain and allow to cool. When cool cut into thin disks.
Finely ground crackers	1		Melt oleo and blend into crackers well.
Melted oleo		4	

Select pan to be used. Cover bottom with layer of cream sauce. Then alternate with potato disks and cream sauce having a layer of cream sauce on top. Cover top with marinated cracker crumbs. Bake in moderate oven.

*****

BROCCOLI WITH HOLLANDAISE SAUCE

Frozen Broccoli: Cook in seasoned boiling water. Cook approximately 5 minutes after water comes back to boil.

Hollandaise Sauce:

Oleo	1	
Flour	1/2	Make into rue.
Hot milk	1 1/2 qts.	Add to above, mixing well.
Eggs	1	
Lemons 4 (juice of)		Add, mixing well.

Yellow coloring

Note: A medium sauce is preferred.

For better results: Make stock of salt meat and water, using portions of it to color broccoli often.

ESCALLOPED EGG PLANT

Egg plant	15 lbs.	Peel and cut into cubes. Boil in plain salted water.
Onions	1 lb	Drain egg plant & saute with onions and bacon fat
Bacon drippings	1 cup	
Eggs	1/2 lb.	After egg plant has been well sauteed, place in mixing bowl and blend with eggs and milk.
Milk	1 qt.	
Crackers	1 lb.	Crumble crackers, put egg plant into pans for baking and sprinkle top with crackers and melted oleo.
Oleo	1/2 lb.	

Bake till done in medium hot oven.

Yield: 4 1/2 pans

*****

ESCALLOPED EGG PLANT WITH TOMATOES

Egg Plant	15 lbs.	Peel egg plant and cut into cubes. Boil in salted water till done, approximately 12 minutes.
Salt	1 oz	
Water (to cover)		
Onions	1/2 lb.	Saute onions in bacon drippings till soft. Add bread cubes, tomatoes, salt & pepper. Cook down. Strain egg plant and add to above.
Bacon drippings	1 cup	
Bread cubes	1/2 lb.	
#10 Tomatoes	1	
Salt & pepper to taste		

Place in greased steam table pan and bake in moderate oven 20 to 35 minutes.

DRESSING

INGREDIENTS	LBS	OZS	METHOD
Corn bread	20		Pour beef stock over corn bread and white bread and mix well.
Bread (dried out)	8		
Beef or chicken stock (3 qts)			
Water (2 gal)			Add rest of ingredients and mix well.
Voltex	2		
Sage		4	
Salt, pepper & accent to taste			
Ground onions	5		
GRound celery	6		

Bake as needed in greased pan.

CHICKEN CROQUETTE

	LBS	OZS	
Chicken skins	4		Pick over skins carefully. Grind skins, chicken meat, potatoes and onions through fine plate, & season.
Chicken meat	1		
Potatoies	3		
Onions	1		

Salt & pepper accen t to taste.

Egg white		8	Add egg white and mix. add crackers till right consistency is obtained.
Crackers as needed			

make into 4 oz croquettes and cook as needed.

DROP DUMPLINGSS

INGREDIENTS	LBS	OZS	METHOD
Flour	15		Place all dry ingredients on machine. Using dough hook start machine on low speed and mix together. Add voltex, shortening and milk. Continue mixing on low speed till well mixed. Approx 3 min.
Baking powder	1		
Sugar		12	
Salt		6	
Voltex	6		
Milk	6		
Shortening	2		

Roll as needed and cut into desired shape. Boil in chicken broth as needed. Make rue of chicken broth thickend with flour water. Color as desired with egg color. Place cooked dumplings in pan add chicken ;meat then the rue.

CHICKEN PIE

Raw diced potatoes	6		Cook onions, carrots, and celery in chicken broth separate from potatoes. Cook potatoes in chicken broth. Cook till just about done.
Cleaned onions	4		
Green peas (drained)	3		
Diced carrots	3		
Celery	1		
Chicken stock (3 gal)			Bring stock to a boil, tighten as needed with flour and water. Add seasoning then add drained cooked vegetables. Add egg color as needed.
Salt & pepper to taste			
Flour	2		

Water as needed for flour wash

For individual chicken pot pie, place one good spoon of above in chicken pie dish then place 1 oz of chicken meat in, then add enough of filling to finish filling the individual pie. Cover with pastry, brush, & bake.

CREAMED OYSTER SOUP

Water	3 gals.	
Salt pork	1 1/2 lbs.	Boil down to good stock.
Onions	2 1/2 lbs.	Saute these ingredients in
Celery	2 1/2 lbs.	oil and butter and add to
Green peppers	1 lb.	above.
Pimentos	1 can	
Oil	1/4 lb.	
Oleo	1/4 lb.	
Oleo	3/4 lb.	Make rue of oleo and flour
Flour	1 lb.	add hot milk, stir well
Milk	6 qts.	and add to above.
Oysters	1 gal.	Cook separate in own liquid add equal amount of water. Strain, pouring liquid into pot, chop up oysters and add.
Salt, Pepper & Accent		Add
Tobasco Sauce---to tangy taste		

Makes 6 gallons.

*****

OXTAIL SOUP

Oxtails	1 1/2 lbs	Simmer oxtails in water slowly
Water	3 gal	2 1/2 hrs. Add barley and all
Salt	2 ozs	vegetables and seasonings.
Pepper	1/2 oz	Continue cooking until all
Bay leaves	3	vegetables are tender,
Barley	10 ozs	approximately another hour.
Onion, diced	3/4 qts	
Celery, diced	3/4 qts	
Carrots, diced	1 1/2 qts	
Rutabagas, diced	3/4 qt	
Worcestershire sauce	2 tblsp	

VEGETABLE SOUP

INGREDIENTS	LBS.	OZS.	METHOD
Cleaned & diced carrots	1	4	Put all vegetables & soup bone
Chopped onions	1	4	on to cook in the gallon of
Cleaned stringbeans	1	4	water. Let come to a good boil.
Cleaned & diced			Add tomatoes & seasoning. Cook
potatoes	1	4	till all vegetables are done.
			When soup comes back to a boil
Leg bones or soup meat			turn fire down.
Salt & pepper & Accent			
#10 Tomatoes (1 can)			

*****

FRENCH ONION SOUP

Cleaned onions	4		Saute onions in oleo till
Oleo		8	lightly browned.
Beef stock	8		Add beef stock, salt & pepper to taste and dash of L & P sauce.
Grated Parmesian Cheese		2	Add to above
Bread cubes			Toast bread cubes, and marinate in oleo. Add to soup as you send to line.

*****

BEEF BROTH & BARLEY

Beef bones	12		Boil to strong stock. Strain.
Cold water 6 gallons			
Celery	1		
Onions	1		
Carrots	1		
Sugar		2	
Salt & pepper to taste			
Barley	1		Add to above stock and let simmer.

Noodles, spaghetti or uncooked rice may be used instead of barley.

SPLIT PEA SOUP

INGREDIENTS	LBS	OZS	METHOD
Water 8 gallons			Put all ingredients in pot & bring to good rolling boil. Strain. Chip up ham and add to soup.
Split peas	6		
Celery	1		
Onions	1		
Potatoes	2		Raw potatoes should be run through grinder and used as tightening agent.
Ham Hock	1	8	
Cream 1 can			Add.

*****

VEGETABLE SOUP

Make good strong stock of beef bones & water using 2 lb. of fresh bones to 1 gal. of water

Beef stock   (4 1/2 gal.)

Carrots	2	Let beef bones & water cook for about two hours, strain pouring 4 1/2 gals. in soup pot, all vegetables and let cook approximately one hour.
Onions	2	
Celery	2	
String beans	2	
#10 Tomatoes (1 can)		Add and let simmer.
Potatoes	2	Add potatoes and about ten minutes later add okra.
Okra	2	
Barley (1 box)		Tighten with barley

Yield: Approximately 4 gallons

CORN CHOWDER

INGREDIENTS	LBS	OZS	METHOD
Salt Pork	1		Saute well in stock pot then
Onions	1		drain off excess grease.
Celery		1/2	
Water 1/2 gal.			Add water and chicken stock.
Chicken Stock 1 gal.			Add potatoes and cook thor-
Raw diced potatoes	3		oughly, but don't overcook.
Cream style corn	3		Add and bring to a boil.
Hot milk 1 qt.			
Soda pinch			
Coffee cream 1 qt.			Remove above from fire, add
Salt as needed			cream and salt and pepper.
Pepper as needed			

Note: Do not overheat soup, or it may curdle.

Variations: Add 2 lbs of grated American cheese to above.
            Add 3 lbs ham (diced) to above.
            Add 1 #10 tomatoes and teaspoon soda to above

Yield: 60 portions

CREOLE CRABMEAT GUMBO

INGREDIENTS	LBS	OZS	METHOD
Hard Shell Crabs (2 doz.)			Method of cleaning hard crabs: Break off claws, then pull belly from shell. Clean and wash belly & chop into about 8 pieces.
Claws			Put on to boil in 3 gal water
Chopped bellies			Put bellies into pot and sprinkle
Oleo	1		with flour, salt and pepper.
Flour	1		Pour melted oleo over this.
Salt & pepper			Saute well to obtain flavor.
Tomatoes #10 (1 can)			Add to above
Celery	2 1/2		Chop together and saute separate
Onions	2 1/2		in a little oil and add to above.
Bell Peppers	1/2		
Garlic (1 pod)			
Oil	1/2		
Okra	8		Saute separate and add to above.
			Now add the stock off the claws and the meat from the largest claws. Allow to simmer.
Rice	1 1/2		Cook separate & add to above.
Bay leaves, Gumbo File, Thyme			Add a pinch of each, stir lightly and allow the spices to be absorbed into gumbo of their own volition.

CRABMEAT GUMBO (Using Canned Crabmeat)

INGREDIENTS	LBS	OZS	METHOD
Ham Hock	2		Put ham hock on to boil in water. Let boil good 1 1/2 hrs.
Water (3 gals)	24		
Celery (cleaned weight)	2		Add herbs to above and let come back to good boil.
Onions " "	2		
Bell Peppers	1		
Garlic (3 sections)			
#10 Tomatoes (1 1/2 cans)			Mash and add allowing to come back to a boil.
Canned Crabmeat	4		Empty into pan and pick out shells then add to above again allowing it to come back to boil.
Shrimp	4		Prepare shrimp. Boil separate in 1 gal. water then add stock and all to gumbo mix. Allow to come back to boil.
Water (1 gal.)			
#10 Okra (1 can)			Drain and wash off all the slimy stuff and add. Allow to come back to a boil.
Cooked Rice	1	8	Add
Corn Starch		4	When above is boiling dissolve cornstarch in small amt. of water and add.
Bay Leaves, Thyme & Bumbo File (pinch of each)			Add by just sprinkling in when gumbo is at a rolling boil. Do not stir.

Turn fire down and allow to simmer.

NOTE: If fresh okra is used, add with herbs.

YIELD: 80 orders.

MANHATTAN CLAM CHOWDER

INGREDIENTS	LBS	OZS	METHOD
Fresh Fish (Cod)	3		Place fish in water. Heat to boiling temp. and let simmer 15 min., remove and flake. Return flaked fish to stock.
Water (3 gal)			
Salt Pork	1		Saute onions & celery in drippings from salt pork.
Onions	1		
Celery	3/4		
Potatoes (diced)	5		Add stock together with flaked fish & potatoes. Let simmer 16 min.
Fish & stock			
Tomatoes #10 (2 cans)			Add all these to above.
Salt & pepper to taste			
Chopped Parsley		3	
L & P Sauce		5	
Chopped Clams (10 7 oz cans) 1/2 gal.			
Thyme (1 tsp.)			
Corn starch	1/2		Tighten above with cornstarch dissolved in sufficient amt. of water.
Water			

YIELD: 6 gals.

Crabmeat (3 15 oz cans)			Grind fish through coarse plate add flaked crab meat hot sauce l & p sauce and salt & pepper. Mix well. by hand.
Cooked f;ish scraps	3		
Hot sauce		10	
L & P sauce		12	
Salt & pepper to taste			
Mashed potatoes	15		
Egg whites	2		
Celery	4		Grind celery, onions, and peppers through chile plate. Place in heavy pot and blanche in oil. Remove from heat, allow to cool and add to crabmeat and fish.
Green onions	3		
Bell peppers	2		
Salad oil		8	

CHAPTER IV

BREADS

	Page		Page
Butter Horns	1	Boston Brown Bread	6
Hard Rolls	1	Bran Muffins	4
Ice Box Rolls	2	Corn Bread	4-5
Soft Rolls	1	Cranberry Bread	7
White Rolls	2	Date Nut Bread	6
Whole Wheat Rolls	2	Dumplings	5-7
Biscuits	2-3	Orange Bread	6

LIST HERE new recipes:

Jalapeno Cornbread   4a

Hard Rolls   1a

BUTTER HORNS

1 1/2 cups hot milk   3/4 t. salt
1/2 cup shortening   1 cake yeast
1/2 cup sugar   2 eggs, well beaten
4 cups flour

Melt shortening in scalded milk. When cool and lukewarm, add sugar and salt. Dissolve yeast in warm water. Add enough flour to make dough a sticky stage. To make rolls, roll out in circle. Brush with melted butter. Cut like pieces of pie. Roll up, begin at large end. Let rise again. Bake 20 minutes.

HARD ROLLS   (Opal Spaulding Recipe)

6 lb. 4 oz. bread flour   4 oz. yeast   )
4 oz. shortening   8 oz. whole eggs   ) Mix well
1 3/4 oz. salt   3 lb. 4 oz. warm water   )
3 oz. sugar

Mix same as white rolls. Let rise to double in size. Punch down and let rise ½ again.

Make into rolls, brush with egg and water mixture. Sprinkle long rolls with poppy seed and round rolls with sesame seeds.

In shaping rolls do not make larger than 1½ oz.

When baking rolls place pan of hot water in oven and allow to steam.

SOFT ROLLS   (N. Jone
By weight recipe

7 lb. 4 oz. flour   2½ oz. malt
2 oz. salt   4½ oz. yeast
12½ oz. sugar   14 oz. shortening
7 oz. skim milk   3 eggs
                            2 qts. iced water

Put on beater and mix for eight minutes. Take off and let proof for 2 hours, first batch 1½ hours.

Yield: 14 dozen
       1¼ oz. for each roll

Chapter IV   Page 1

August 8, 1966

HARD ROLLS

HERBERT KNIGHT
McALLEN

Yield:
5 doz. 1 1/2 oz. rolls

3 lb. 2 oz. flour
2 oz. shortening
7/8 oz. salt
1 1/2 oz. sugar
2 oz. yeast
3 eggs
1 lb. 10 oz. water

After rolls are made out, brush with egg and milk so poppy seed will stick.

Top with poppy seed or sesame seed.

Chapter IV   Page 1a

JOSEPH OWEN LUBY SR.'S ORIGINAL COOKBOOK

WHITE ROLLS (15-16 Doz.)

3½ quarts milk) Heat
1¼ quarts water)
3 lbs. shortening
1½ cups sugar
½ cup salt
3 eggs
6 yeast cakes
9 sifters flour (16 qt.)

WHOLE WHEAT ROLLS

5 eggs
1 cup sugar
2 serving spoons salt
1 cup granma molasses
4 yeast cakes or 2-2/3 oz.
1 lb. shortening

1 qt. milk
1 qt. water
5 cups white flour
10 cups whole wheat flour
5 cups Graham flour

Let rise

ICE BOX ROLLS

Dissolve 1 yeast cake in ½ cup cold sweet milk. Cream 3 t. sugar and 3 t. (heaping) shortening, add ½ pint of sweet milk, 1 t. salt and heat just enough to melt shortening. Add ½ pint cold milk, add the ½ cup milk with dissolved yeast cake. Stir in flour until stiffer than cake dough. Fold in 3 stiffly beaten egg whites. Leave in moderate room temperature for about two hours, mix with enough flour that it can be handled nicely and it may be made out into rolls and allowed to rise 2 hrs. or may be left in refrigerator several days by working down twice a day. (If cheese rolls are desired, add grated cheese before making into rolls).

BISCUIT RECIPE (EL PASO)

9 pints flour, then sift
2/3 cup Fleishmans baking powder
1 soupspoon salt
2/3 teaspoon soda
2 quarts buttermilk
1 quart sweet milk
3 heaping cookspoons shortening

Put dry ingredients in last sifting. Bake 10 to 12 minutes at 400 F.

Brush tops with melted oleo just before they are done. Put back in oven for a minute or so.

Yields 4 pans of twenty-five 2½ inch biscuits. Pans are 10½ by 16 inches.

Chapter IV   Page 2

BISCUIT MIX

8 qt. flour
1 C. B. P.
½ C. Sugar
¼ C. Salt
3 heaping cookspoons shortening
Pinch soda

This is a single mix. We make a double batch. Add enough milk (we use bt. milk) to make it right consistency.

For 3 pans we use 1½ qt. bt. milk (5 - 7 pan)

BISCUITS (16 biscuits)

2 cups flour
½ tsp. salt
4 tsp. baking powder
¼ tsp. cream of tartar
2 tsp. sugar
½ cup shortening
1 cup milk

BISCUITS --- Larger amounts

10	20 cups flour
2½	5 tsp. salt
20 tsp.	2/3 cup baking powder
2½	5 tsp. cream of tartar
2½	5 cups shortening
5	10 cups milk
10 tsp.	¼ cup sugar

BISCUITS (Ida's Recipe)

7 cups flour
7 soupspoons baking powder
4 cookspoons shortening
1 cookspoon salt
1 cookspoon sugar

BRAN MUFFINS

18	36 eggs
1	2 measuring cups baking powder
2/3	1 3/4 cans sugar (#10 can)
½	1 can shortening (#10 can)
7	14 qts. sifted flour
1	2 boxes bran
1	2 tbsp. salt

Enough milk to make soft batter. Fold bran in carefully.

BRAN MUFFINS (13 doz.)

1½ cups sugar	1½ cans (#10)
1½ cups lard	1 can (#10)
3 eggs or 6 egg yolks	3 dozen
1 tsp. salt	2 tbsp.
3 cups milk	1 gal.
6 tsp. baking powder	2 cups
6 cups flour	14 quarts
6 cups bran	3 boxes

Before adding bran reserve half of batter for blueberry muffins. Do not add bran too far in advance or it will get too soggy.

CORN BREAD

½ can (#10) egg yolks or 3 doz. whole eggs
4 measuring cups baking powder
2 tbsp. baking soda
5 gallon meal
2½ gallon flour
2 gallon buttermilk
2 gallon sweet milk
¼ cup salt
½ can #10 melted shortening
4 cups sugar

DRY MIX CORN BREAD   EL PASO

6 quarts flour	to 1 batch:
10# white corn meal	30 eggs
2 cups baking powder	4 quarts sweet milk
1 cup salt	4 quarts bt. milk
pinch soda	8 quarts mix
1-3/4 cups sugar	3 heaping cookspoons melted shortening

Chapter IV

December 29, 1965

JALAPENO CORN BREAD

JIMMY WOLIVER

6 lbs. corn meal	1 gal. buttermilk
3 lbs. flour	1 qt. sweetmilk
9 oz. baking powder	40 chopped Jalapenos (fine)
12 oz. sugar	1-2½ can diced red pepper
2 oz. salt	(or pimentos)
1 tsp. soda	18 eggs
	1 qt. Wesson Oil
	1 #10 can cream style corn

Cream oil, sugar and eggs on beater. Add wet and dry ingredients as conventional cake method. Then combine and add Jalapenos, corn and peppers. Mix lightly.

Chapter IV   Page 4a

CORN BREAD

Mix:
6 Qt. flour
1 10# white meal
2 C Baking Powder
1 C Salt
Pinch Soda
2 C Sugar (I prefer less)

To 1 batch:
30 eggs
 4 Qt. sweet milk
 4 Qt. bt. milk
8 Qts. mix
3 heaping cookspoons melted shortening.

DROP DUMPLINGS

6 cups flour
6 tbsp. shortening
6 tsp. baking powder
3 eggs
3 tsp. salt

Add milk until soft; then knead and cut in squares. Steam in boiling broth 5 minutes.

Do not lift cover until done.

DUMPLINGS   (Ida's recipe)

3	4½	9 cups flour
2/3	1	2 rounding cookspoons baking powder
1½	2½	5 level cookspoons shortening
2	3	5 eggs
2 tsp.	1	2 level cookspoons salt

Just enough milk to make a stiff dough

BAKED DUMPLINGS

10 cups flour
 7 eggs (beaten slightly)
10 soupspoons baking powder (not too full)
 3 soupspoons salt
10 soupspoons melted oleo
 8 cups milk

Beat well and drop by spoonfulls on top of chicken and bake.

Chapter IV   Page 5

BOSTON BROWN BREAD

6 cups Graham flour
2 cups Bran
7 t. soda
1 t. salt

2 cups molasses Mary Jane
2½ pints sour milk (Buttermilk)
3 cups raisins

Fill coffee cans 2/3 full and cook in boiling water 3 hours.

DATE NUT BREAD

1½ cups dates (cut fine)
1½ cups boiling water
2 T. oleo
1½ cups sugar
1 t. salt
Warm the above. When cool, add to batter and bake in loaf pans

1 egg, well beaten
2 3/4 cups flour
1 t. soda
1 t. baking powder. (Bake in moderate oven)
½ cup nut meats
½ t. vanilla

DATE NUT BREAD (4 loaves)

6 cups dates, cut fine
6 cups boiling water
6 eggs
6 cups sugar
8 T. butter

11 cups flour
4 t. soda
4 t. cream of tartar
2 cups nut meats
2 T. vanilla

Bake 1 hour.

ORANGE BREAD

Cut up peeling of 4 large oranges into narrow strips. Cover with water and add ½ teaspoon soda and cook 15 minutes. Draw off water and cook in clear water 15 minutes. Repeat this 3 or 4 times. Then drain off water and add 1 large cup sugar and allow to simmer until preserved.

Batter:
2 eggs well beaten
2/3 cup sugar
½ teaspoon salt
1 cup sweet milk

2½ cups flour
3 teaspoons baking powder
2 tablespoons melted butter

Mix above ingredients well and add 2 cups orange peel (leave syrup in it), and ½ cup chopped nuts. Let rise 30 to 40 minutes. Bake in loaf pan in moderate oven.

Chapter IV

CRANBERRY BREAD — ASA HUBBARD

Mix together:

4 cups sifted flour
1 teaspoon salt
3 teaspoons baking powder
1 teaspoon soda
2 cups sugar

Add to above:

4 tablespoons melted crisco in a little boiling water
Add juice of 2 large oranges to crisco making liquid to 1½ cups

Add to above grated peel of the 2 oranges
2 cups of cranberries (raw) cut in halves
1 cup chopped nuts (pecans)

Bake in oven 325 degrees for 1 hour.

DUMPLING RECIPE (Charles Johnston)

Sift together well:

24 cups pastry flour
4 tablespoons salt
8 tablespoons baking powder
Work in one cup oleo into the above flour mixture
12 cups milk

Method: Make a well in sifted dry ingredients. Fold milk in. Do not stir or beat. Then drop by spoons in boiling liquid. Cover and cook.

May 20, 1964

PIONEER DUMPLINGS — LOTTIE CHAPPEL

2½ cups Pioneer Biscuit Mix
4 tsp. melted shortening
2 eggs
3 serving spoons of whole milk

Combine in order given.

Drop by teaspoon or cut into approximately 1¼" by 4" rectangular or parallelogram shaped strips into boiling chicken or beef broth. Cover tightly and simmer without removing cover for five (5) minutes. Serve on top of cut chicken or with Beef Short Ribs. Also may be served with ¼ or ½ Broiled Chicken.

Chapter IV

CINNAMON OR BUTTER ROLLS

INGREDIENTS	LBS	OZS	METHOD
Flour	10		Place ingredients in mixing
Sugar	1		bowl and with dough hook start
Salt		4	mixing on low speed.
Powdered milk		14	
Shortening		12	Add to above and let mix about
Voltex		12	1 minute.
Water	5		
Egg Shad (1 lid)			
Yeast		10	Dissolve yeast in water and add
Water	2		to above. Continue mixing for
			about 6 minutes.

Place in greased dish pan and let rise about 1 hour, punch and take in 15 minutes. For butter rolls, roll out and spread with melted oleo then make up as desired. For cinnamon rolls, roll out, spread with melted oleo and then cinnamon sugar mix and raisins, then make up as desired.

*****

EGG BREAD

Eggs 6			Beat eggs well,
Sugar (3 small veg. bowls)			
Salt		6	
Melted oleo	2		
Yellow coloring (2 bottle caps)			
Water 2 qts.			
Yeast		8	Add: Mix ingredients together
Flour			Add flour until dough pulls
			away from sides of bowl.

*****

DINNER ROLLS

INGREDIENTS	LBS	OZS	METHOD
Flour	15	3	Place all ingredients in mixing
Sugar	1	11	bowl and mix together by hand.
Salt		4 1/2	Then by dough hook.
Powdered milk		13 1/2	
Voltex		18	Add to above and let mix about
Shortening	1	11	1 minute.
Water (4 1/2 qts)			Dissolve yeast well in water and
Yeast	1	2	then add to above mixing well
			on low speed for approx 7 minutes.

Place in greased dish pan and let rise 1 hour. Punch and take in 15 minutes.   YIELD: 24 doz. 1 1/2 oz. rolls

WHOLE WHEAT ROLLS

INGREDIENTS	LBS	OZS	METHOD
Bread flour	3		Scale all dry ingredients into
Whole wheat flour	1	11	mixing bowl and using dough
Bran flour		6	hook begin mixing on low speed.
Brown sugar		12	Add shortening. Let mix about
Powdered milk		4 1/2	1 minute.
Salt		1 1/2	
Shortening		12	
Water (1 1/2 qts.)			Dissolve yeast in water and add
Yeast		6	to above. Continue mixing approx. 6 minutes.

Scrape into greased pan. Allow to rise. Knock down. When it rises again punch and scale into 1 1/2 oz. portions.

YIELD: Approx. 9 doz.

*****

BUTTERMILK BISCUITS

Flour	12 cups	Place all ingredients in pan
Baking Powder	8 tbsp	and mix together well.
Soda	5 tbsp tsp.	
Salt	1/4 cup	
Sugar	1/2 cup	
Buttermilk	10 cups	Add to above and by hand mix
Melted shortening	3 cups	gently.

Roll out and cut as desired.

*****

OLD SOUTHERN SPOONBREAD

White cornmeal	1 1/2		Sift together into mixing
Salt		1	bowl.
Boiling water	1 qt.		Add to above making stiff dough.
Oleo		1/4	Melt oleo and add with egg yolks
Beaten egg yolks	(6)		to above.
Buttermilk	1 qt.		Stir soda into buttermilk, Add
Soda	1 tbsp		to cornmeal mixture and stir till smooth
Egg whites	(6)		Beat the whites of the 6 eggs. Fold into above mixture.

Pour into greased baking pan and bake in hot oven (400°) 40 to 45 min.

Excellent with butter or gravy.

RICH DINNER ROLLS

INGREDIENTS	LBS. (1 quart)	OZS.	LBS. (1 gallon)	OZS.	METHOD
Bread flour	3	2	12	8	Dissolve yeast thoroughly
Water(variable)	2		8		in part of the water.
Yeast		1 1/2		6	
Yeast food		1/16		1/4	Add to remainder of ingredients
Sugar		6	1	8	mix to a smooth plastic dough.
Salt		1		4	
Dry milk solids		3		12	
Shortening		6	1	8	

Bring dough from mixer at 80° F. Give first proof 1 hr. 45 min., second proof 55 min. to bench in 30 min. Make up in desired shapes, proof and bake at 425° F.

*****

CORNBREAD

INGREDIENTS	LBS	OZS	METHOD
Flour	5		Blend ingredients together
Shortening	2	4	thoroughly.
Baking Powder		9	
Sugar	2		
Salt		1	
Corn meal	4	12	
Eggs, whole	1	4	Mix eggs and milk. Add and
Milk, liquid-variable	9		mix to a smooth batter.

Spread in greased bun pans, scaling about 6 lbs. br bun pan.
Bake at 425° F. for 25 to 30 min.

NOTE: 4 3/4 ozs. powdered eggs and 15 1/4 ozs. water may be used in place of the 1 lb. 4 ozs. eggs.

MINCEMEAT GINGERBREAD

INGREDIENTS	LBS	OZS	METHOD
Shortening		10	Scale the ingredients into mixing bowl. Mix at medium speed four to six min. Scrape down bowl and paddle at least once during this stage to obtain a smooth batter.
Granulated sugar		14	
Molasses	1	14	
Cake flour	2	8	
Baking powder		2	
Dry milk solids		2 1/2	
Cinnamon		1/4	
Ginger		1/4	
Salt		3/4	
Water		4	
Whole eggs		10	Add eggs and water, continue to mix at low speed 4 min. or until a smooth batter is obtained. Scrape down bowl at least once during this stage.
Water	1	10	
Mincemeat	1	6	Bring to a boil and hold 1 min. Cool and fold into above mix.
Water		10	

Bake at 350° F. for approximately 21 minutes.

*****

BLUEBERRY MUFFINS

	LBS	OZS	METHOD
Granulated sugar	3		Cream together thoroughly
Shortening	2		
Whole eggs	2		Add eggs slowly, then milk while creaming.
Liquid milk	2		
Cake flour	5		Sift together. Add and mix in.
Cream of tartar		2	
Soda		1	
Blueberries, fresh or frozen	4		Fold in by hand

Bake at 375 to 400° F.

GLEAM RICH SWEET DOUGH

INGREDIENTS	LBS.	OZS. (1 quart)	LBS.	OZS. (1 gallon)	METHOD
Sugar	1		4		Place all the dry ingredients
Salt		1		4	including the Gleam, in the
Spice	to taste		to taste		mixing bowl. While mixing at
Bread flour	4		16		medium speed add the eggs and
Shortening	1	8	6		water in which the yeast has
Milk powder		4	1		been dissolved. Mix to a
Whole eggs		12	3		smooth dough. This usually
Water	2		6		requires 2 to 3 min. mixing.
Yeast		8	2		
Flavor	to taste		to taste		Bring dough from mixer at 85° F.

Allow the dough to ferment to a three-quarters to a full rise then fold. The fermentation time should be adjusted to meet your shop conditions.

After folding, let dough loosen up then take to bench and make up into desired pieces. Proof to about double size and bake.

*****

APPLE PECAN MUFFINS

INGREDIENTS	LBS.	OZS.	METHOD
Sugar mix	2 1/2		Cream well at medium speed
Brown sugar	1 1/2		
Shortening	1 1/4		
Salt		1/2	
Soda		1/4	
Whole eggs		14	Add slowly and cream well
Water (1 qt.)			
Powdered milk		4	
Pastry flour	4		
Baking powder		1	
Chopped apples	2		Stir in by hand

Deposit into cupcake tins (greased or paper lined) and sprinkle with sugar mix and 1/4 lb. chopped pecans.

Yield: 12 doz.

Bake at 370° F.

BRAN MUFFINS

INGREDIENTS	LBS.	OZS.	METHOD
Sugar	1	4	
Butter		2 1/2	
Shortening		2 1/2	
Salt		1/4	
Soda		1	Blend above ingredients together
Whole eggs		8	well and cream.
Molasses		9	
Honey		9	Add slowly and mix smooth.
Fresh buttermilk	2	12	Add slowly and mis smooth.
(1 qt. and not quite 1/2)			
Cake flour		10	Blend together well and add
Bread flour		10	slowly mixing well
Bran	1	8	
Soaked raisins	as desired		Add and mix well.

Yield: 60 muffins

*****

WHOLE WHEAT ROLLS
(Cloverleaf style)

Whole wheat flour	1 3/4		Dissolve yeast in part of water.
Bread flour	1 3/4		Put rest of water in bottom of
Sugar	1/4		mixing bowl, pour powdered milk
Salt		1 1/2	on top of water, beat, add salt
Yeast		2 1/2	and sugar. Mix together two
Powdered milk		2	flours, add to above. Pour
Shortening		2	yeast water over top of this.
Water	2 1/4		Mix for about one minute, then
			add shortening. Mix till ready.
			(about 5 minutes.

Yield: 54 rolls.

*****

PARKERHOUSE ROLLS

Roll mix	4		Dissolve yeast in water. Place
Yeast		1 1/2	R mix and yeast water in mixing
Water	3/4 qt.		machine and mix 4 min. Take to
			bench. Mold into evenly rounded

ball. Allow to proof. Punch, round into 1 1/2# balls. Allow to proof again and then make up into desired rolls.

BRAN MUFFINS

INGREDIENTS	LBS.	OZS.	METHOD
Bran muffin mix	1		Mix together and drop into
Water		10	heavy iron molds and make.
Raisins	1/4		

*****

BLUEBERRY OR PECAN MUFFINS

Plain muffin mix	1		
Water		10	
Blueberries or			
Chopped pecans	1/4		

*****

CORN STICKS OR MUFFINS

Cornbread mix	6		Mix together and bake in hot
Water	6		greased corn stick irons.
Oil	1 1/2		

*****

BISCUITS

Biscuit mix	1 1/2	
Water	1 1/4	

*****

BISCUITS

6 cups flour
12 tsp. baking powder
     salt
6 tbls. shortening

Enough sweet milk to make a dough not too stiff.

*****

BOSTON BROWN BREAD

6 cups whole wheat or graham flour
2 cups bran
7 tsp. soda
1 tsp. salt
2 cups molasses
2 1/2 pts. sour milk or buttermilk
3 cups raisins
Fill containers 2/3 full and cook in boiling water for 3 hours

CORNBREAD

2 cups baking powder
2 cookspoons salt (level)
1 1/2 dozen egg yolks or 32 oz. frozen whole eggs.
1 1/2 cups of sugar
5 sifters corn meal
2 sifters flour
1/2 gal. buttermilk
1 gallon sweet milk
1 qt. melted shortening

Cream eggs, sugar, salt, soda and add meal and flour and baking powder together alternately with the milks. Add shortening after the above mixture is well mixed.

*****

BUTTER ROLLS

6 qts. hot milk
1 1/2 qt. melted shortening
1 #2 can sugar
3 cookspoons salt
8 yeast cakes (In cold water, increase to 10)
8 dippers frozen whole eggs

Add enough flour to make correct dough.

*****

CINNAMON ROLLS

INGREDIENTS		LBS.	OZS.	METHOD
Flour		3 3/4		Put sugar, salt, flour, shortening, mace, powdered milk and vanilla in mixing bowl. Mix slightly. Then add yeast dissolved in the qt. of water together with the eggs and mix 5 minutes. Put into slightly greased pan and let rise for approximately one hour or till' double in size, punch, allow 15 minutes more for proofing then take to bench. Then proceed to make up.
Sugar			10	
Salt			2	
M. F. B.		3/4		
Brown eggs	(8)			
Drop of Vanilla				
Yeast			7	
Powdered milk		1/4		
Water	1 qt.			
Raisins		2		
Butter		1/4		
Pinch of Mace				

CLOVERLEAF ROLLS

2 Quarts:

2 qts water (warm)
8 ozs powdered milk
5 ozs yeast
3/4 lb. lard
3 oz. salt
10 ozs. sugar
7 lbs. hard flour

Yield: 10 1/4 dz. rolls

***

4 Quarts:

4 qts water (warm)
1 lb. powdered milk
9 ozs yeast
1 1/2 lbs. lard
6 ozs. salt
1 1/4 lb. sugar
14 lbs. hard flour

Yield: 21 doz. rolls

3 Quarts:

3 qts water (warm)
12 ozs. powdered milk
7 ozs. yeast
1 lb. lard
4 1/2 ozs. salt
15 ozs. sugar
10 1/2 lbs. hard flour

Yield: 15 3/4 doz. rolls

***

5 Quarts:

5 qts water (warm)
20 ozs. powdered milk
12 ozs yeast
30 ozs lard
7 1/2 ozs salt
1 1/2 lbs sugar
17 1/2 lbs. hard flour

Yield: 26 doz. rolls.

*****

BUTTERMILK BISCUITS

INGREDIENTS	LBS.	OZS.	METHOD
Flour	2		
Baking powder		4	
Salt		1	
Sugar		4	Mix together well
Shortening (M.F.B.)		8	Mix in well
Buttermilk (1 qt.)	2		
Water (1/2 pt.)			Mix in lightly

Yield: 35 to 1 lb. of flour.

BLUEBERRY MUFFINS

INGREDIENTS	LBS.	OZS.	METHOD
Sugar	5		Cream together well using cake paddle.
Cake shortening	2	8	
Cake flour	5		In separate pan mix together by hand the cake flour, salt, soda and baking powder. Add to above and after a few turns of the paddle add the honey and buttermilk.
Salt		1/2	
Honey	1		
Soda		1	
Baking powder		1	
Buttermilk	2	8	
Voltex	3		Add to above in two parts mixing well and scraping down after each.
Drained Blueberries	4		Toss blueberries in flour and add to above.
Flour		8	

Take up in 3 gallon crock.

Note: For chocolate muffins add 1# cocoa to flour and mix as usual.

CHAPTER V

PASTRY, PUDDINGS AND CUSTARDS

PIES	Page
Pastry	1
Pattie Shells	1
Graham Cracker Crust	1
Gingersnap Crust	1
Fillings:	
Butterscotch Filling	2
Chocolate Filling (10 Pies)	2
Cream Filling	2
Lemon Fillings	2-3
Apple, Swedish	27
Apple, Swiss	8
Apples for Open Face Pie	4
Apricot, Dried, Cream Pie	4
Blackbottom Pies	5
Boston Cream Pies	5-6
Buttermilk Pie	6
Butternut Brownie Pie	6
Butterscotch Pies	6-7
Butterscotch Filling	7
Caramel Fudge Pie	7
Cheese Pies	
Cream Cheese Pie or Cake	11
Cream Cheese Pie, (Evans)	19
Lemon Cream Cheese Cake	11
Raspberry Cheese Pie	11
Raspberry Cheese Pie, Uncooked	11
Cherry, Bing Chiffon Pie	4
Chess Pie (11 Pies)	9
Chocolate Pies	
Angel	27
Chiffon	9
Filling for 10 Pies	10
Ice Box Pies	10
Marshmallow Ice Box Pie	9
Chocolate-Toffee-Coffee Pie	8
Cream Filling	11
Coca-Coffee Chiffon Pie	10
Coconut, Fresh, Ice Box Pie	12
Custard, Egg, Pies	12
Fresh Fruit Pies, Glazed	13
Graham Cracker Crust	11
Grape Pie (Concord)	13

	Page
Lemon Pies	
Butter or Lemon Chess	13
Chiffon Pie (1 Pie)	14
Filling	13-14
Ice Box Pie (1 Pie)	14
Lime Light Pie (6 Pies)	19
Luby's Special Pies (12 Pies)	15
Macadamia Nut Cream Pie	25
Molasses Pies	15
Orange Chiffon Pie	15
Orange Ice Box Pie	16
Pecan Pie (Andy)	16
Pineapple Chess Pie	16-26
Prune Whip Pies	17
Pumpkin Pie	17-17
Pumpkin Chiffon Pie	24
Raisin Candy or Peanut Brittle	17
Rum Pie	18
Sour Cream Pie	18
Sour Cream Raisin Pie	26
Spanish Cream Pie	18
Strawberry, Frozen, Pie	18
Strawberry, Glaze Pie (6 Pies)	19
Sweet Potato Pies	19
PUDDINGS AND CUSTARDS	
Boiled Custard	21
Bread Pudding	20
Brown Sugar Pudding	20
Butterscotch Pudding	20
Cake Pudding	20
Carmel Sauce for Carmel Custard	25
Date Pudding (2 Pans)	21
Grapenut Pudding	21
Lemon Boston Pudding	22
Ozark Pudding	22
Rice Pudding	22
Tapioca Pudding	23
GLAZES	
Strawberry	22-28
Peach	28

LIST HERE new recipes:

Oatmeal Pie	17a	The Millionaire	30
Harvest Pudding	23	Praline "Philly" Pie	31
Pecan Pastry	29	Peach Dandy	31
Cheese Pastry	29		

PASTRY

6 lbs shortening
½ cup salt
1 cup sugar
6 scoops flour
6 dippers (12 oz.) ice water

PATTIE SHELLS

4 cups boiling water
4 cups sifted flour
1 lb. butter
12 eggs

Melt butter in boiling water. Add flour and cook until mixture leaves side of pan. Put in beater and add eggs one at a time, beating constantly. Bake in greased hot muffin tins. Serve with chicken a-la-king.

GINGERSNAP CRUST

14 gingersnaps per crust
4 tbsp. melted oleo

Bake 10 minutes in a 300 degree oven and cool.

GRAHAM CRACKER CRUST

4 cups of graham cracker meal
1 cup of sugar
1 serving spoon of cinnamon
½ cup of oleo melted

Mix above and press into pie tins. Cook in 300 degree oven for 15 to 20 minutes.

BUTTERSCOTCH FILLING

- 5 quarts milk
- 10 cups brown sugar
- 3 cups flour
- 1 cup cornstarch
- 18 eggs

Heat milk in double boiler. Mix sugar, flour, cornstarch. Add to eggs and mix. Pour into hot milk and stir constantly.

CHOCOLATE FILLING (10 pies)

- 1½ cups cocoa (10 sq. choc.)
- 4 quarts milk
- 3 cups sugar
- 2 rounding cups flour
- 1½ tsp. salt
- 9 egg yolks
- 10 sqs. butter
- 1 cookspoon vanilla

Add cocoa to dry ingredients. Pour slowly into hot milk in top of double boiler, stirring constantly. Add well beaten egg yolks and cook 2 minutes. Add butter and vanilla.

CREAM FILLING

1½	3 gallons sweet milk
5	10 cups sugar
9	18 egg yolks
3½	7 cookspoons cornstarch
1½	3 cookspoons flour
1	2 tsp. salt
1½	3 cookspoons vanilla

Heat milk in top of double boiler. Beat egg yolks until light. Mix dry ingredients together and add to eggs. Pour mixture slowly into hot milk stirring constantly until thick. Remove from fire. Add vanilla.

LEMON FILLING   2 Gal.

- 5 quarts hot water
- 12½ cups sugar
- salt

Bring to a boil. Dissolve one box cornstarch and 2/3 box flour, (measure in cornstarch box), in cold water. Add to mixture in double boiler and stir constantly until thick. When clear and thick, take off stove and add grated rind of seven lemons and juice of 24 lemons, 18 egg yolks beaten light, 2 serving spoons oleo and ½ tsp. egg coloring.

Chapter V   Page 2

LEMON FILLING

20 cups water put in pot to boil
24 lemons (juice)
Grated rind of 7 lemons
1 Box cornstarch
10 cups sugar
12 egg yolks beaten
Add to thickened lemon filling. Add ½ pound oleo.

PIES

APPLES FOR OPEN FACE PIE

Wash and prepare long pan of fresh apples, pour in pan to cook. When apples begin to boil, add 1 cup sugar (#2 1/2).
Mix 2 cooksp. sugar and 1 cooksp. cornstarch, nutmeats and cinnamon with 1 cup of warm water; add to apples. Cook several min. and remove from fire. Pour into unbaked shells and sprinkle with a little genesee pudding powder and small hunks of butter.

DRIED APRICOT CREAM PIE

2 Cups milk	¼ t. salt
1 Cup sugar	1 t. vanilla
1 T. butter	4 T. cornstarch and sugar
3 Egg yolks	1½ cups apricot puree

Scald milk, butter and salt. Combine cornstarch and sugar, add to scalded milk. Beat egg yolks and add to mixture. When thick add apricot puree.

MERINGUE:

Add salt to egg whites, beat stiff, add sugar in 1 T portions. After last sugar, add 1/2 cup puree. Spread on pie and bake slowly until brown.

BING CHERRY CHIFFON PIE
(Makes 9 inch pie)

2 cups (#303 can) Bing Cherries	1 cup undiluted Carnation Milk
1 pkg. (3 ounces) lemon flavored gelatin	¼ cup lemon juice
¼ cup sugar	1 9-inch crumb crust*

FILLING:

Drain Bing cherries thoroughly and save 1 cup of syrup. Pit and dice cherries. Heat syrup. Dissolve gelatin and sugar in hot syrup. Cool until gelatin is consistency of unbeaten egg whites. Add diced cherries. Chill Carnation in refrigerator tray until soft ice crystals form through milk (15 to 20 minutes). Whip until stiff (about 1 minute). Add lemon juice and whip very stiff (about 2 minutes longer). Fold whipped Carnation into chilled cherry mixture. Spoon into crumb crust. Chill about 2 hours or until firm.

*CRUMB CRUST:

Combine 1½ cups graham cracker crumbs, 2 tablespoons sugar with 1/4 cup melted butter. Line sides and bottom of 9 inch pie plate.

BLACKBOTTOM PIES

7	9 tbsp. (envelopes) gelatine	21	27 egg whites
1-3/4	2-1/4 cups cold water	1-1/8	2 1/4 tsp. cream
21	27 egg yolks slightly beaten		of tartar
3-1/2	4-1/2 cups sugar		
3/4	1-1/8 tsp. salt		
1 scant	1 rounding cup cornstarch		
10	13 sqs. unsweetened choc. melted		
3-1/2	4-1/2 tsp. vanilla		
	Rum extract to taste		

Soften gelatine in cold water. Combine cornstarch, sugar and salt; add to beaten yolks. Gradually stir into hot milk in double boiler. Cook until mixture coats the spoon stirring constantly. Remove from heat. Measure about 12 cups custard and add melted choc. and vanilla. Beat well. Pour into chilled ginger snap crusts. Chill. To remaining custard add softened gelatine and rum extract. Stir well while still warm to dissolve gelatin. Cool. Beat egg whites with cream of tartar until like meringue. Add the sugar gradually and beat only until thoroughly mixed. Fold this into cooled custard. Pour over chocolate layer in crust. Chill thoroughly. Just before serving, spread with whipped cream and sprinkle with coarsely grated sweet chocolate.

GINGERSNAP CRUST:

14 gingersnaps per crust
5 tbsp. melted oleo
Bake 10 minutes in a 300 degree oven and cool.

BOSTON CREAM PIE (12 pies)

12 eggs separated
12 cookspoons hot water
2 cups sugar
6 tsp. baking powder
3 cups flour
3 tbsp. vanilla
2½ cookspoons cocoa (or 4 squares choc.)
Salt

Separate eggs, beat yolks until very light, add hot water. Add sugar gradually. Add flour, baking powder, and cocoa sifted together. Fold in stiffly beaten egg whites. Bake in moderate oven in pie pans. When baked, spit cake thru center, put cream filling between layers and ice with chocolate powdered sugar icing.

BOSTON CREAM PIE

6 cups flour
2 cups sugar
1 cup egg yolks

Beat yolks till very light. About 15 minutes.

12 cookspoons hot water.

Vanilla

BUTTERMILK PIE

2/3 cup sugar
2 tablespoons flour
3 egg yolks
3 tablespoons butter
2 teaspoons lemon juice
1-2/3 cups buttermilk
3 egg whites
few grains salt

Baked pie shell.
Combine sugar, flour, and salt. Add beaten egg yolks, melted butter, and lemon juice and mix well. Stir in buttermilk. Fold in stiffly beaten egg whites. Pour in baked pie shell and bake in moderate oven (350°) about 35 minutes or until set.

BUTTERNUT BROWNIE PIE

Beat:
9 egg whites
1-1/4 teasp. baking powder
3/4 tsp. salt
Add 3 cups sugar slowly, beating until stiff. Fold in 3 cups (42) graham crackers rolled fine. Fold in 2 cups chopped pecans and 3 teasp. vanilla. Bake in greased pie tin at 350 degrees for 25 minutes. Cool and put in ice box. Serve whipped cream on top.

BUTTERSCOTCH PIE (1 Pie)

1 cup brown sugar (Pressed down)   1 tablespoon butter
2 tablespoons flour   Pinch of salt
1 cup hot water   ½ teaspoon vanilla
2 eggs

Method: Mix sugar and flour and salt. Add hot water, stir to dissolve. Place on fire and cook until thick, stirring constantly. Then add the beaten yolks of 2 eggs and cook two more minutes. Remove from fire, add butter and ½ teaspoon vanilla. Place in baked pie shell. Make meringue of 2 egg whites, ¼ cup sugar, ½ teaspoon vanilla and brown in oven.

Chapter V   Page 6

BUTTERSCOTCH PIE (1 pie)

1 cup brown sugar (pressed down)
2 tablespoons flour
1 cup hot water
2 eggs
1 tablespoon butter
Pinch of salt
½ teaspoon vanilla

Method: Mix sugar and flour and salt. Add hot water, stir to dissolve. Place on fire and cook until thick, stirring constantly. Then add the beaten yolks of 2 eggs and cook two more minutes. Remove from fire, add butter and ½ teaspoon vanilla. Place in baked pie shell. Make meringue of 2 egg whites, ¼ cup sugar, ½ teaspoon vanilla and brown in oven.

BUTTERSCOTCH FILLING

5 quarts milk
10 cups brown sugar
3 cups flour
1 cup cornstarch
18 eggs

Heat milk in double boiler. Mix sugar, flour, cornstarch. Add to eggs and mix. Pour into hot milk and stir constantly.

CARAMEL FUDGE PIE
Yield: 8 pies

3 lb. powdered sugar
2 lb. oleo
1 lb. Karamelicious
   Beat above until fluffy.
Then add:
1 lb. voltex (1 lb is equal to one pint) (voltex is 1 egg plus one egg yolk)
   Beat until fluffy.
Then add:
2 lb. cold cream filling
   Beat until fluffy.
   Fold in chopped toasted almonds. Top with whipped cream and toasted almond slivers. Let set in refrigerator before serving.

CHOCOLATE-TOFFEE-COFFEE PIE (ICE BOX)   .25¢

English Toffee Pastry Shell
  Mix with enough regular pastry for eight pies the following
  ingredients:
    1 cup brown sugar
    8 squares unsweetened chocolate (grated)
    2 tablespoons vanilla
    1/2 cup chopped pecans or walnuts

Chocolate Coffee Filling
    Cream, two pounds Oleomargarine
    Add, 6 cups sugar slowly and beat until light
    Stir in, 8 squares melted and cooled unsweetened chocolate
      squares
    Add, 16 whole eggs, beating on high speed one at a time
    Add, 16 teaspoons instant coffee

Whipped Cream Topping
    Whip 2 quarts heavy cream
    Fold in, 16 teaspoons instant coffee
    Fold in, 12 tablespoons confectioners powdered sugar

NOTE: The Chocolate Coffee filling must be poured into the shells
      only after they have cooled completely.
      A portion of the pastry shells should be saved and cooked
      apart so that it may be used later to crumble on top of
      the pie as a garnish.

SWISS APPLE PIE

Use regular Apple Pie Filling and add a handful of Cheddar Cheese
40 sq. and work it into pie filling. This should be made into
an open face apple pie. Sprinkle crushed ginger snaps over the
top. About a minute or two before removing from oven, take out
and sprinkle a little more grated cheese on the top to give color.
We charge .22¢ per serving.

Chapter V   Page 8

CHESS PIE (11 Pies)

2 lbs. oleo (colored)
8 cups sugar
8 rounding soupspoons flour
24 egg yolks, dropped in one at a time
Beat on 3.
Add 14 cups hot milk, beating on 1. Then fold in the 24 stiffly beaten egg whites.

CHOCOLATE CHIFFON PIES

About

12 pies	6 pies
12 tbsp.	6 tbsp. gelatin
2 cups	1 cup water
3½ qts.	7 cups milk
5 1/3 cups	2 2/3 cups sugar
1 tsp.	½ tsp. salt
28 oz.	14 oz. semi-sweet chocolate
16	8 egg yolks
4 tsp.	2 tsp. vanilla
16	8 egg whites

Soak gelatin in water. Cook milk, half of sugar, salt and chocolate in top of double boiler until smooth.

Beat egg yolks slightly and add to chocolate mixture, stirring constantly, until dissolved. Add vanilla, cool until it begins to congeal; fold into stiffly beaten egg whites to which the remaining half of sugar was added. (Like meringue) Place in baked pastry shells and chill. Then top with whipped cream and sprinkle with grated sweet chocolate.

CHOCOLATE MARSHMALLOW ICEBOX PIE

1 four ounce bar German chocolate
1 lb. marshmallows
1½ cups milk

Melt above ingredients in double boiler. When melted remove from fire and <u>chill with ice.</u> Fold in 1 pt. whipping cream. Pour into baked pastry shells. Place in ice box until firm. Top with whipped cream before cutting. Yeild: 3 pies.

CHOCOLATE ICEBOX PIES

9 qts. milk
2 boxes bitter chocolate (16 sqs.)
24 whole eggs
13 cups sugar
1 3/4 box cornstarch
1 lb. oleo
2 cookspoons vanilla

Heat milk. Beat eggs till fluffy. Mix cornstarch and sugar, then add to eggs on beater. Add chocolate and butter and vanilla to hot milk. When chocolate is thoroughly melted, add egg mixture to hot milk and keep stirring until done. Top with whipped cream. Sprinkle with grated dot chocolate. Use baked Graham cracker crust.

CHOCOLATE FILLING (10 Pies)

1½ cups cocoa (10 sq. choc.)   1½ tsp. salt
4 quarts milk   9 egg yolks
3 cups sugar   10 sqs. butter
2 rounding cups flour   1 cookspoon vanilla

Add cocoa to dry ingredients. Pour slowly into hot milk in top of double boiler, stirring constantly. Add well beaten egg yolks and cook 2 minutes. Add butter and vanilla.

COCA-COFFEE CHIFFON PIE

6 envelopes plain Knox gelatin
1½ cups cold water
3 cups strong coffee
15 sqs. unsweetened chocolate
18 egg yolks
3 cups sugar
1½ tsp. salt
3 tsp. vanilla
6 tbsp. orange rind

18 egg whites   ) beat as meringue and fold into chocolate
 3 cups sugar   ) mixture last.

Soften gelatin in cold water 5 minutes. Heat coffee and chocolate together until chocolate is melted. Beat smooth with egg beater. Sitr in gelatin until dissolved. Add to slightly beaten egg yolks combined with the 3 cups sugar, salt, vanilla and orange rind. Chill until thick enough to mound slightly when dropped from spoon. Beat egg whites until stiff. Add sugar gradually. Fold into gelatin mixture. Pour into baked shells and chill until firm. Top with whipped cream.

Chapter V   Page 10

CHEESE PIES

CREAM CHEESE PIE OR CAKE:

3 lbs. cream cheese, beat well on beater. Add 4 cups sugar, 2 cookspoons of flour and 1 cookspoon of vanilla. Add 8 whole eggs and 1 quart of half and half. Beat for about one minute. Pour into graham cracker shells and bake 15 to 20 minutes at 350 degrees. Sprinkle graham cracker crumbs over top.

RASPBERRY CHEESE PIE:

Same as cheese pie above, except do not sprinkle cracker crumbs over top. When pie has baked and cooled, spread with fresh frozen raspberries and top with whipped cream.

UNCOOKED RASPBERRY CHEESE PIE:

Use cream cheese pie recipe above but leave out the eggs and flour. This uncooked recipe yields less pies.

LEMON CREAM CHEESE CAKE:

3 lbs. cream cheese. Beat well in mixer. 22 whole eggs; add one at a time while cheese is whipping. 5 cups sugar; add all at one time while cheese and eggs are in beater. Continue beating until well blended. Add 1 quart plus one cup of whipping cream. Pour into beater and beat until mixture begins to be a little light or fluffy. Add one serving spoon of vanilla and 8 oz. of fresh lemon juice to above mixture.

Pour into cracker crumb crusts or baked pastry shells. Bake 15 to 20 minutes at 350 degrees. Yield: About 10 pies.

GRAHAM CRACKER CRUST:

4 cups of graham cracker meal
1 cup of sugar
1 serving spoon of cinnamon
½ cup of oleo, melted

Mix above and press into pie tins. Cook in 300 degree oven for 15 to 20 minutes.

CREAM FILLING

1½	3 gallons sweet milk
5	10 cups sugar
9	18 egg yolks
3½	7 cookspoons cornstarch
1½	3 cookspoons flour
1	2 tsp. salt
1½	3 cookspoons vanilla

Heat milk in top of double boiler. Beat egg yolks until light. Mix dry ingredients together and add to eggs. Pour mixture slowly into hot milk, stirring constantly until thick. Remove from fire. Add vanilla.

Chapter V   Page 11

FRESH COCONUT ICEBOX PIE

4½ qts. milk
4 cups sugar
5 heaping cooksp. flour
27 egg yolks

Heat milk in double boiler. Beat egg yolks, add sugar and flour (mixed together) beat well. Pour egg mixture into hot milk (stirring constantly). When thick, add fresh grated coconut. Pour into baked pie shell. Place in icebox to cool. Top with whipped cream and cut in 6 pieces.

EGG CUSTARD PIE   (6 Pies)

3 quarts whole milk
6 rounding cookspoons sugar
18 whole eggs

1½ cookspoon flour
1 cookspoon vanilla
¼ tsp. nutmeg

Beat eggs <u>only until mixed.</u> Mix sugar, flour, nutmeg and add to eggs. Then add milk and vanilla. Pour into unbaked pie shells.

EGG CUSTARD PIE   (6 Pies)

18 eggs
3 cups sugar
2½ quarts milk
soupspoon vanilla
pinch of salt

Beat eggs, add sugar, salt, vanilla and milk. Bake in unbaked shell.

QUICK EGG CUSTARD PIE

9 eggs
1 pt. sugar
3 pts. sweet milk

Dash salt
Dash nutmeg
Egg coloring

Beat eggs slightly, mix in sugar, mixing thoroughly. Add salt, coloring and spice. Mix well and pour into shells. Bake at 350° for 15 to 20 minutes. Makes three pies.

GLAZED FRESH FRUIT PIES

5 cups sugar
5 cups boiling water
5 rounding serving spoons cornstarch
3 serving spoons red Jello powder for fresh raspberry or strawberry pie

Mix sugar, cornstarch and Jello and dissolve in good 1/2 cup hot water. Cook until real clear, remove from fire and add 5 sqs. butter. Add 1 1/2 serving spoons red coloring. Stir well before chilling. When cold, stir well before glazing pie; it will be more creamy. Fill baked pie shell about 1/2 full of cold cream filling. Prepare fresh strawberries or raspberries by adding sugar and then drain well before adding to pie. Put thin layer of glaze over top of berries. Top with whipped cream. Cut in 6 slices. Fresh peach pie can be made by using 3 serving spoons lemon Jello and egg coloring.

GRAPE PIE (Concord)

Stem and wash grapes, separate pulp from hull. Cook separately. Run pulp through colander and remove seeds. Mix with hulls; sweeten and thicken slightly with cornstarch; let cook a little longer and pour into unbaked pie shells.

LEMON BUTTER PIE (or Lemon Chess)

6 Pies	1 Pie
18	3 eggs, well beaten
9	1½ cups sugar
6	1 level tbsp. flour
6	1 tsp. vanilla
9	1½ tbsp. lemon juice
36	6 tbsp. buttermilk
3	½ cup melted butter

Add ingredients in the order given above. Mix the sugar and flour together before adding to the eggs. Bake in unbaked shell.

LEMON FILLING

20 cups water, put in pot to boil   1 box cornstarch
24 lemons (juice)   10 cups sugar
Grated rind of 7 lemons   12 egg yolks, beaten

Add to thickened lemon filling ¼ pound oleo.

LEMON FILLING (2 Gal.)

5 quarts hot water
12½ cups sugar
salt

Bring to a boil. Dissolve one box cornstarch and 2/3 box flour (measure in cornstarch box) in cold water. Add to mixture in double boiler and stir constantly until thick. When clear and thick, take off stove and add grated rind of seven lemons and juice of 24 lemons, 18 egg yolks beaten light, 2 serving spoons oleo and ½ tsp. egg coloring.

LEMON CHIFFON PIE (1 Pie)

3 eggs   3 tsp. boiling water
1 cup sugar   1 lemon (juice and rind)

Beat egg yolks until creamy, add lemon juice and grated rind; add 1/2 cup sugar and beat until well mixed. Add boiling water. Cook in double boiler until mixture is like jelly. Set aside to cool.

Beat egg whites until stiff. Add cooked lemon mixture to egg whites, blending thoroughly. Pour into pastry shell (use graham cracker crust). Bake in oven until browned. Make cracker crust as you do for cheese cake.

LEMON ICEBOX PIE (1 Pie)

3 eggs to one can condensed milk
¼ cup lemon juice

Beat egg yolks until thick. Add milk, then lemon juice. Pour into pie pan that has been lined with vanilla wafers. Top with egg whites beaten stiff and sweetened. Brown in oven. Set in icebox.

LUBY'S SPECIAL PIES (12 Pies)

8	5 quarts milk (top)
26	18 whole eggs
8	4½ cups sugar
1½	1 tsp. salt
8	5 rounding cookspoons cornstarch
4	3 serving spoons vanilla

Heat milk in double boiler. Beat eggs until <u>very light</u> on beater. Mix sugar, salt and cornstarch, add to beaten eggs. Pour slowly into hot milk, stirring constantly. When thick, remove from fire and add vanilla. Pour into baked pie shells and set in icebox to cool. When cold, top with whipped cream, and add grated sweet chocolate over top.

MOLASSES PIE (6 Pies)

1/2 gallon light syrup
18 eggs
Juice of 2 lemons
6 soupspoons melted butter

3 rounding soupspoons flour
1 soupspoon vanilla
3/4 cup sugar

Beat about five minutes on No. 3.

MOLASSES PIE (6 Pies)

6 level cookspoons flour
18 eggs
1 tsp. nutmeg
Juice of two lemons
Pinch of salt
1 cookspoon vanilla
12 cups molasses

ORANGE CHIFFON PIE

1 envelope plain gelatin
1 cup of water
Dash of salt

3/4 cup sugar
3 eggs
1 - 6 oz. can concentrated orange juice

Combine water, salt, gelatin and ½ cup of sugar in top of double boiler. Stir until blended. Slowly add to the 3 slightly beaten egg yolks. Return to top of boiler and cook, stirring constantly, until gelatin is dissolved and mixture begins to thicken. Remove from heat and add 6 oz. of concentrated orange juice, blend well. Chill until mixture begins to thicken slightly.

Beat egg whites until they stand in peaks. Add remaining ¼ cup of sugar while beating, 2 tbsp. at a time.

Fold egg whites into orange mixture. Put into 9 inch pastry shell. Chill until firm. Top with thin layer of whipped cream.

Chapter V

ORANGE ICEBOX PIE

1 envelope plain gelatin
1 cup water
Dash of Salt
3/4 cup sugar
3 eggs
1 six oz. can conc. orange juice

Combine water, salt, gelatin and 1/2 cup of the sugar in top of double boiler. Stir until blended. Slowly add mixture to the 3 slightly beaten egg yolks. Return to top of double boiler and cook until mixture coats spoon, stirring constantly. Remove from heat and add orange juice, blending well. Chill until mixture begins to thicken slightly. Beat egg whites until they stand in peaks. Add remaining 1/4 cup of sugar to whites while beating. Fold whites into egg-orange mixture. Put into 9 inch pastry shell. Chill until firm. Top with layer of whipped cream.

PECAN PIE

Beat 4 eggs slightly
Add 1 cup white sugar
    1 cup white corn syrup
    1/8 tsp. salt
    3 tbsp. melted shortening
    3/4 cups whole pecan nut meats
    1-1/2 tsp. vanilla

Fill pie shell and bake in moderate oven 350° about 1 hour.

PINEAPPLE CHESS PIE

2 Cups sugar
2-1/2 Cups pineapple juice
4 level serving spoons flour
6 eggs
1-1/4 cubes butter

Cream butter and sugar, egg yolks, flour and then add pineapple juice. Mix well, put in unbaked pie shells and bake about 45 min. and cool a little. Add sliced pineapple over top and meringue made with egg whites.

Chapter V

PRUNE WHIP PIES

8 cups chopped cooked prunes
Juice of 2 lemons
20 egg whites
2 tsp. cream of tartar
4 cups sugar

Whip egg whites until they peak, add cream of tartar and sugar gradually; beat 2 minutes. Fold in chopped prunes. Pour into baked pie shells and bake in oven until browned.

PUMPKIN PIE

12 Pies	4 Pies
2½	3/4 cup sugar
1	1/3 cup flour
1½	½ serving spoon cornstarch
1	1/3 box brown sugar
1½	½ tsp. nutmeg
3	1 tsp. cinnamon
1	1/3 tsp. salt
12	4 eggs (beat well)
3	1 can pumpkin (#2½)
15	5 cups milk
2	2/3 cups dark syrup

RAISIN CANDY PIE OR PEANUT BRITTLE PIE

2/3 cup light or dark raisins
1 envelope (1 tablespoon) plain gelatin
¼ cup cold water
1-3/4 cups milk
½ cup sugar
2 tablespoons cornstarch
½ teaspoon salt
2 eggs
½ teaspoon vanilla
½ cup whipping cream
1 cup ground or coarsely crushed peanut brittle
1 baked and cooled 9-inch pie shell

Rinse and dry raisins; chop coarsely. Soften gelatin in cold water; scald milk. Blend sugar, cornstarch and salt with beaten eggs and vanilla, until smooth. Stir into hot milk and cook over hot water until thick and smooth, about 15 minutes. Stir occasionally. Add gelatin, stirring until dissolved. Remove from heat and cool. When mixture begins to thicken and jell fold in stiffly beaten cream, raisins and peanut brittle. Turn into baked pie or tart shells and chill until firm. Garnish top with additional whipped cream and peanut brittle, if desired. (This pie is served the day it is made.)

Note: We chop raisins quite fine and use only ½ cup crushed peanut brittle.

PUMPKIN PIE MIX

16 eggs, slightly beaten
1 #10 can pumpkin
3 lbs. sugar
4 tsp. salt
8 tsp. cinnamon
3 tbsp. Pumpkin Pie Spice Mix
8 tall cans Evaporated milk

Mix in order given. Makes 8 pies.

OATMEAL PIE

Yield: 16 pies

1 gallon granulated sugar
1 tablespoon salt
2 lbs. melted oleo
32 eggs, whole
½ gallon milk
2 tablespoons vanilla

3/4 gallon Dark Karo Syrup   )
3/4 gallon Angel Flake Coconut   ) Fold in
3/4 gallon uncooked oatmeal   )

Mix dry ingredients, add eggs, beat slightly. Add wet ingredients then fold in oatmeal and coconut. Bake at 350° for about 45 minutes.

RUM PIE

5 qts. milk
18 eggs beaten very light
5 cups sugar
5 serving spoons cornstarch

Stir constantly while cooking. Add 4 serving spoons rum when you take it off stove. Pour into graham cracker crusts and set in ice box to cool. When cool cover with grated sweetened chocolate. Chopped toasted pecans may also be sprinkled over top if desired.

SOUR CREAM PIE

3 eggs
1 T. cornstarch
1 T. melted butter
1 T. lemon juice
1 cup sour cream
1 cup chopped cooked pitted prunes
1/2 t. salt

Combine well beaten yolks, cornstarch, salt and butter. Mix well, add prunes, lemon juice and sour cream. Sweeten to taste. Pour in lined pastry pie pan. Bake 450 degrees about 30 minutes. Remove from oven, cover with meringue made of egg whites and 3 T. sugar. Bake in slow oven 325 degrees for 20 min. Raisins may be used instead of prunes.

SPANISH CREAM PIE

2/3 cups sugar
1 1/2 cups milk
1 1/2 heaping T. cornstarch
Vanilla

Let cool. Spread whipping cream on top and grated chocolate. Set in ice box.

FROZEN STRAWBERRY PIE

1 gallon strawberries
3-1/4 cups sugar
1-1/2 cups cornstarch

Let berries, sugar and red coloring come to a boil; add cornstarch which has been dissolved in a little cold water. Cook until thick and cornstarch is done.

STRAWBERRY GLAZE PIE (6 pies)

5 pints berries - washed

5 cups sugar   )
1-1/4 cups cornstarch   )
2 serving spoons red coloring)

Combine above ingredients and cook until clear. Remove from fire and cool. Wash and slice 5 pints of strawberries and mix gently with cooked mixture. Pour into cooked pie shells, and top with whipped cream.

SWEET POTATO PIES

2 cups sweet potatoes
2 cups sugar
2 T. flour
2 tsp. butter
4 eggs
Nutmeg
1 Pt. milk

CREAM CHEESE PIE

Cream together 1 lb. oleo, 4 whole eggs, 2 lb. sugar then add 2 tablespoons plain gelatin dissolved in 6 oz. water. Mix 2 minutes then add 3 lbs. Cream Cheese and cream for 4 minutes, and last fold in 1 quart unseasoned whipped cream and place in shells. (Either graham cracker or regular pie dough shells with graham cracker crumbs rolled in.) Sprinkle graham cracker crumbs on top.

LIME LIGHT PIE (6 pies)

6 Cans Eagle Brand Milk
1-1/2 Cups Lime Juice
5 cups Drained Crushed Pineapple
24 drops Green Food Coloring

Roll out pastry in chocolate wafer crumbs for pie shells. Bake the shells off. Mix Eagle Brand milk, lime juice and half of the pineapple with a wire hand whip. In separate container add food coloring to the remaining half of the pineapple and stir until dark green in color. Add the two mixtures together and fill pie shells. After chilling, top with whipped cream and sprinkle with chocolate wafer crumbs.

BREAD PUDDING

12 eggs
3 cups sugar
16 slices bread
4 quarts milk
1 tsp. vanilla
nutmeg
1 cup raisins

Dots of butter on top.

BROWN SUGAR PUDDING

1 cup brown sugar
2 cups water, boiling
2 tbsp. butter

Mix above ingredients in pan in which it is to be baked. Mix 1 cup flour and 1/2 cup water. Add to this batter either nuts, apples, pineapple or raisins. Drop by spoonfuls into first mixture and bake in oven.

BUTTERSCOTCH PUDDING

6 qts. milk - heat in double boiler
1½ boxes brown sugar
¼ lb. butter
9 cooksp. pudding powder

Melt sugar and butter, then pour into hot milk. Make paste of powder and small amount of sweet milk. Then pour into hot milk. Cool and serve with whipped cream.

CAKE PUDDING

Use day old cake and crumble in bottom of serving pan and pour a thick chocolate or vanilla cream sauce over this and then another layer of cake and one of sauce. Chopped pecans, coconut or mixed fruit can be used on top; then serve with thin sauce in orders.

BOILED CUSTARD

5 quarts whole milk (heat in double boiler)
18 egg yolks
6 whole eggs
2½ cups sugar
2 heaping cookspoons cornstarch
3 serving spoons vanilla

Beat eggs until light. Mix cornstarch and sugar and add to eggs. When milk is hot pour egg mixture slowly into milk. Remove from fire and add vanilla.

Serve in sherbet dishes.

DATE PUDDING (2 pans)

1 lb. dates cut fine
2 heaping t. soda
3 cups boiling water, pour over the above and let stand.
2 cups sugar
2 cooksp. butter
3 eggs well beaten
4 scant cups flour
1 rounding t. baking powder

Cream butter and sugar, add eggs and flour with baking powder and add to date mixture. Pour into greased baking pans and sprinkle with 1 cup chopped pecans. Bake in moderate oven. Serve with butter sauce

BUTTER SAUCE

2 cups brown sugar
1 heaping cooksp. cornstarch
1 1/2 cups water
1/4 lb. butter
1 t. vanilla
2 cooksp. vinegar (or enough to cut sweet).
Mix sugar, cornstarch and water. When hot add butter, vanilla and vinegar. Cook until thick and clear.

GRAPENUT PUDDING

12 eggs
1-1/3 cups sugar
2 quarts milk
1 cookspoon vanilla
½ pkg. grapenuts over top when half done

Cook in pan in larger pan with about 1 inch of water.

LEMON BOSTON PUDDING

2 eggs
1 Lemon
1 cup sugar

1/3 cup flour
1 cup sweet milk
1 1/2T. melted butter

Beat 2 egg yolks, adding the sugar, flour, milk and butter, then add the beaten whites of eggs. Pour in baking dish, putting in pan of hot water to bake. Bake in moderate over 1/2 to 3/4 hour.

OZARK PUDDING

1 egg, well beaten
3/4 cup sugar
3 tablespoons (rounded) flour)
Pinch of salt   )   Sift together
1½ teaspoon baking powder   )

3/4 finely chopped apple
½ cup chopped nuts

Add sugar gradually to egg. Then add sifted ingredients. Mix well. Add apples and nuts. Bake in a greased square pan at 325 degrees for 30 minutes. Serve with vanilla sauce or whipped cream.

RICE PUDDING

12 Eggs
3 Cups sugar
4 Cups cooked rice
4 Quarts milk
1 tsp. vanilla
Dash of nutmeg

Dots of butter over top.

STRAWBERRY GLAZE

1½ cups fruit juice
1½ cups water
1 cup sugar
6 tablespoons cornstarch (level spoons)

Bring to boil and add red color and one square butter.

TAPIOCA PUDDING

4 quarts milk, scalded

1 cup Tapioca   )
1 cup sugar   )   Slowly add to scalded milk
Pinch of salt   )

4 egg yolks   )
1 cup sugar   )   Beat until very light

Add egg yolks and sugar to milk mixture and cook from 3 to 5 minutes, until thick. Remove from fire. Add 2 tbsp. vanilla and fold in 4 beaten egg whites.

HARVEST PUDDING

CAKE:

1½ cups sugar
2 cups flour
2 tsp. soda
2 eggs
1 - 303 can fruit cocktail (well drained)

Mix sugar, flour, soda and add eggs. Add juice from 2 cups of fruit cocktail. Mix till smooth, then fold in drained fruit cocktail. Pour into greased and floured pan, 9" x 13". Sprinkle ½ cup chopped pecans mixed with ½ cup brown sugar on top. Bake at 325 degrees for 40 minutes.

SAUCE:

1 cup sugar
1 - 13 oz. can milk (Pet)
1 stick oleo
1 tsp. vanilla

Boil 8 minutes, add vanilla. Pour over cake while both are still hot.

PUMPKIN CHIFFON PIE

Step 1

1¼ Cup Sugar (Super fine granulated preferred)
1 Cup Whipping Cream
½ Teaspoon Cinnamon
½ Teaspoon Vanilla

Sift then measure sugar. Whip cream, adding sugar, cinnamon and vanilla. Gently stir until mixture is stiff. Set in refrigerator until ready to use.

Step 2

Add 1 envelope unflavored gelatin to 1/4 cup cold water.
3 Eggs separated
1/3 Cup Granulated Sugar
1¼ Cup Pumpkin
½ Cup Milk
¼ Teaspoon Salt
1 Teaspoon Cinnamon
¼ Teaspoon Ginger
¼ Teaspoon Allspice
¼ Teaspoon Nutmeg
¼ Cup Powdered Sugar

Beat egg yolks slightly. Add granulated sugar and beat until well mixed. Add pumpkin, milk, salt, and spices. Cook over medium heat, stirring until it has boiled 2 minutes. Remove from heat and stir in softened gelatin. Let mixture cool. Beat egg whites adding ¼ cup powdered sugar, until egg whites are stiff. Beat cooled pumpkin mixture until smooth and then fold in stiff egg whites. Pour about half into pie crust - then spread a layer of whipped cream, then add a layer of pumpkin mixture over the whipped cream. Chill in refrigerator and top with whipped cream before serving.

Chapter V

MACADAMIA NUT CREAM PIE

1 cup fresh milk	1/3 cup fresh milk
¼ cup sugar	1 whole egg (1 yolk will do)
¼ cup chopped macadamia nuts	1 oz. cornstarch
pinch of salt	1/3 cup egg whites
1 teaspoon vanilla	½ cup sugar

Baked Pie Shell

Combine first five ingredients in top of double boiler and scald over hot water. Beat egg (or yolk) and add 1/3 cup milk and cornstarch. Beat egg whites until fluffy and then gradually add the ½ cup sugar, beating constantly until egg whites are stiff. When first mixture is scalding hot, add cornstarch mixture and stir constantly until mixture thickens. (About 4 minutes) Remove from fire and carefully fold in the egg white mixture. Pour into baked pie shell and cool. Before serving, top with a thin layer of whipped cream and sprinkle with chopped toasted macadamia nuts. The ¼ cup chopped macadamia nuts weighed 1½ oz. ½ oz. of chopped nuts were toasted and sprinkled on top of pie. The eggs used were Grade A 'large'. 3 egg whites equaled 1/3 cup. I made one pie with the whole egg and the other with the yolk and could detect no difference in color, texture, taste or volume.

I could not possibly put all the filling into one pie shell and believe a double recipe would make 3 generously filled pies.

Nuts can be purchased from: Alexander Spaulding - 3030 Audley Street Houston 6, Texas.   1 doz. 6 oz. cans - $9.60.

CARMEL SAUCE FOR CARMEL EGG CUSTARD

Heat 8 qt. stock pot (empty) over hot flame until <u>hot</u> - then pour in 8 cups of sugar. Stir often until sugar has melted (with a brown color, do not allow to burn as this will make syrup bitter). Bring 5 cups of water to boil in separate pan. Remove melted sugar from fire. Then add water slowly (be very careful with amount of water added; if you are not, sugar may foam over side of pot). After adding water, place back over fire (this time use slow flame) and cook until drops can be dropped into glass of water, going to bottom of glass without separating. Then pour up and let cool in refrigerator. Pour full teaspoon in cup custard cups. Finish filling with regular custard filling.

Cook same as cup custard. When done, turn upside down in fruit dish and serve. (If carmel should be too thick after sitting in refrigerator, hot water may be added to thin down).

SOUR CREAM RAISIN PIE

1 cup sour cream
2/3 cup sugar
3 tbsp. corn starch
2 egg yolks
½ cup milk
½ cup raisins

Bring above to a boil and cook until thick. (We cooked this in our steam kettle.)

Then mix: ½ cup milk
            1 tsp. cinnamon
            Pinch of cloves

Add above to hot mixture. Cool and then put into baked shells and top with meringue.

PINEAPPLE CHESS PIE
(1 Pie)

½ cup butter (melted)
2 cups sugar
4 egg yolks, beaten
1 small can pineapple (6 oz. can)
4 egg whites

Cream sugar and butter. Add slightly beaten egg yolks and pineapple and mix thoroughly but very little as too much mixing will cause the egg yolks to break down and will not thicken. After you have mixed this mixture, beat the egg whites and fold the first mixture into the beaten egg whites. Pour into a raw shell and bake at 350° for 45 minutes. Be sure to let pie set awhile before serving.

12 PIES

3 lbs. oleo
24 cups sugar
48 egg yolks
1 #10 can pineapple
48 egg whites

SWEDISH APPLE PIE

(Four Pies)

3/4 cups sugar
2 eggs - beat well

Add: 3 medium apples diced
     1 tsp. soda
     ½ tsp. cinnamon
     ½ tsp. nutmeg
     Pinch salt

Add: 1 cup flour
     1 tsp. vanilla
     ½ cup nuts

Mix well in order given. Bake 30 minutes in 350 degree oven.

SAUCE

½ cup white sugar
½ cup brown sugar
½ cup canned milk
2 tbsp. butter

Cook in double boiler until thick. Remove and cool. Top with whipped cream and then add cooled sauce.

CHOCOLATE ANGEL PIE

(Four Pies)

I. Beat 8 egg whites (save yolks) with 2 tbsp. vinegar, 1 tsp. salt, 1 tsp. cinnamon until soft mounds form.

II. Add: 2 cups sugar gradually, beating until meringue stands in stiff glossy peaks. Spread on bottom and sides of baked pie shell.

III. Bake at 325° for 15 - 18 minutes until lightly browned - cool.

IV. Filling: Add 3 slightly beaten egg yolks and 1 cup water to 24 oz melted semi-sweet chocolate pieces. Spread 3 tbsp. chocolate mix over each pie shell.

Combine 1 qt. whipped cream, 1 cup sugar, 1 tsp. cinnamon. Spread half of whipped cream. Mix evenly over the 4 pie shells. Combine remaining whipped cream with remainder of chocolate mix. Spread over whipped cream in pie shell. Chill at least 4 hours before serving.

Chapter V

GLAZE FOR FRESH STRAWBERRY OR PEACH PIE

9 cups sugar
6 cups water (Fruit juice is better. Anything from
           Salad Dept. except pineapple juice.)
1½ cups white Karo
1½ cups tapioca flour
Red color
Few grains salt

Reserve part of liquid to mix with tapioca flour. Bring other ingredients to boil. Add flour and water mixture. Bring back to boil. Let cool before use. May be made up day in advance. Try this with chilled ripe peaches. Omit red color and use peach juice.

PECAN PASTRY
FOR REGRIGERATOR PIES
(EXCEPT THOSE CONTAINING NUTS)

Cream w/paddle - 1 lb. oleo

ADD: 4 cups flour
       3/4 cup powdered sugar
       2 tbsp. water
       2 tsp. vanilla

Blend well and add: 2 cups chopped pecans

Roll out and fit into shells.

CHEESE PASTRY

Put on beater and mix the following:

1# oleo
12 oz. cream cheese
4 cups flour

THE MILLIONAIRE

9--9 Inch Pies

3 lbs.		Powdered sugar	**First Stage**
1 lb.	4 oz.	Kneedit margarine	Cream, fast, 3rd speed
1 lb.		Rich eggs	3 speed machine, 10 min.
	1 oz.	Vanilla	
			Second Stage
2 lb.		Whip, cream, 1qt.	Whip firm
	5 oz.	Powdered sugar	
		2 tsp. clear Gelatine, dissolved in 4 oz. water	
			Third Stage
2 lb.		(1 qt.) crushed pineapple	Fold into whip cream
	6 oz.	Chopped pecans	

SPECIAL INSTRUCTIONS: Divide First Stage evenly in baked pie shells. Refrigerate till set well. Top with whipped cream mixture, spread evenly over set pies, refrigerate again.

SUGGESTIONS: The first part of this pie can be made into a light chocolate or Egg Nog Pie with the addition of a little nut meg and rum flavor. This pie tops them all.

For the richest pie, top again with whipped cream. Keep refrigerated.

PRALINE "PHILLY" PIE

8 Pies

  6 lbs. cream cheese
4½ cups dark brown sugar
  2 tablespoons vanilla
12 eggs
  3 cups chopped pecans

Combine softened cream cheese, sugar and vanilla, mixing until well blended. Add eggs, one at a time, mixing well after each addition. Fold in chopped pecans. Pour into graham cracker crust. Bake at 325° for 35 minutes. Cool. To garnish, brush with maple syrup. Top with pecan halves.

PEACH DANDY

8 Pies

STEP I

2 cups egg whites
2 2/3 cups white karo

Beat egg whites until foamy. Gradually add karo and continue beating until stiff peaks form.

STEP II

1 - 24 oz. pkg. lemon gelatin
8 cups boiling water
6 lbs. frozen peaches
½ cup lemon juice

Place gelatin in large pan, then add boiling water and stir until dissolved. Then add peaches (should be frozen solid). Stir until thawed.

STEP III

Fold in egg whites and chill until mixture thickens slightly. Use graham cracker crust.

PUMPKIN PIE

INGREDIENTS	lBS	OZS		METHOD
Granulated Sugar	4		)	Sift and mix together.
Cake flour		2	)	
Salt		1	)	
Nutmeg		1/3	)	
Cinnamon		1/3	)	
Eggs	3		)	
Syrup		8	)	
Pumpkin (1 no 10 can)			)	Add
Milk (2 qts)			)	Add
Margarine		8	)	

EGG CUSTARD

	lBS	OZS		METHOD
Sugar	4		)	Get together with paddle
Cake Flour		8	)	
Milk Powder	1	4	)	
Salt		1	)	
Vanilla to taste			)	
Eggs		4	)	Add well
Melted Butter		1	)	Add
Water		10	)	Add

Bake in hot oven 400°

PECAN PIE STOCK

INGREDIENTS	LBS	OZS		METHOD
Granulated Sugar	10	8	)	Put sugar, flour & salt in & water mixing machine with paddle & mix 5 min., med. speed.
Bread Flour	1	10	)	
Salt		3	)	
Boiling Water	5		)	
Eggs	5		)	Add eggs and mix on medium speed for 5 minutes.
Glucose or White Syrup	5 quarts		)	Add and mix on low speed to incorporate.
Wesson Oil	1	4	)	

Bake at 365°

Keep on hand.
Stir when used.
Sprinkle pecans over pies.

PASTRY FOR PIES

INGREDIENTS	LBS	OZS		METHOD
Pastry Flour	12		)	Use paddle in machine.
M.F.B.	18		)	
Pastry Flour	12		)	Scrape well and add. Get to a mass.
Cold Water	10		)	Dissolve and add.
Salt		14	)	
Brown Sugar	1	8	)	Mix till dry
All Purpose	6		)	

PRALINE PECAN PIES

INGREDIENTS	LBS	OZS	METHOD
Whole eggs (Voltex)	1	8	Beat well.
Flour		1	Mix flour together with milk until smooth paste is obtained. Add to above
Liquid milk (1/2 qt.)	1		
White Karo syrup	5		Add syrup, vanilla, salt and then oleo. Be sure that all ingredients are thoroughly mixed.
Vanilla (1/2 tsp)			
Salt (1/4 tsp)			
Melted Oleo		4	
Pecans		12	Chop pecans but not too fine. Distribute over 4 uncooked pie shells. Add syrup mix.

Bake in moderately slow oven, 325° F for approximately 35 min.

Yield 4 pies.

CHEESE PIES

Oleo	1		
Sugar	2	8	Cream till smooth.
Vanilla (2 tsp)			
Eggs (voltex)		8	Add and blend.
American cheese		12	Fold in
milk		8	Add and mix till smooth.

Bake in moderate oven slowly as this pie will burn if cooked too fast

Yield: 4 pies.

FRUIT CHEESE CUSTARD PIE

Sugar	1	12	
Bakers cheese (dry)	4		
Cornstarch		1 1/2	Mix smooth, slowly adding eggs
Durkee's betrkake	1		
Salt		1	
Vanilla		1	
Eggs	3		Disolve, add slowly. Mix to a smooth solution. Handle like custard
Powdered milk	1		
Warm water	8		

MAKEUP DIRECTIONS: Line deep pie tins with pie dough. Fill the shells as for custard with dipper, stirring soulution while filling pies. Bake in 380° to 400° oven. When cold spread desired pie fruit filling around edge to form ring about 1 1/2 in wide. Garnish edge with coconut. These pies can also be sold plain, or stable fruit may be placed on the bottom of pie shells before filling with custard

APPLE PIE

Sugar mix as follows:

10 lb sugar

1 oz nutmeg

1 oz cinnamon

1) Take 1 #10 can of apples and divide into five pie shells.

2) Take 2 1/2 lbs of sugar mix, add to it 2 oz of corn starch and mix well, then pour over each pie 8 oz of sugar mix.

3) Take 1/2 lb of oleo and divide evenly over the apples & sugar mix.

4) Top, wash with a mix of 1lb of oleo blended with one egg, allow to stand at least 5 minutes.

5) Bake at 400° for one hour.

Do not vary from this temp. or time as it is necessary for a perfect pie.

Recipe:

       1 #10 can apples

       2 1/2 Sugar mix

       1/4 lb oleo

       2 oz corn starch

LEMON CREAM PIES

INGREDIENTS	LBS	OZS.	METHOD
Water (3 qts)	6		Put all ingredients into kettle and bring to a good boil.
Sugar	5		
Corn syrup	1	8	
Salt		1/2	
Grated lemon rind		2 1/2	
Corn starch	1	2	Thicken the above with disolved corn starch and allow
Water (1 qt)	2		to cook thick and clear.
Eggs	1	8	remove mix from fire and add eggs slowly stirring them with
Oleo		6	a wire whip to keep from lumping. Add oleo then lemon juice.
Lemon juice	1	8	

Remove filling from kettle and place into another container and allow to cool. When cool stir the mix up well and put into precooked shell and put in ice box till serving time. Garnish with whipped cream

Yield"   8 pies or 70 tarts.

When making tarts top with meringue and brown in oven.

PATTY SHELLS

Oleo	1		Put oleo and water in pot and bring to a boil. Add flour
Water	2		and stir to a paste.
Flour 4 cups			
Eggs (18)			Empty the above into mixing bowl and using cake paddle drop one egg at a time continue mixing till all eggs are added. Spoon into muffin tin and bake off.

LEMON CREAM PIE

INGREDIENTS	LBS	OZS	METHOD
Grated lemon rind		3	
Water (2 1/2 qts)	5		
Lemon juice (1 qt)	2		Bring to a boil.
Sugar	5		
White karo	1		
Salt		1	
Starch	1	4	Thicken above with starch mixture, stirring constantly.
Water	1		Allow to cook thick and clear.
Whole eggs		2	When mix has finished cooking, remove from fire. Beat whole eggs and add slowly so as not to lump. After adding the eggs break butter into small pieces and mix thoroughly with wire whip.

Yield" 11 cream pies.........12 meringue

Use pre-baked pie shells

Cover this pie with whipped cream. One qt of cream will covere 15 pies.

FRUIT PIES (not packed in syrup)

INGREDIENTS	LBS	OZS	METHOD
Caned fruit	(1 no. ten can)		Place the fruit in a seive to allow all the liquid to drain. If less than a quart drains add water to make 1 qt. Hold out enough juice to dissolve the cornstarch. Place the remainder in a kettle and bring to a boil.
Liquid (juice & water)	2		
Cornstarch		4	Add cornstarch soulution and cook thoroughly until the paste is thick and clear.
Salt		1/4	
Sugar		8	Add sugar and salt and breing to a vigorous boil. Stir to prevent scorching. remove from fire and pour over drained fruit, mixing the two together thoroughly.

Allow to cool before pouring into the pie. Do not cool in reefer as it will tend to cloud the mixture and ruin the color.

Properly made, the fruit and filling should have a nice shiny appearance, and have a syrupy consistency. It will have body enough to prevent soaking or boiling in a reasonable perion of time.

To make the filling thinner increase the sugar slightly or decrease the starch. To make it thicker decrease sugar and increase starch slightly.

Bake pies for 25 to 30 min at 450°

PINEAPPLE PIE

Crushed pineapple	1 #10 can
Sugar	1 lb 8 oz
Corn syrup	8 oz
Salt	1/4 oz
Corn starch	3 oz
Water	8 oz
Sugar	1 lb

METHOD

Place the contents of a # 10 can of crushed pineapple in a kettle on the stove and add 1 lb 8 oz sugar, 8 oz corn syrup and 1/4 oz salt. Bring to a boil, disolve 3 oz cornstarch in 8 oz water and add to boiling fruit mix and cook until thick and clear. then add the additional one lb of sugar, stir in well and cook to a good boil. Thoroughly cool at room temp. before putting in pie bake at 425° F

*For frogen pineapple adjust the sugar to allow for the sugar in which the frozen pineapple is packed.

+SOUTHERN PECAN PIE

INGREDIENTS	LBS	OZS	METHOD
Sugar	1		
Margarine		4	Mix well together
Flour		4	
Salt		1/16	
Whole eggs		14	Add to above slowly and mix smooth.
Corn syrup	3		Add and mix smooth.
Lemon juice		1	
			Sprinkle pecans on bottoms of unbaked shells. Pour in about one lb of mixture in each shell, Bake at 385° to 410° until done

CUSTARD PIE FILLING

INGREDIENTS	LBS	OZS	METHOD
Sugar	1	8	
Egg White stabilizer		1/4	Mix together.
Salt		1/8	Add to above and stir well to be sure sugar is dissolved and eggs well broken up.
Whole eggs	1	3	
Whole Milk	4	4	Add slowly the mild and vanilla and stir in well.
Vanilla		1/2	

Pour into unbaked pie shells in the oven, dust with nutmeg and bake at 450° for 25 to 30 minutes

PIE DOUGH

	LBS	OZS	
Pastry flour	1	12	Dissolve salt in water then add to flour & mix to a smooth (Thin) paste either by hand or machine.
Water	3		
Salt		4	
Pastry flour	8	4	Cut velvet into flour either by hand or machine then add flour-water paste and mix just until it doughs up. Roll out and handle in usual way.
Velvet shortening	6	8	

CUSTARD PIE FILLING

	LBS	OZS	
Sugar	1	8	
Egg white stabilizer		1/4	
or Tapioca flour		1/2	Mix together
Salt		1/8	Add to above and stir well to be sure sugar is dissolved & eggs well broken.
Whole eggs	1	3	
Whole milk	4	4	Add slowly the milk and vanilla and stir in well. Pour into unbaked pie shells in the oven, dust with nutmeg and bake at 450° for 25 to 30 minutes.
Vanilla		1/2	

PINEAPPLE CHEESE PIES

INGREDIENTS	LBS	OZS	METHOD
Cottage cheese	2	8	Beat until creamy
Sugar	2		
Cornstarch		3	Add and blend thoroughly.
Eggs (Voltex)	1	8	Beat eggs slightly, add milk
Vanilla		1	and vanilla. Add oleo. Combine
Liquid Milk (1 1/2 qts)	3		with the first mixture.
Oleo (melted)		3	
#2 crushed pineapple (3)			Put one cup of crushed pineapple
Cinnamon 1 1/2 tbsps			in bottom of unbaked pie shell. Pour in cheese filling. Sprinkle cinnamon over entire surface of pie.

Bake in moderate oven.   Yield: 5 pies.

PINEAPPLE PIE

Crushed pineapple	7		
Granulated sugar	2		
Salt		1/2	
Water	1		Bring to a boil.
Water	1		Mix the cornstarch in the water
Cornstarch		5	and add the egg yolks. Stir
Egg yolks		4	into the above boiling mixture. Cook until clear

Pour while hot into baked pie shells. Cool and top with whipped cream.

FRUIT PIES

(Canned fruit not packed in syrup)

INGREDIENTS	LBS	OZS	METHOD
Canned fruit	6	10	Place the fruit in a sieve to allow all the liquid to drain from it. If less than a quart drains, add water to the juice to make 2 lbs. or one quart. Hold out sufficient juice to dissolve the cornstarch. Place the remainder in a kettle and bring to a boil. Add cornstarch solution and cook thoroughly until the
Liquid (juice & water)	2		
Cornstarch		4	
Salt		1/4	
Sugar	2	8	

paste is thick and clear. Add sugar and salt and bring to a vigourous boil. Stir to prevent scorching. Remove from fire and pour over drained fruit, mixing the two together thoroughly with a wooden paddle or spoon. Allow to cool before pouring into the pie. Do not cool in refrigerator. If this mix is placed in refrigerator while it is hot the color is destroyed and the fruit will look cloudy.

Properly made, the fruit and filling whould have a nice shiny appearance and have a syrupy consistency. It will have body enough to prevent soaking or boiling in a reasonable period of time.

To make the filling thinner increase the sugar slightly or decrease the starch. To make it thicker increase the starch or decrease the sugar slightly.

Bake pies 25 to 35 minutes at 450° F.

CHOCOLATE CHIFFON PIE

INGREDIENTS	LBS	OZS	METHOD
Sugar	1		Place in copper kettle and
White syrup	1		bring to rolling boil.
Water (1 1/2 Qts)	3		
Kolishus		12	
Salt		1/2	
W-13		8	Dissolve W-13 in water and stir
Water (1/2 qt.)	1		into above. Allow mix to come back to a boil and cook until thick and clear
Egg Whites (1qt)	2		Place eggwhites in machine and
Sugar	1 1/2		beat dry stiff adding sugar a little at a time.

Yield: 12 pies

Place mix in cooked pie shells and place in ice-box. When cold and set, top with whipped cream and serve.

*****

LUBYS SPECIAL LEMON PIE FILLING

INGREDIENTS	LBS	OZS	METHOD
Water (3 qts)	6		Place all ingredients in copper
Sugar	6		kettle, bring to a rolling boil.
Salt		1/2	
Grated lemon rind		1/2	
Water (1 qt)	2		Stir together till smooth and add
W-13	1		to above. Allow to come back to
Voltex	1		second boil and then remove from fire.
Lemon juice		24	Mix into above with hand whip,
Melted oleo		4	mixing till smooth.

Yield: 18 pies

*****

LEMON CHESS PIE

INGREDIENTS	LBS	OZS	METHOD
Shell eggs (36			Beat on #3 speed until light.
Sugar	7		Add to above and beat on #3
Flour		6	speed until light and fluffy.
Vanilla		1	
Lemon juice		16	Add to above and beat on #3
Buttermilk	2	4	speed until light and fluffy
Melted oleo	3		

Take up in 3 gallon crock. Whip again before pouring into shell.
Bake in moderate oven about 35 to 40 minutes.

RUM ICE BOX PIE

INGREDIENTS	LBS	OZS	METHOD
Water (2 qts)	4		Place all ingredients in copper
Sugar	1	8	kettle and bring to a boil, being
Salt		1/2	sure to stir good before mix
Egg color (1/2 lid)			gets hot
W-13		10	Dissolve W-13 in milk and stir
Milk (1 pt)	1		into above. Cook till thick and clear.
Nutmeg (4 pinches)			Add nutmeg and rum and stir
Rum		6	well.
Egg whites	2		Start eggwhites on high speed
Sugar	2		and as they begin to rise add sugar very slowly. Beat till medium stiff.

Remove the eggwhites from the machine and add the hot cooked rum mix. Mix in by hand easily buy well. Put filling in precooked pie shell and refrigerate. Top with whipped cream when cold.

Yield: 10 pies.

******

SYRUP PIE

	LBS	OZS	METHOD
# 10 syrup (2)			Place all ingredients in mixing machine except flour and vanilla.
Voltes	2	8	Begin mixer on low speed. After mixing few minutes add flour.
Butter (2 1/2 cups)			Blend together, remove from machine and fold in vanilla.
Lemon juice		2	
Nutmeg (2 tsp)			
Flour	1	8	
Vanilla (1 cookspoon)			

Yield: 3 gallons

Bake in moderate oven.

For syrup pecan pies add pecans to syrup mixture after filling pies two thirds full.

PUMPKIN PIE

INGREDIENTS	LBS	OZS	METHOD
Brown sugar	2		Sift brown & granulated sugar into mixing bowl then add rest of ingredients. Mix together.
Granulated sugar	2		
W-13		12	
Nutmeg 4 tbsp			
Ginger 1 tbsp			
Salt 1 tbsp			
Cinnamon 2 tsp			
# 10 Pumpkin 2 cans			Add pumpkin to above and mix.
White syrup	3		Add syrup to above and mix.
Milk (6 qts.)			Add milk to above and mix.
Voltex	3		Allow all the above to stand for an hour then add eggs and mix. Pour into raw shells and bake at 425°. Pies will puff over in center done.

LEMON CHIFFON PIE

Ingredients	LBS	OZS	METHOD
Water (2 qts)	4		
Sugar	1	8	Place on stove and bring to a boil.
Lemon rind		1 1/2	
Yellow coloring (few drops)			
Salt		1/2	
Corn starch		12	Dissolve cornstarch in water and lemon juice and stir into boiling mix above. Cook until thick and clear.
Lemon juice	1		
Water		8	
Egg whites	2		Beat until medium stiff and then fold in lemon mix easily but well.
Sugar	2		

Yield: 8 pies

Pour into pre-baked shells and put in ice box to cool.

EGG WHITE MERINGUE

INGREDIENTS	LBS	OES	METHOD
Egg whites	2		Put eggwhites in mixing bowl and start mixing with wire whip on
Sugar	2		high speed. Add sugar gradually. beat till medium stiff.
Powdered sugar]	1		Turn machine to low speed and gradually add powdered sugar then
Vanilla as desired			Vanilla. After sugar and vanilla has been added turn back on high and mix approximately one minute.

Note: when cream pies are topped bake in moderate oven.

PECAN CRUMB PIE

Egg whites		24	Beat medium stiff on high speed with wire whip
Baking powder (2 tsp)			
Salt (2 tsp)			
Sugar		4	Add slowly and beat until stiff but not dry.
Graham cracker crumbs (8cups)			
Pecans (chopped fine)(8 cups)			Mix together while dry, fold in above mixture by hand, adding small amounts at a time.
Vanilla (8 tsp)			Add last and mix well by hand.

Divide evenly into 10 lightly greased pie tins and bake 25 min at 350°

Remove and let come to room temp DO NOT REFRIGERATE

When cool top with whipped cream and grated sweet bakers chocolate.

FRENCH LEMON PIE

INGREDIENTS	AMOUNT	METHOD
Sugar	12 1/2 cups	
Flour	1 1/4 cups	
Salt	1 1/2 Tsp.	
Soft oleo	2 1/2 cups	
Whole eggs	30	
Water	5 cups	
Lemon rind	10 tsp.	
Lemons	10	peeled and sliced paper thin

Place above ingredients in <u>unbaked</u> pastry shell and cover with pastry rolled paper thin, sprinkle top with cinnamon and sugar mixture. Bake in moderate oven.

****

LEMON CHESS PIE

Eggs	36	Beat well.
Sugar	6 lb	Add
Flour	12 tbls.	Add
Butter milk	2 lb. 4 oz.	
Lemon juice	18 tbls	
Melted oleo	3 lb.	Add butter milk, lemon juice,
Vanilla	(to taste)	lemon and oleo. Then vanilla.

Beat until all foam disappears.

Makes 8 pies.

CHOCOLATE CREAM PIE

INGREDIENTS	LBS	OZS	METHOD
Sweet milk	(5 1/2 qts)		Bring to a boil in a copper kettle
Sugar	5	4	
Salt		1	
Kiloshus	1	8	
Sweet milk	(1 1/2 qts)		Mix well in separate pan and to above. Bring to a second boil and remove from fire. Add 2 lids of vanilla. Pour into crock and whip with hand whip till smooth and fluffy.
W-13		10	
Voltex	2	4	

******

LUBYS SPECIAL CREAM PIE FILLING

Sweet milk	6	6	Bring to a boil in a copper kettle.
Sugar	2		
Salt		1/4	
Sweet milk	2	2	Mix in separate pan and add to above. Bring to a second boil and remove from fire. Add 3 lids of 2x vanilla and mix well with hand whip.
Corn starch		7	
Whole eggs	1	4	

Take up in 3 gallon crock and allow to cool.

Use this filling as a base for coconut cream, pecan cream, cherry cream, etc.

******

BUTTERSCOTCH CREAM FILLING

Sweet milk	6		
Sugar		12	
Brown sugar	2		Place all ingredients in copper kettle. Stir together with wire whip and bring to a rolling boil.
Karmelishus		6	
Oleo	1		
Salt		1/2	
Sweet milk		8	Stir together till W-13 is dissolved. Add to above and bring back to a boil. Remove from fire at once. Beat with hand whip till smooth.
W-13		5	
Butterscotch pudding powder	1 cup		
Voltex	1	2	

EAGLE BRAND MILK

3 # POWDERED MILK

4 1/2 # sugar

1 1/2 pints warm water

Whip low speed 3 to 5 minutes until smooth.

Add 1 pint of warm water

Add to above and whip 12 minutes on high speed.

Add 1 1/4# fresh lemon juice

Add to above and mix 10 minutes on high speed.

LUBY'S SPECIAL FILLING

5 qts whole milk

2 qts half and half

1 tablespoon salt

6 cups sugar

1 lb cornstarch

36 egg yolks (fresh shell eggs)

H eat 7 qts liquid and salt in kettle. Beat egg, sugar, starch at high speed on mixer until light and fluffy. Add this mixture to scalded milk, beat until thick. Then add 2 cookspoons of vanilla and 1/4 lb. oleo.

EGG CUSTARD

INGREDIENTS	LBS	OZS	METHOD
Whole eggs	3	6	
Milk	6 qts		
Sugar	6 cups		
Vanilla	2 cookspoons		
Nutmeg	1 spoon		

Mix at low speed.   Yield: 14 pies

*****

CORNBREAD

Cornmeal	3 fill in pots
Flour	" " "
Salt	1 hand full
Sugar	1 hand full
Baking powder	3 cookspoons
Eggs	1 qt.

Milk or water   Mix and Bake

*****

DUMPLINGS

Flour	14 cups
Baking Powder	1 cup
Sugar	1 cup
Salt	1/2 cup
Shortening	1/2 cup
Eggs	2 1/2 dippers (8oz dipper)
Milk	1 qt.

*****

DRESSING

Salt	2 hands full	
Pepper	1 " "	
Sage	3 " "	
Whole eggs	1 1/2 qt.	
Celery	2 stalks	Chopped fine
Onions	4 large	Chopped fine

Soak bread in chicken broth. Mix well & bake in greased pan.

CHEESE PIE

INGREDIENTS	LBS	OZS	METHOD
Grated cheese	1	8	
Margarine		8	
Hard wheat flour		8	Rub together
Salt		1/4	
Granulated sugar	6		
Egg yolks	3		Add and cream in
Whole milk	10		Add and cream in until smooth.

Handle same as custard pie. If desired, whole eggs can be used. Use 4 lbs whole eggs and reduce milk by 1 lb. Makes 10 - 8 in. deep pies.

*****

MERINGUE FOR PIES

Egg whites	2		Blend together at medium
Fine granulated sugar	2		speed until light and fluffy.
Fine granulated sugar	1		Add slowly to above and mix in
Vanilla to taste			at low speed, just until sugar is uniformly distributed.

NOTE: It is sometimes advisable to use a meringue stabilizer.

*****

CRUMB TOPPING FOR PIES
(Streusel)

INGREDIENTS	LBS	OZS	METHOD
Granulated sugar	8	10	
Salt		1 3/4	
Nutmeg		1/2	
Cinnamon		1/2	Cream together
Shortening	3	10	
Margarine	3		
Cake flour	10		Add and rub together until crumbly.

APPLE SLICES

INGREDIENTS	LBS.	OZS.	METHOD
Solid pack apples	12	8	Drain apples, then add enough water to the juice to make total of 2 qts.
Cornstarch		8	Dissolve starch in about 12 oz of juice and water mix, bring remainder to a boil then add starch solution and cook until clear.
Sugar	3	8	Add to starch solution and again bring to a boil.
Corn syrup		8	
Salt		1/4	
Margarine		4	Add and put in. Cool filling before putting in bun pan.
Cinnamon		1/8	
Nut meg		1/16	
			Use about 3 lb pie dough for lining 18" X 26" bun pan, fill with 12 lb apple filling then cover with 3 lb streusel and sprinkle on top about 6 oz sugar. Or in place of streusel, put on a top crust and ice with water icing or put lattice covering on top with pie dough.

STREUSEL TOPPING

	LBS	OZS	
Granulated sugar	1		
Shortening	1		Cream together.
Cinnamon		1/4	
Mace		1/4	
Salt		1/2	
Lemon and vanilla		1	
Yellow color (5 drops)			
Bread flour	1		Rub in.

EGG NOG PIE

INGREDIENTS	LBS	OZS	METHOD
Water	9		Place in kettle and stir. Bring to boil
Salt		3/4	
Granulated sugar	4	8	
Powdered milk	2	4	
Nutmeg		3/4	
Whole milk	3		Dissolve starch in milk. Add to yolks and whip frothy. Add to boiling first part. Cook smooth and remove from fire.
Starch		6	
Egg yolks	1	8	
Water	1	8	Dissolve gelatin and add to cooked mix while hot. Mix thoroughly. Allow to cool slightly.
Gelatin		3	
Egg whites	3		Whip whites to stiff wet peak. Fold cooked part in by hand, Pour into baked pie shells and chill until firm. Top with whipped cream and sprinkle with nutmeg.
Granulated sugar	1	8	
Rum flavor	to taste		

ORANGE COCONUT CREAM PIE FILLING

	LBS	OZS	
Whole milk	3	12	Bring to a boil.
Granulated sugar	1	14	
Salt		3/4	
Orange peel (ground fine)		5	
Milk	1	4	Dissolve starch in milk. Stir in yolks. Add slowly to first part. Stir constantly. Cook smooth. Remove from fire
Starch		6	
Egg yolks		13	
Shortening		5	Add and mix in.
			Pour into baked pie shells while hot. Allow to cool. Top with meringue and sprinkle top with shredded coconut.

BUTTERSCOTCH PIE FILLING

INGREDIENTS	LBS	OZS	METHOD
Margarine	1		Cook to 280° in kettle
Brown sugar	2	8	
Whole milk	6	6	Mix flour into milk thoroughly.-
Voltex		8	
Whole eggs		8	Add to above while
Cake flour		6	stiring slowly. Dissolve starch in
Starch			milk. Add eggs and mix thoroughly.
Whole milk			Add slowly to cooking syrup. Stir
			constantly. Cook clean, remove from heat
margarine		4	Add and mix in.
Vinalla			
			Pour into baked shells. Top as desired.

CUSTARD PIE FILLING

INGREDIENTS	LBS	OZS	METHOD
Whole milk	2		Bring to a boil
Whole milk		8	Dissolve starch in milk. Add to
Starch		3	Above, stir in, and remove from fire.
Yolks		13	Place in mixing bowl and whip
Whole eggs	1	7	until frothy. Add cooked mix
Sugar	1	8	above and mix briskly.
Salt		1/8	
Nutmeg		1/4	
Margarine		3	Heat just o a boil, cool and add
Whole milk	4		to above, mix thoroughly.

CHOCOLATE CREAM PIE

INGREDIENTS	LBS	OZS	METHOD
Whole milk	5	4	
Sugar	2	10	
Margarine		#3	Bring to a boil.
Salt		1/2	
Chocolate (bitter)		12	
Whole milk	1	10	Dissolve starch in milk, add yolks
Starch		6	and mix smooth. add to boiling
Vanilla		1	mix above, stirring constantly.
Voltex	1	2	Cook smooth
			Pour into baked shells. Top with
			meringue or whipped cream as desired.

LEMON PIE FILLING
(Can be used for cake filling)

INGREDIENTS	LBS	OZS	METHOD
Water	6		Bring to a boil
Sugar	6		
Salt		1/2	
Grated lemon rind		3	
Water	2		Dissolve starch in water, stir
Starch	1		in eggs, add to above and cook clear.
Whole eggs	1		
Margarine		4	Add and mix in.
Lemon juice	1		
			Pour into baked shells. Top as desired.

PUMPKIN PIE

	LBS	OZS	METHOD
Brown sugar	2		Sift brown and grainulated sugar
Granulated sugar	2		into mixing wowl then add rest
W-13		12	of ingredients. Mix together
Nutmeg (4 tbsp)			
Ginger (1 tbsp)			
Salt (1tbsp)			
Cinnamon (1tsp)			
# 10 pumpkin	2 cans		Add pumpkin to above mix.
White syrup	3		Add syrup to above mix.
Milk	12		Add milk to above mix.
Voltex	3		Allow all the above to stand for an hour then add eggs and mix. Pour into raw shells and bake at 425°. Pies will puff over in center when done.

OLD FASHIONED CHESS PIE

INGREDIENTS	LBS	OZS.	METHOD
Oleo (room temp.)	4		Place all ingredients and using wire whip on low speed cream together till well mixed, about 2 minutes. Do not over cream.
Sugar	5		
Voltex	2	8	
Flour		10	
Scalded milk (4 qts)	8		Add scalded milk
Egg White (1 qt)			Beat eggwhite till slightly less than medium stiff. Pour chess mixture over this and fold in.
Vanilla 2 teaspoons			Fold in.

YIELD: 3 gallons

Baking temperature - 350 to 375°

TAPIOCA PUDDING

INGREDIENTS		LBS	OZS	METHOD
Milk	(3 qts)			Warm milk, do not let boil.
Sugar	2 cups			Mix together and add to above,
Tapioca	1 1/2 cups			cook over medium fire till
Milk	1 cup			clear and slightly thickened.
Voltex			1	Pour into pan and refrigerate. Serve in parfait, top with whipped cream and a cherry slice.

CHAPTER VI

CAKES
FROSTINGS AND FILLINGS

CAKES	Page
1-2-3-4 Cake	3
Angel Food Cake	2
Apple, Roman, Cake	1
Applesauce Cake	2
Banana Cake	2
Blackberry Jam Cake	3
Boston Cream Cake (Evans)	12
Butter Cake	3
Carrot Cake	12a
Cheese Cake	4
Cream Cheese Cake or Pie	4
Creole Cake	4
Devils Food Cake (Large Cake)	5
Devils Food Cake	5
German Chocolate Cake	5
Gingerbread	6
Gum Drop Cake	7
Lady Baltimore Cake	7
Lemon Cake	7
Lemon Cream Cheese Cake	8
Milky Way Cake	1
Mohogany Cake	8
Orange Cup Cake and Sauce	8
Pineapple Cake	9
Prune Cake	9
Royal Polynesian Cake	11
Short Cake	10
Sour Cream Cake	10
Spice Cake	10
Waldorf Astoria Cake	11
White Cake	10

FROSTINGS AND FILLINGS:	Page
Butter Icing	14
Caramel Nut Icing	14
Chocolate Wonder Frosting	14
Frosting and Filling	14
Frosting	13
Fudge Icing	13
Filling for German Chocolate	5
Lemon Filling for Cake	15
Prune Cake Icing	9
Seven Minute Frosting	13
Seven Minute Icing	13
Frosting for Waldorf Astoria	11

LIST HERE new recipes:

14 Karat Gold Cake	12b	Prune cake	17a
Icing for 14 Karat Gold Cake	12b		
Chocolate Banana Cake	12a		
Cheese Cake	4a		
Cream Filling	15		
Cranberry Cake	16		
Cranberry Cake Icing	16		
Chocolate Cheese Brownie	17		

ROMAN APPLE CAKE

1 cup margarine	1 tsp. baking soda
1 cup sugar	1 tsp. baking powder
½ cup brown sugar	3 tsp. cinnamon
2 eggs	¼ tsp. salt
1 cup sour milk	2½ cups sifted all purpose flour
	2 cups chopped raw peeled apples

Cream margarine and sugar. Add eggs one at a time and blend well. Sift all dry ingredients together and add alternately with sour milk. Add apples last.

Pour batter into bean pan or two eight inch square pans.

Then mix: ½ cup brown sugar
1 tsp. cinnamon
½ cup finely chopped pecans

Sprinkle above mixture over batter. Bake about 40 minutes at 350 degrees.

Cut cake into squares. May be served plain or topped with whipped cream that has been mixed with equal amount of apple butter.

MILKY WAY CAKE

Combine: 8 Milky Way bars (cut up) with one stick oleo. Melt over boiling water. Cream 2 cups sugar with 2 sticks oleo and 4 beaten eggs.

Add: Milky Way mix and mix well and add 1½ cup buttermilk with 2½ cups flour, ½ tsp. soda (sift with flour). Add alternatel with milk and add 1 tsp. vanilla and 1 cup chopped pecans.

FILLING: 2½ cups sugar
1 can evaporated milk
  Cook to soft boil
1 stick oleo
1 cup marshmallow
1 small pkg. chocolate chips
  Beat until creamy

ANGEL FOOD CAKE

1 cup sifted Swandsown cake flour
1½ cups sugar
1¼ cups (10-12) egg whites
¼ teaspoon salt
1¼ teaspoon cream of tartar
1 teaspoon vanilla
¼ teaspoon almond extract

Sift flour once, measure, add 1/2 cup sugar and sift together three times. Place egg whites and salt in large mixmaster bowl and beat at No. 8 speed until foamy. Add cream of tartar and beat until stiff enough to hold up in definite peaks, but not dry. Continue beating, adding remaining sugar rapidly a tablespoon at a time. Beat only until sugar is just blended. Remove bowl from mixer. Add flavoring. Then sift in dry ingredients, a small amount at a time, folding in each addition with a wire whisk or spoon. Turn into ungreased 10 inch tube pan. Bake in moderate oven 375°, 30 to 35 minutes. Invert pan until cake is cold. Spread with strawberry fluff topping or 7 minute icing.

APPLESAUCE CAKE

3/4 cup shortening
1-2/3 cup sugar
2 eggs
3 cups applesauce
2 cups raisins
1 cup chopped nut meats

3½ cups cake flour
3 tsp. soda
1 tsp. cinnamon
½ tsp. cloves
1 tsp. allspice

Cream shortening and sugar. Add eggs, then applesauce. Sift dry ingredients together, and add to mixture. Stir in floured raisin and nuts.

BANANA CAKE

3/4 cups shortening
1½ cups sugar
3 eggs
3 cups cake flour
1½ tsp. soda

1½ tsp. baking powder
2 tsp. vanilla
3/4 cup buttermilk
4 very ripe bananas, mashed

Cream shortening and sugar. Add eggs one at a time. Dissolve soda in buttermilk. Add alternately with flour and baking powder. (Sifted 3 times.) Add bananas and vanilla.

Chapter VI

BLACKBERRY JAM CAKE

3/4 cup oleo
1½ cups sugar
4 eggs, separated
1 cup buttermilk with
1 tsp. soda dissolved in it
3 cups sifted flour
1 tsp. baking powder
1 cup blackberry jam
1 cup raisins
1 cup chopped pecans

Cream oleo and add sugar. Beat egg yolks lightly and add to oleo and sugar. Add flour which has been sifted with baking powder alternately with buttermilk. Add jam, raisins and nuts.

BUTTER CAKE

1 scant cup butter (scant ½ lb.)
2 cups sugar
1 cup milk
3 cups flour
3 tsp. baking powder
5 egg whites, beaten stiff
1 tsp. vanilla

Bake in Angel Food cake pan. Ice with butter icing.

1-2-3-4 CAKE

1 cup shortening
2 cups sugar
3 cups flour
4 eggs
3 tsp. baking powder
1 cup milk

Cream shortening and sugar. Add beaten eggs. Add sifted dry ingredients alternately with milk.

CHEESE CAKE

2 Cakes	1 Cake
72	36 Graham crackers
2	1 cup sugar
2	1 tsp. cinnamon
1	½ lb. oleo (melted)

Crumble crackers, add sugar, cinnamon and oleo. Line angel cake tins. Reserve 2/3 cup for top.

Filling

3	1½ lbs. cottage cheese
2	1 cup evaporated milk
8	4 eggs
8	4 tbsp. (rounding) cake flour
1	½ tsp. salt
4	2 tbsp. lemon juice
2	1 rind of lemon
2	1 cup sugar

Cream cheese thoroughly. Add cream, eggs, one at a time, sugar, salt and flour mixed together. Then lemon juice and rind and 1 tsp. vanilla. Pour into pan. Sprinkle remaining crumbs on top. Bake in moderate oven one hour or until set. When cool, loosen edge and remove from pan.

DO NOT CUT UNTIL COLD

CREAM CHEESE PIE OR CAKE

3 lbs. cream cheese, beat well on beater. Add 4 cups sugar, 2 cookspoons of flour and 1 cookspoon of vanilla. Add 8 whole eggs, and 1 quart of half and half. Beat for about one minute. Pour into graham cracker shells and bake 15 to 20 minutes at 350 degrees. Sprinkle graham cracker crumbs over top.

CREOLE CAKE

4 cups sifted cake flour
4 tsp. baking powder
1 tsp. salt
1 cup shortening
2 cups sugar
1 sq. unsweetened chocolate (or 3 T. cocoa)
2 eggs well beaten
1½ cups milk
2 tsp. vanilla

Sift dry ingredients together 3 times. Cream shortening and sugar, add melted chocolate (or cocoa is sifted with flour). Add eggs. Then flour and milk alternately. Add vanilla last.

CHEESE CAKE

(10 Pies)

6# cream cheese
3# sugar
1 1/2 oz. vanilla
1 1/4 pint whole eggs
1 1/2 oz. lemon juice
1 qt. egg whites

Cream cheese and sugar until well mixed. Then add whole eggs, lemon juice and vanilla and mix well. Beat egg whites until stiff. Fold into above mixture by hand. Bake in 350° oven 35 minutes or until done.

CRUST:

3 1/2# vanilla wafer crumbs
6 oz. sugar
18 oz. melted oleo

Chapter VI   Page 4a

GERMAN CHOCOLATE CAKE

2½ cups flour	1 teaspoon soda
2 cups sugar	1 pkg. chocolate (German's Sweet 4 oz.)
1 cup M.F.B.	½ cup boiling water
4 eggs	1/8 teaspoon salt
1 cup buttermilk	1 teaspoon vanilla

Cream sugar and shortening, add 3/4 cup of the buttermilk and 2 cups of the flour, alternately. Then add 4 beaten egg yolks. Add soda to the ¼ cup of buttermilk, and the other ½ cup of flour. Add melted chocolate (melt in the ½ cup boiling water), and vanilla. Last fold in stiffly beaten egg whites. Bake at 350 degrees for about 25 minutes.

FILLING FOR GERMAN'S CHOCOLATE CAKE

1 cup whipping cream	1 cup sugar
(or whip topping)	3 egg yolks
1 cup cocoanut	¼ lb. margarine
1 cup nuts	

Beat the 3 egg yolks slightly, add sugar, cream and margarine in pan. Cook until thick. Take off fire and add nuts and cocoanut. Beat until cool. Spread on cake.

(Double the recipe will make three cakes using 9" pan.)

DEVILS FOOD CAKE (Large Cake)

6	3	cups cake flour
6	3	eggs
5	2½	cups sugar
2	1	cup shortening
1	½	cup cocoa
1 qt.	2	cups sour cream or buttermilk
4	2	tsp. soda
4	2	tsp. vanilla

Cream shortening and sugar and cocoa. Beat 5 minutes. Add egg yolks and beat well. Add flour and milk and soda alternately. Fold in beaten egg whites. Vanilla.

DEVILS FOOD CAKE

3/4 cup shortening	1 cup sour cream
2 cups sugar	1 cup water
4 eggs	3 sq. Bakers chocolate
3 cups cake flour	1 tsp. vanilla
1 tsp. baking powder	Pinch of salt
2 tsp. baking soda	

Cream shortening and sugar. Add eggs. Add dry ingredients (sifted 3 times) alternately with sour cream. Add cooled melted chocolate. Mix thoroughly and bake at 375 degrees F.

GINGERBREAD

3 cups sifted flour
2 tsp. soda - level
3 rounding soupspoons cocoa
1 tsp. cinnamon
1 tsp. cloves
1½ soupspoons ginger

Sift all dry ingredients together 4 times.

1 cup sugar
1 cup shortening
1 cup molasses
1 cup buttermilk
3 eggs

Cream sugar and shortening, add egg yolks and cream well. Add molasses, then buttermilk, then flour mixture. Fold in beaten egg whites.

GINGERBREAD

2 cups molasses
2 cups sour milk
2 cups sugar
2 cups butter or oleo
6 cups flour
6 eggs (beaten separately)

2 tbsp. ginger
2 tsp. cinnamon
2 tsp. cloves
4 tsp. soda
6 tbsp. cocoa
1 tbsp. nutmeg

Cream butter and sugar and add molasses, egg yolk and milk. Then sift flour, spices and cocoa together and fold in beaten egg whites.

GINGERBREAD SUPREME

½ cup sugar
1½ cup sifted cake flour
½ tsp. baking soda
½ tsp. salt
½ tsp. ginger
¼ tsp. allspice
½ tsp. baking powder

1 tsp. cinnamon
¼ cup shortening, melted
¼ cup maple syrup
½ cup sour milk
1 egg, well beaten
1 cup black walnut meats, broken (optional)

Sift first eight ingredients together. Combine shortening, maple syrup, sour milk and egg. Add liquid mixture to dry ingredients, beat well and pour into greased pan. Sprinkle walnuts and additional cinnamon over top and bake in moderate oven (350 degrees) about 30 minutes. Cut into squares, top with whipped cream and garnish with a dash of nutmeg. Makes one 8 by 8 inch cake.

GUM DROP CAKE

1 cup figs (grind)
1 cup raisins
1 cup hot water
1 tsp. soda (cook this and let cool)

3 eggs
1 cup sugar
½ cup lard
gum drops
1½ cup flour
1 tsp. baking powder

Cream shortening and sugar, add beaten eggs and then sifted flour and baking powder. Add fruit and gum drops. Bake in greased pan.

LADY BALTIMORE CAKE

3/4 cup shortening
2 cups sugar
3 cups sifted cake flour
3 tsp. baking powder
½ tsp. salt

½ cup milk
½ cup water
1 tsp. vanilla
6 egg whites beaten stiff

Cream shortening and sugar until fluffy. Sift dry ingredients three times. Combine liquids. Add flour mixture alternately with liquids, beating until smooth after each addition. Fold in stiffly beaten egg whites. Bake in floured tins.

FILLING FOR LADY BALTIMORE CAKE

3 pineapple rings cut fine
½ cup pineapple juice

Cook pineapple and juice slightly. Then thicken. Add ½ cup raisins, chopped and 1/3 cup pecans.

LEMON CAKE

1 1/8 cup shortening
1 1/2 cups sugar
6 egg yolks
1 1/8 cups milk

4 1/2 cups flour (scant)
4 1/2 tsp. baking powder
1 1/2 tsp. lemon extract
Little egg coloring

FILLING:

Rind and juice of 1 1/2 lemons
3 egg yolks
1 1/2 cups sugar
1 1/2 cups water

3 sqs. butter
3 tbsp. cornstarch
Little egg coloring

Chapter VI

LEMON CREAM CHEESE CAKE

3 lbs. cream cheese - beat well in mixer.
22 whole eggs - add one at a time while cheese is whipping.
5 cups sugar - add all at one time while cheese and eggs are in beater.
   Continue beating until well blended.
Add 1 quart plus one cup of whipping cream. Pour into beater and beat until mixture begins to be a little light or fluffy. Add one serving spoon of vanilla and 8 oz. of fresh lemon juice to above mixture.

Pour into cracker crumb crusts or baked pastry shells. Bake 15 to 20 minutes at 350 degrees. Yield: about 10 pies.

MAHOGANY CAKE

2½ cups cake flour (sifted)
3 tsp. baking powder
½ tsp. salt
2/3 cups butter or shortening
2 cups sugar
3 eggs, well beaten

1 cup chopped nuts (walnuts or pecans)
3 sqs. chocolate (unsweetened) melted
1 cup riced potatoes
2/3 cup milk
1 tsp. vanilla

Sift flour, salt and baking powder together 3 times. Cream butter, add sugar gradually, cream until light. Add eggs and beat well; add nuts and chocolate and blend, then potatoes and beat thoroughly. Add flour after each addition until smooth. Add vanilla. Bake in Angel Food cake tin or 2 sq. cake tins. (Greased).

ORANGE CUP CAKE AND SAUCE

1/3 cup shortening
1 cup sugar
1 cup milk
2 cups cake flour
2 eggs

3 tsp. baking powder
¼ tsp. salt
rind of 1 orange and
juice of 2 oranges

Makes 18 cakes

SAUCE:

1 cup sugar
4 egg yolks
grated rind of 1 orange
juice of 2 oranges

Cook until thick. When cool, add 1 pt. of whipped cream and ½ cup chopped nut meats.

PINEAPPLE CAKE

3/4 cup shortening
1 7/8 cups sugar
1½ tsp. vanilla
1¼ cups crushed pineapple and juice
3½ cups cake flour

3½ tsp. baking powder
pinch salt
1/3 cup water
5 egg whites

Cream shortening and sugar, add crushed pineapple and juice, vanilla. Then add dry ingredients alternately with the water, blending well after each addition. Fold in stiffly beaten egg whites.

PRUNE CAKE

½ cup shortening
1½ cups sugar
3 large eggs
2¼ cups sifted cake flour
½ tsp. salt
1 tsp. soda

1 tsp. baking powder
1 tsp. cinnamon
1 tsp. nutmeg
1 tsp. allspice
1 cup buttermilk
1 cup cooked prunes, mashed

Cream shortening, add sugar and cream until fluffy. Blend in well beaten eggs. Sift flour, salt, soda, baking powder and spices together. Add to creamed mixture alternately with buttermilk. Blend in prunes.

Bake in well greased and floured pans (3 eight inch or 2 nine inch pans).

Bake 30 to 40 minutes at 350 degrees.

PRUNE CAKE

1 cup sugar
3/4 cup shortening
2 eggs
2 cups flour
2 tsp. soda

1 tsp. ginger
1 tsp. nutmeg
1 tsp. cinnamon
½ cup buttermilk

Mix above ingredients in conventional manner. Then stir into batter 1 cup chopped prunes, 1 layer of dates out of a seven ounce package and 3/4 cup chopped nuts. Bake 40 to 45 minutes at 325 degrees.

ICING FOR PRUNE CAKE:

2 eggs, beaten
1 cup cooked chopped prunes
½ cup buttermilk

1 cup sugar
1 tbsp. butter

Cream sugar and butter. Then add beaten eggs, buttermilk and chopped prunes. Mix well. Cook and stir until mixture is thick. A few nuts may be sprinkled on iced cake if desired.

SHORT CAKE

3 tbsp. shortening
¼ cup salt
1 can sugar (#2½)
2 scoops flour
3 dippers ice water
5 heaping tsp. baking powder

Cream salt and sugar with shortening. Add flour and baking powder, mixed, slowly to creamed mixture. Then add ice water.

SOUR CREAM CAKE

2 cups brown sugar
½ cup granulated sugar
1 cup shortening (if rich cream is used, 3/4 cup shortening is enough)
2 cups sour cream
3 cups cake flour

3 eggs
2 tsp. soda (level)
1 tsp. baking powder
2 tsp. vanilla

SPICE CAKE

3 cups sifted flour
3 tsp. baking powder
½ tsp. baking soda
1 tsp. salt
1 tsp. ginger
1 tsp. cinnamon
1 tsp. allspice

½ tsp. cloves
2 tsp. nutmeg
3/4 cup chortening
1 cup firmly packed brown sugar
3 eggs separated
1 cup chopped raisins
1 cup sour milk

Mix and sift flour, baking powder, soda, salt, spices, cream shortening. Gradually beat in brown sugar, add well beaten egg yolks then raisins, add flour alternately with sour milk, fold in stiffly beaten egg whites. Bake in moderate oven.

WHITE CAKE

1 cup shortening
2 cups sugar
4 cups flour (scant)
4 tsp. baking powder

1 cup milk
2 tsp. vanilla
8 egg whites, beaten until stiff

WALDORF ASTORIA CAKE

½ cup shortening
1½ cups white sugar
2 eggs
1 tsp. salt
1 cup buttermilk
2¼ cups sifted cake flour
1 tsp. baking soda
1 tsp. vinegar
2 oz. red coloring
1 tsp. vanilla
2 rounded tsp. cocoa

METHOD: Mix vinegar and soda in small cup and let set. Cream sugar, shortening and eggs. Make paste of cocoa and a little of the red food coloring and add to creamed mixture. Then add rest of red coloring, buttermilk, salt and flour alternately. Add vanilla. Lastly add soda and vinegar, stirring mixture before adding it. When well mixed, pour into two 9 inch layer cake pans. Bake at 350 degrees for 30 minutes. Cool thoroughly and split in half horizontally. (Cool in refrigerator.)

FROSTING:
1 cup milk
3 rounded tbsp. flour
Cook until thick, then cool stirring while it cools
1 cup white sugar
1 cup butter
Cream these two until very fluffy, and add the flour mixture 1 tbsp. at a time, beating all the time. Keep in refrigerator. Will keep fresh one week. We have tried this and had very good luck.
Suggested price .25¢ a slice.

ROYAL POLYNESIAN CAKE

2 lbs. 8 oz. sifted cake flour
3 lbs. 4 oz. white sugar
1 lb. 4 oz. cake shortening
1¼ oz. salt
4½ oz. powdered milk
2½ oz. baking powder
8 oz. drained crushed pineapple
10 oz. soft ripe bananas
14 oz. cold pineapple juice
¼ oz. rum flavor
1¼ oz. grated orange peel

Mix all together for 4 minutes on 1st speed. Then add 1 lb. 12 oz. of whole eggs, 1 pt. of cold water. Add and mix 3 minutes on 1st speed. (This makes 15 lbs. batter.)

SUGGESTED FROSTING:
German Chocolate Icing with chopped maraschino cherries added.
Suggested price .25¢.

BOSTON CREAM CAKE

5 lb. regular yellow cake mix

<u>Mix as directed.</u>
Scale off at 14 oz. per layer and cook in chess pie tins (7 layers). When done, split each layer and place cream filling between. Then either take blueberries, strawberries, cherries or pineapple and thicken the syrup (the consistency of filling) and cover the top except about one inch circle around edge and save that space for whipped cream.

NOTE: Cream should be put on first. Cool fruit and spread in middle. We charge .25¢

CARROT CAKE

2 cups regular flour
2 cups sugar
2 teaspoons soda
2 teaspoons cinnamon
1 teaspoon salt

Sift all above ingredients together. Beat 4 eggs and add 1½ cup salad oil and 3 cups grated fresh carrots. Mix this mixture with dry ingredients above. Bake in two cake pans at 350 degrees.

ICING:

6 oz. cream cheese
1 box powdered sugar
2 oz. oleo
2 teaspoons vanilla
1 cup chopped pecans

Mix all above ingredients.

CHOCOLATE BANANA CAKE

2 cups sugar
1 cup shortening
2 eggs, well beaten
2 large mashed ripe bananas

Cream the sugar, shortening, eggs and bananas.

Sift together:
½ cup cocoa
2½ cups flour
2 tsp. soda
¼ tsp. salt

Add alternately to the banana mixture with ½ cup buttermilk. Then add 1 cup boiling water. Mix well. Batter will be very thin. Bake in well greased and floured 9" x 13" baking dish. Bake in slow oven at 300 degrees about 1 hour.

CHOCOLATE ICING:

1½ cups sugar
½ cup cocoa
½ cup milk
1 stick oleo
1 tsp. vanilla

Bring to boil for 1 minute the sugar, cocoa, milk and oleo. Remove from heat and add 1 tsp. vanilla. Beat until creamy, then pour over cake. Spread with spatula as you pour.

14 KARAT GOLD CAKE

3 lbs. sugar
¼ oz. cinnamon
3/4 oz. baking soda
¼ oz. baking powder
3/4 oz. salt
2 lbs. 8 oz. cake flour
Scale into bowl.

2 lbs. 8 oz. Wesson Oil
14 oz. egg yolks
Add to above and whip with paddle.

3 lbs. 8 oz. carrots (ground fine)
3/4 oz. vanilla
Add to above, whip until fairly light.

1 lb. egg whites
8 oz. sugar
½ oz. cream of tartar
Whip stiff and fold into above, make similar to Orange Chiffon.

Baking Temperature: 350° to 365°

Special Instructions: Wash pans and do not grease. Put in 9" pan. Invert after baking. (Makes three cakes - 2 layer.)

ICING FOR 14 KARAT GOLD CAKE

2 lbs. cream cheese
4 lbs. powdered sugar
1 lb. Kneedit Margarine
Cream until light.

14 oz. Angel Flake Cocoanut
8 oz. pecans
8 oz. black raisins
1 oz. vanilla
Fold into above.

Chapter VI

FROSTING

2 unbeaten egg whites
1½ cups sugar
5 tbsp. water
1½ tsp. white Karo syrup
1 tsp. vanilla

Put egg whites, sugar, water and syrup in top of double boiler. Beat with rotary egg beater until mixed. Place over rapidly boiling water. Beat constantly for 7 min. or until frosting stands in peaks. Spread over cake. Melt 2 sqs. of chocolate with 2 tsp. butter when frosting is set. Pour chocolate mixture over cake, then let run over sides.

FUDGE ICING

2 cups sugar
1 tsp. vanilla
3/4 cup unsweetened condensed milk
3 sqs. melted unsweetened chocolate
3 tbsp. butter

Bring sugar and milk to a good boil. Add melted chocolate and butter (melted together). Boil until soft ball forms in cold water. Let cool, add vanilla and stir constantly until it forms a cream. Spread on cake while warm.

SEVEN MINUTE FROSTING

2 egg whites
1½ cups sugar
¼ tsp. cream of tartar
1/3 cup cold water
dash of salt
1 tsp. vanilla

Place all ingredients except vanilla in top of double boiler. Cook, beating constantly until forms peaks (about 8 min.). Remove from fire, beat until spreading consistency. Add vanilla.

SEVEN MINUTE ICING

2 unbeaten egg whites
1 cup sugar
3 tbsp. cold water

Put in double boiler and beat with egg beater to consistency of whipped cream. Add 10 marshmallows and beat until melted. Add 1 tsp. vanilla. Spread on cake.

BUTTER ICING

2 cups of 4 x sugar
4 squares of butter
2 egg yolks
1 tsp. vanilla
2 tbsp. cream

CARAMEL NUT ICING

3 Layers	2 Layers
3	1½ cups packed brown sugar
½	¼ tsp. salt
4	2 tbsp. butter
2	1 tbsp. cream
1	½ cup granulated sugar
1½	3/4 cup top milk
1	½ cup nut meats

Combine all ingredients except cream. Cook till it forms a soft ball in cold water. Remove from fire and cool. Add cream and beat until thick enough to spread. Add nuts. Spread on cake. Add more cream if it begins to thicken too much.

CHOCOLATE WONDER FROSTING

2 small pkgs. cream cheese   4 sqs. chocolate, melted
6 tbsp. milk   pinch of salt
4 cups confectioners sugar #1 box

Soften cheese with milk. Add sugar 1 cup at a time, blending after each addition. Add chocolate and salt and beat smooth. More milk may be added if necessary.

FROSTING AND FILLING

3 cups sugar   1 tsp. vanilla
1 cup water   ½ cup chopped figs
¼ tsp. cream of tartar   1 cup raisins
3 egg whites, stiffly beaten   1 cup nuts

Boil sugar, water and cream of tartar together until small amount forms a soft ball when tested in cold water. Pour hot syrup gradually over stiffly beaten whites, beating constantly. Add vanilla. Divide mixture in half. Add fruit and nuts to 1 portion and spread between layers. Frost top and sides with remaining part.

LEMON FILLING FOR CAKE

Rind and juice of 1½ lemons
3 egg yolks
1½ cups water
1½ cups sugar
3 sq. butter
3 tbsp. cornstarch
Egg coloring

CREAM FILLING

Heat in double boiler:
1 gallon whole milk
¼ lb. oleo

Beat:
18 whole eggs

Then add:
5 cups sugar
½ lb. cornstarch
1½ tsp. salt

Pour the above into hot milk. Stir and cook until thick.

Then add:
2 serving spoons vanilla

Coloring may be added, if needed.

CRANBERRY CAKE

1 cup butter
2 cups sugar
4 eggs
2 cups strained cranberry sauce
4 cups sifted flour
3 cups chopped seedless raisins
2 teaspoons soda
1 teaspoon salt
2 teaspoons cinnamon
1 cup chopped nut meats

METHOD:

Cream butter and sugar thoroughly. Add beaten eggs, then add cranberry sauce, which has been whipped with a fork until light. Blend together thoroughly. Sift flour, measure. Add soda, salt and spices and sift together. Add nut meats and raisins, which have been washed, dried and chopped. Add this mixture to cranberry mixture and beat together. Turn into a greased and floured bean pan and sprinkle with one tablespoon sugar. Bake in a slow oven, 325 degrees, about a hour. Serve in squares.

NOTE: Top with whipped cream and garnish with a cranberry or use the recipe for icing below.

CRANBERRY CAKE ICING

2 cups cream cheese
4 cups powdered sugar
½ cup mashed cranberries

Cream, add enough cranberry sauce to spread to desired consistency.

CHOCOLATE CHEESE BROWNIE

```
8    pkgs. German Chocolate (Sweet) 32 oz.
2½   cups oleo
1½   pounds cream cheese
8    cups sugar
24   eggs
4½   cups unsifted cake flour
4    tbsp. vanilla
4    tsp. baking powder
2    tsp. salt
4    cups chopped nuts
2    tsp. almond extract
```

First Step
Melt chocolate and 1½ cups oleo over low fire and cool. Cream cheese and 1 cup oleo until smooth. Then add 2 cups sugar, beat until light and fluffy. Then stir in 8 eggs, ½ cup flour and vanilla.

Second Step
Beat remaining eggs until fluffy and gradually add remaining sugar and beat until thickens. Fold in baking powder, salt and remaining flour and cool chocolate mixture, nuts, extract.

Third Step
Measure 8 cups chocolate mixture and set aside. Spread remaining chocolate in greased pie pans. Then pour cheese mixture over chocolate. Then drop chocolate mixture into cheese and make a marble effect with spoon. Bake at 350° for 40 minutes.

PRUNE CAKE

1 cup Wesson oil 2 cups granulated sugar	Combine oil and sugar.
3 eggs	Add eggs one at a time, mixing well.
2 cups flour (all purpose) 1 teaspoon cloves 1/2 teaspoon salt 1 teas. soda 1 teas. all spice 1 teas. cinnamon	Sift together flour, soda, salt and spices. Add to mixutre alternating with buttermilk
1 cup buttermilk	
1 teaspoon vanilla	Add to mixture.
1 cup cooked chopped prunes	Fold in prunes.

Bake in lightly greased 9 x 12 pan at 325 degrees for 1 hour and 10 min. Remove cake from oven. Puncture cake and add the following sauce:

1 cup sugar 1/2 cup buttermilk 1 teaspoon soda	Combine sugar, buttermilk, soda and Karo. Bring to a soft boil. Remove from heat and add butter.
1 stick (1/2 cup) Oleo	

CHAPTER VI

BUTTER COCOANUT

INGREDIENTS	LBS	OZS		METHOD
Sugar	6		)	Mix together
Cake flour		8	)	
Milk powder		8	)	
Salt		3/4	)	
Vanilla	3 tsp.		)	
Eggs - voltex	2	8	)	Add well
Melted butter	1	6	)	Add
Syrup	1	4	)	Add
Water - boiling	4		)	Add
Chopped Cocoanut - fine	2		)	Add

Bake at 350°

CANDY HOME MADE ICING

	LBS	OZS		
PET MILK (4 cans)			)	Boil until thickens
Sugar	3	8	)	
Margarine (kneeded)	1		)	
Voltex		10	)	
Chopped cocoanut		14	)	Add
Chopped pecans		12	)	

REFRIGERATED CHEESE CAKE

I. MIX AND LET SET 15 MINUTES BEFORE STARTING BATCH:

    2 heaping teaspoons gelatine
    6 oz. cold water

II. CREAM LIGHT:

    2 pound granulated sugar
    1 pound yellow margarine

III. ADD GRADUALLY   BEAT LIGHT:

    4 eggs

IV. WHIP IN UNTIL ALL IS SMOOTH

    3 pound Philadelphia Cream Cheese (Break-up in pieces before adding)

V. ADD GELATINE MIXTURE TO CREAMED MASS ALONG WITH WHIPPED CREAM MIS #VI. BELOW:

VI. WHIP STIFF:

    1 quart whipping cream
    6 oz. sugar

FOLD ALTOGETHER UNTIL WELL MIXED

2 Oz. to 6 Oz. **Drained,** mashed pineapple may be added for additional flavor

PREPARE PIE CRUST AS FOLLOWS:

   Roll regular pie dough out in crushed Graham Crackers.

Formula mades about 10 - 8" pies - sprinkle crushed Graham Crackers - Crumbs on top.

Refrigerate all these pies.

Sell at $1.00 to $1.50 each.

A very ruck item that should be sold in 24 to 36 hours. They keep several days but will start to pull from sides after 48 hours.

CHEESE CAKE

INGREDIENTS	LBS	OZS	METHOD
Graham Cracker Crumbs	2		) Blend together smoothly on a mixer using cake paddle. Grease seven (7)
Granulated Sugar	1		) 8 inch deep pie tins well and press crumb mixture firmly and evenly on the
Oleo (room temperature)	1		) bottom and sides of the tin. Shape to the pan but do not pack. There is enough for eight tins but save the amount of the 8th tin to sprinkle on top of the finished cake. Bake crusts in slow oven 300° for 5 minutes then allow to cool thoroughly.

PART II MIDDLE LAYER

Loaf Cream Cheese (room temp)	6		) Measure out all ingredients except egg yolks and whites
Granulated Sugar	1	8	) and blend together till smooth, using cake paddle
Vanilla		2	) on low speed. Scrape. Next mix in egg yolks and continue
Grated Lemon Rind		1	) on low speed for approx. 5 minutes scraping down
Lemon Juice		8	) twice. Beat eggwhites stiff and fold into above mixture.
Egg Yolks		12	) Scale mix into seven cooled crusts 21 ozs. each. Bake
Salt		1	) for 45 minutes in cool oven 275° to 300°. Remove from
Egg Whites		12	) oven and cool thoroughly.

PART III TOPPING FOR CHEESE CAKE

Sour Cream (thick)	3		) Blend together. When cakes have cooled thoroughly then
Powdered Sugar		5	) spread two good cook-spoons of this sour cream mix on
Vanilla		1	) each and spread over top surface. Return to oven and bake for 10 minutes at 300°.

After cooling again the cake should be chilled in ice-box and served cold. Sprinkle top with remainder of graham cracker mixture and cut as desired.

FONDANT BUTTER CREAM ICING

INGREDIENTS	LBS	OZS	METHOD
Fondant	5		) Cream on low speed till smooth.
Oleo	1		)
Cake Shortening	1	8	)
Fondant	5		) Add fondant to above 1 lb. at a time. Then add salt & vanilla and continue creaming till light. If icing needs thinning use evaporated milk.
Salt		1	)
Vanilla		1	)

FONDANT CHOCOLATE ICING

INGREDIENTS	LBS	OZS	METHOD
Sugar	1	12	) Dissolve sugar in water then bring to a boil making a simple syrup.
Water	1		)
Fondant	6		) Place fondant, kolishus, salt and vanilla in mixer and add above syrup. Mix only to a smooth mass.
Kolishus	1	8	)
Salt		1	)
Vanilla		1	)

WHITE CREAM ICING

INGREDIENTS	LBS	OZS	METHOD
Cake Shortening	2		)
Salt		1	) Mix on low speed for 5
			minutes then whip on
Liquid Mild	1	4	) second speed 10 to 15 minutes.
Vanilla		1	)
Powdered Sugar	8		)

YIELD: Approximately 12 lbs.

Variations:

Butter Cream Icing: Use 1 lb. oleo in place of 1 lb. cake shortening.

Add any of the following ingredients to 10 lbs of white cream icing:

```
    1 lb. chopped nuts ------------------ Nut Icing
    1 lb. ground raisins ---------------- Raisin Icing
    1 lb. candied fruits ---------------- Candied fruit Icing
    1 lb. almond paste or flavour ------- Almond Icing
    1 lb. jam or marmalade -------------- Jam or Marmalade Icing
    5 lbs. Fondant ---------------------- Fondant Icing
   10 ozs cocoa plus 4 oz water --------- Cocoa Icing
   12 ozs Kolishus --------------------- Chocolate Icing
    8 ozs crushed peppermint candy ------ Peppermint Icing
    1 to 3 lbs chopped nuts, cherries &
              raisins ------------------- Lady Baltimore Icing
```

NEW YORK STYLE CHEESE CAKE

INGREDIENTS	LBS	OZS	METHOD
Cheese Cake Base		20	) Put cheese cake base, egg yolks and milk in mixing
Egg Yolks (3)			) bowl and whip till smooth. (About 1 minute)
Sweet Milk		18	)
Cream Cheese	1		) Add cream cheese and after a few rotations of the whip
Sweet Milk		18	) add the sweet milk gradually. Whip to a smooth consistency. Approximately two minutes.
Cheese Cake Whip		12	) In a separate mixing bowl, whip the cheese cake whip
Boiling Water		12	) and boiling water to a stiff meringue. Approximately 3 minutes. Fold the two mixes together by hand.

For graham cracker crust mix together 2 lb crushed graham crackers and 1/2 lb of warm oleo.

Divide crust equally into 7 pie tins, fill with cheese cake mix and top with krunchies. Refrigerate 1 hour.

BUTTERMILK DEVILS FOOD CAKE

INGREDIENTS	LBS	OZS	METHOD
Cake Flour	4	10	Weigh all dry ingredients into mixing bowl and start machine on low speed. Add cake shortening and after a few turns of the paddle add buttermilk slowly. Scrape down, mix on low speed for 4 minutes scraping down at least twice.
Cocoa		1	
Salt		2 1/2	
Soda		2 1/2	
Sugar	6	14	
Cake Shortening	2	11	
Buttermilk	3	5	
Voltex	3	11	Stir together. Then add slowly in two parts. Scrape down. Mix on low speed 3 minutes.
Buttermilk	3	5	
Vanilla		1	

Yeild: 25 lbs.

Baking temperature: 360° to 370°

.APPLE SAUCE CAKE.

INGREDIENTS	LBS.	OZS.		METHOD
Swansdown Cake Flour	5		)	
Quick Blend	2	4	)	
Sugar	4	8	)	
Soda		1	)	Blend together 3 to 5 minutes on medium speed.
Baking Powder		2	)	
Cinnamon		1/2	)	
Cloves		1/2	)	
Salt		3	)	
Voltex	1	4	)	
Raisins (Soak)	2	4	)	
Apple Sauce	3		)	
Apple Sauce	2	8	)	Add and mix smooth.
Vanilla		1	)	

Baking: 375° to 400:

Suggested Icings: Lady Baltimore

Apple Jelly Cream (Add 1 lb. of apple jelly to 8 lbs. of cream of fondant base).

YELLOW LAYER CAKE

INGREDIENTS	LBS.	OZS.	METHOD
Quick-Blend	2	4	)
Swans Down Cake Flour	5		)
Sugar	6	4	)
Baking Powder		5	)
Salt		3	) Mix for 7 minutes at medium speed.
Powdered Milk		3	) Add to the above in 3 parts and mix for 3 minutes at low speed.

Total Weight: 22 lbs.

Baking Temperature: 375°

Variations:

Fruit Layers: Add   4 ozs. finely chopped prepared fruit to each 4 lbs. of cake batter and mix till smooth.

Honey Layer Cake: Add 4 ozs. honey and 1/4 oz. of mixed spices to each 4 lbs. of batter.

Cocanut Layer Cake: Add 3 ozs. cocanut to each 4 lbs. of batter.

Nut Layer Cake :   Add 4 ozs. finely ground, roasted nuts and 1/4 ozs. cinnamon to each 4 lbs. of batter.

WHITE LAYER CAKE

INGREDIENTS	LBS.	OZS.	METHOD
Cake Flour	5		)
Quick-Blend	2	4	)
Sugar	6		)
Powdered Milk		8	) Mix for 1 min., at medium speed.
Salt		2	)
Baking Powder		5	)
Egg Whites	3	12	)
Flavor (as desired)			)
Water	3	8	) Add in 3 parts; scrape down once after the first portion of water has been added. Mix at low speed.

Yeild: 21 1/2 lbs.

Baking Temp.:   360° to 375°.

Variations: Same as for YELLOW LAYER CAKE or any good, practical, variation.

Chocolate chip layers: Add 4 ozs. of grated sweet chocolate candy to each 4 lbs. of mix.

DEVILS FOOD LAYER CAKE

INGREDIENTS	LBS.	OZS.		METHOD
Quick-Blend	2	8	)	
Cake Flour	5		)	
Sugar	7	4	)	
Cocoa Powder (Dutched)	1	6	)	Mix for 7 minutes at medium speed.
Powdered Milk		8	)	
Baking Powder		3 1/2	)	
Soda		1	)	
Salt		1	)	
Whole Eggs	4		)	
Water	1	4	)	
Vanilla (as desired)			)	
Water	4	4	)	Add slowly to above and mix for 3 minutes at low speed.

Yeild: 26 1/2 lbs.

Baking Temp.:   360° to 370°

NOTE!"   If a closer grain is desired 2 lbs. of egg-whites may be substituted for 2 lbs. of whole eggs.

Pan Grease:
    Quick-Blend   1 lbs.)
    Bread Flour   3 ozs.)   Mix together till smooth.
    Cocoa Powder   1 ozs.)

CHOCOLATE LAYER CAKE

INGREDIENTS	LBS.	OZS.		METHOD
Quick-Blend	2	8	)	
Melted Bitter Chocolate	2		)	Mix till smooth (about) 1 min., and scrape.
Sugar	4		)	
Sugar	3	8	)	
Cake Flour	5		)	
Powdered Milk		8	)	
Baking Powder		3 1/2	)	
Soda		1	)	Add to above and mix for 6 min. at medium speed.
Salt		2	)	
Whole eggs	3	8	)	
Water	1	12	)	
Vanilla	4	4	)	Add slowly to above and mix for 3 min. at low speed.

Yeild: 27 1/2 lbs.

Baking Temperature: 360° to 370°

NOTE!: Melt chocolate in double boiler.

Honey, butterscotch, molasses coffee or cinnamon may be added to vary the flavor of the chocolate.

DEVIL FUDGE CAKE

INGREDIENTS	LBS.	OZS.	METHOD
Cake Flour	2	)	Mix from 3 to 5 min. Scrape down at least once.
Quick-Blend	1	6)	
Sugar	2	12)	
Cocoaa (Dutches)		8)	
Salt		1 1/4)	
Soda		1/2)	Add to above and mix for 3 to 5 min. scraping once.
Baking Powder		2)	
Cinnamon		1/4)	
Powdered Milk		6)	
Water	1 1/4	)	
Voltex	2	)	Add to above in 2 parts. Mixing to smooth batter.
Water	2	)	
Vanilla (to taste)		)	

Mixing speed: For the whole operation use second speed.
NOTE!:   Use cocoa and grease as for DEVIL FOOD CAKE.
Baking time: 30 minutes at 360° to 370°.
Yeild: 11 1/2 lbs.

CHOCOLATE BAVARIAN CAKE

Scale the devil fudge batter into pans using 16 ozs. to the layer. After baking, cool, then top with Bavarian Cream made from the following formula.

INGREDIENTS		LBS.	OZS.	METHOD
Liquid Milk	(8 cups)	1	)	
Whole Eggs	(fresh)		3)	Beat eggs with sugar
				Stir in hot milk, cooking over boiling water till thick. Dissolve gelatin in the water and stir into mix.
Gran. Sugar	(1 cup)		8)	
Gelatin	(2 tablespoons)		3/4)	
Water	(1 tablespoon)		1)	
Vanilla	(1 tablespoon)		)	Cool the above and stir in vanilla.
Whipped Cream	(1 cup)		8)	When mixture starts to set add the whipped cream.

Finish: Spread the following on the cooled fudge cake about 1/2 inch high. To keep the edges smooth and even during the time it takes the cream to set fasten a high paper collar around the edge of the cake and place in cool refridgerator.

Y E L L O W P O U N D C A K E

INGREDIENTS	LBS.	OZS.		METHOD
Quik-Blend	3		)	
Cake Flour	5		)	
Sugar	6		)	
Salt		1/2	)	Start mixing at low speed until ingredients are smooth, then shift to medium speed and mix for 7 min.
Powdered Milk		4)	)	
Voltex	3	8	)	
Water	1	4	)	
Flavor (as desired)			)	
Baking Powder		1/2	)	
Water	1		)	Add and mix for 3 min. at low speed.

Total Weight: 20 1/4 lbs.
Baking Temp: 340°

WHITE POUND CAKE

INGREDIENTS	LBS.	OZS.	METHOD
Quick-Blend	3		)
Cake Flour	5		)
Sugar	6	4	)
Salt		2 1/2	) Start mixing at low speed until ingredients are smooth, then shift to medium speed and mix for 5 minutes.
Baking Powder		2	)
Cream of Tartar		1/2	)
Water	2	12	) Stir together and add in 2 parts, mix for 5 min. at low speed.
Egg Whites	3		)

Yeild: 21 1/2 lbs.

Baking Temp.: 340°

FRUIT CAKE

INGREDIENTS	LBS.	OZS.	METHOD
Flour	5	)	Blend together 3 to 5 min. using 2nd speed.
M.F.B.	3	)	
Sugar	6	)	
Baking Powder		1 1/2)	
Salt		1 1/2)	
Nutmeg		1/2)	
Whole Eggs	3	)	
Powdered Milk		6)	
Water (3/4 qt.)		)	
Brandy (1 pint)		)	Add and blend 5 to 8 min. using 2nd speed.
Vanilla		1)	
Citrus Fruit	12	)	Fold in.
Chopped Pecans	8	)	
Chopped Floured Raisins	2	)	

Line 10 inch angel food pans with paper fillers. Grease well and fill with 5 # of batter, decorate with pecan halves and citrus fruits. Bake 3 to 5 hours. Oven temperature should be 300°. Turn over on moist cloth 5 minutes after removing from oven.

Yeild: 8 - 5# FRUIT CAKES.

VANILLA CHIFFON CAKE

INGREDIENTS	LBS.	OZS.	METHOD
Cake Flour	1	11	
Baking Powder		1 1/2	)
Salt		3/4	) Blend by sifting into mixing bowl.
Granulated Sugar	2	5	)
Quick-Blend		14	) Place in mixing bowl with dry ingredients.
Voltex Eggs		14	) Use wire whip and mix together on medium speed
Water	1		) until smooth.
Water		5	) Add to above in several parts. Be careful not to overmix this part of the cake.
Egg Whites	1	12	) Beat stiff, then add the batter mixture in a steady stream to the egg whites as fast as the white will take it. Mix only enough to thoroughly blend the two.

Scale into angel food pans immediately. Bake at 350° for 50 min. turning upside down immediately upon removal.

For tropical Chiffon use 1 lb. and 2 qt. of brown sugar in place of the same amount of granulated plus 1/4 oz. allspice, 1/4 oz. nutmeg and 1/8 oz. cloves.

For orange Chiffon use 7 oz. of orange juice and 2 oz. orange rind in place of 5 oz. water. Leave out vanilla.

For Golden Chiffon use 3 oz. water, 2oz. lemon juice and 2 oz. grated lemon rind in place of 5 oz. of water.

CARAMEL CAKE

INGREDIENTS	LBS.	OZS.	METHOD
Cake Flour	5		)
Quick Blend	2	4	)
Brown Sugar	6		) Blend together 3 to 5 minutes at medium speed.
Salt		3	)
Baking Powder		4	)
Powdered Milk		6	
Water	1	8	)
Voltex	2	4	) Add and mix smooth.
Water	2	4	)
Maple Flavor		1	)

Yeild: 19 1/4 #

Baking temp.: 375° to 400°

SUGGESTED MAPLE CREAM ICING

Ingredient	LBS.	OZS.	METHOD
Brown Sugar	3	12	)
Liquid milk	1	12	) Heat to boiling point. Cool to temperature of 70° to 75°.
Salt		3/4	)
Quick-Blend		14	) Whip together. Add gradually to above syrup. Continue beating about 5 minutes.
Butter or Oleo	1		)
Fondant	3	12	)

B A N A N N A C A K E

INGREDIENTS	LBS	OZS		METHOD
Cake Flour	4	8	)	
Quick Blend	1	12	)	
Sugar	6		)	Blend together 3 to 5 minutes. on medum speed. Be sure that banannas are well seived after the fashion of banana puree for a baby.
Baking Powder		4	)	
Salt		3	)	
Ripe Bananas (Seived)	4		)	
Whole Eggs	3	8	)	
Liquid Milk	2		)	Add and mix smooth.
Vanilla or Banana Flavor		1	)	

YIELD: Aprox. 22 lbs.

Baking Temp: 375° to 400°

Note: Use fully ripe bananas as they have a richer, sweeter flavor.

Note: Make Fondant Cream, Boiled, Plain creamed or butter creamed icing with an addition of 1 lb. mashed ripe bananas to each ten pounds of icing also use banana flavor if obtainable.

PRUNE CAKE

1 1/2 cup shortening
2 cups sugar
6 eggs well beaten
2 cups ground cooked prunes
3 cups sour cream
4 cups flour   MAKES 6 LAYERS
2 tsp soda
4 tsp cinnamon
1 tsp all spice
pinch of salt

GINGER BREAD

1 CUP molasses   3 cups flour
1 cup sour milk   3 eggs beaten separately
1 cup sugar   1 tbl sp ginger
1 cup shortening   1 tsp cinnamon and cloves
                              2 tsp soda
                              3 tbl sp cocoa

DROP DUMPLINGS

3 cups flour
1 tsp salt
2 eggs beaten lightly
7 tsp baking powder
milk to make soft dough
1/4 cup shortning

Drop dumplings into boiling broth from spoon. Place cover on tight allowing no steam to escape. Do not uncover for 20 minutes.

WHOLE WHEAT ROLLS

2 Qts milk
3 Qts water
3 Eggs
1 Cooks spoon salt
2 Yeast cakes
1 Cooks spoon sugar
1/2 cup molasses
3 Cooks spoons shortening (melted)
1/2 sifter bran
2 Scoops whole wheat flour

SPICE CAKE

4 cups brown sugar
1 Cup butter
6 Eggs
3 Cups sour cream
3 Tsp soda
1 Tsp nutmeg
7 Cups flour

Cream butter. add sugar and add egg yolks beaten LIGHtly add sour cream. Sift dry ingredients and add alternately with sour cream to first mixture. Makes 6 layers

LADY BALTIMORE CAKE

3/4 cup butter or shortening
2 cups sugar
3 cups sifted cake flour
3 tsp baking powder
1/2 tsp salt
1 cup milk
1 tsp vanilla
6 egg whites

Cream shortening and sugar together until fluffy. Sift flour salt, baking powder together 3 times. Combine milk and vanilla. Add small amounts of flour to creamed mixture alternately with milk mixture, beating until smooth after each addition. Beat egg whites until stiff but not dry and fold into mixture. Bake in greased and floured 9 in. layer tins. Makes 2 layers

M A HOGANY CAKE

5 cups sifted cake flour
6 tsp baking powder
1 tsp salt
1 1/3 cup shortening
4 cups sugar
6 eggs well beaten
2 cups chopped nuts
6 squares melted chocolate
2 cups riced potatoes
  1/3 cup milk
1 tsp vanilla

Sift flour, salt and baking powder together three times. Cream butter, add sugar gradually. Cream till light. add eggs and beat well; add nuts and chocolate and blend; then potatoes and beat well. add flour after each addition until smooth. Add vanilla.

Makes 6 layers.

DEVIL'S FOOD CAKE

6 eggs
5 cups sugar
2 cups shortening
6 cups cake flour
16 tbspn cocoa
4 cups sour cream
4 tsp soda
4 tsp vanilla

Cream shortening, add sugar and cocoa. beat 20 min. Add egg yolks and beat 5 min. Add flour and sour cream and soda alternately. Beat egg whites until firm, then fold in

Makes 6 layers.

SWEETHEART CAKE

8 eggs (seperated)
1 1/4 cups sugar
1 cup flour
1 tsp cream of tarter

Beat egg yolks, add sugar and flour and beat well. Beat egg whites till they form peaks. Fold egg yolks mixture into whites. Bake in biscuit pan in moderate oven. Use as strawberry or peach short cake.

WHITE CAKE

2 cups shortening
4 cups sugar
8 cups cake flour
8 tsp baking powder
2 cups milk
2 tsp vanilla
16 egg whites

CHOCOLATE FILLING

10 squares unsweetened chocolate
3 qts milk
3 1/2 cups sugar
2 rounding cups flour
1 1/2 tsp salt
9 egg yolks
1/4 cup butter
1 cooks spoon vanilla

Add chocolate to milk on top of double boiler. When chocolate is melted beat with beater until blended. Combine sugar, flour and salt. Add to hot mixture, stirring constantly. Add well beaten egg yolks. Add vanilla and butter.

CREAM FILLING

6 qts milk
6 cups sugar
15 egg yolks
10 cooks spoons flour
1/4 lb butter
1 cooks spoon vanilla
Put milk in double boiler. Beat eggs lightly, add just a little milk (1 cup) to mix withffour and sugar.

S P I C E   C A K E

INGREDIENTS	LBS.	OZS.		METHOD
Cake Flour	5		)	
Quick Blend	2	4	)	
Sugar	3		)	Blend together 3 to 5 min. at medium speed.
Brown Sugar	3		)	
Salt		4	)	
Baking Powder		4	)	
Powdered Milk		6	)	
Water	1	8	)	
Voltex	2	4	)	
Spice Mix		1 3/4	)	
Water	2	4	)	Add and mix smooth.
Vanilla		1	)	

Note: Spice Mix: 4 ozs. cinnamon
1 ozs. Mace
1/2 ozs. Ginger
1 ozs. Nutmeg
1/2 ozs. Allspice

Make up, mixing together well, using 1 3/4 ozs. mix for each 5 lb. batch of spice cake.

Icing Suggestion: Mocha Butter Cream or Mocha Fondant, made by adding strong coffee in place of milk.

Jelly Cream or Jelly Fondant Icing: Add 1 lb. of jelly or marmalade to 10 lns. of creamed of fondant icing.

C R E A M E D I C I N G

INGREDIENTS	LBS.	OZS.		METHOD
4x Sugar	3	8	)	
Quick-Blend	2	8	)	Cream light.
Powdered Milk		8	)	
Whole Eggs		8	)	
Water		8	)	
Vanilla (as desired)			)	Add slowly and cream lightly.
Salt (as desired)			)	

Fondant Cream Icing

Fondant	4		)	
Quick-Blend	3		)	Cream light.
Whole eggs or whites		8	)	
Water		4	)	Add slowly and cream lightly.
Vanilla (as desired)			)	
Salt (as Desired)				

Glossy chocolate icing

Fondant	6		)	
Vanilla (as desired)				
Salt (as desired)				Melt chocolate, place all ingredients in bowl and
Quick blend		8	)	mix smooth.
Bitter chocolate	1	4	)	
Boiling water (variable)		5	)	Add and mix smooth

CAKE ICINGS

Types of icings:

1) Fudge type icing

2) Cream icing

3) Fondant cream icing

4) Marshmellow icing

Note: There are two types of marshmellow icings:
1) Egg white type

2) gelatin type

Proper use of icings:

    Ice cakes carefully to give best appearance and flavor.
Have cakes cooled to room temp. before icing.
Use a liberal quanity of icing.
Use ingenuity and imagination plus basic formula.

Storage:

    Store all icings, except marshmellow, in refrigerator when not in use. Cover with wax paper to prevent crusting. Icing stored under 60° F. will keep fully a week.

Make up marshmellow icing as needed because this icing toughens on standing. Leftover marshmellow icing may be added to fresh batch.

WHITE CREAM ICING

INGREDIENTS	QTS	OZS	METHOD
Quick blend	2		)
Salt		1	) Mix on low speed about 5 minutes.
Liquid milk	1	4	) Whip at medium speed 10 to 15
Vanilla		1	) minutes to desired lightness.
4x sugar		8	)

Yield: Approx. 12#

Variations:

    Butter cream icing   Use 1 lb of butter in place of 1 lb of Quick blend.

    Add any of the following ingredients to 10 lbs of white cream icing

1 # chopped nuts	Nut icing.
1 # ground raisins	Raisin ining
1 # Candied fruits	Fruit icing
1 # Almond paste and almond flavor	Almond icing
1 # Jam or marmalade	Jam or marmalade icing
5 # Fondant	Fondant icing
10 oz cocoa, plus 4 oz water	Chocolate icing.
12 oz melted bitter chocolate	Chocolate icing.
8 oz pepermint candy (crushed)	Pepermint icing.
3 # chopped nuts, cherries, raisins.	Lady Baltimore icing.
4 oz ground fresh fruit.	Fresh fruit icing.

Variations of icings is a truly imaginative task and there is not a limit to them as long as the basic icing is kept in mind.

CHOCOLATE FUDGE ICINGS

INGREDIENTS	LBS	OZS		METHODS
Sugar		12	)	
Oleo		4	)	Combine. Boil at 244° F
Salt		1/2	)	
Water		4	)	
Cream of tarter (1/2) tsp				
Sugar	2	8	)	Cream together, add above
Quick blend		10	)	syrup quickly, beat together
Milk		3	)	
Milk		3	)	Stir in and beat icing
Melted better chocolate		6	)	to desired consistency.
Vanilla		1/2	)	

Yield: Approximately 5 lbs.

Chocolate Malted Milk Cream Icing

INGREDIENTS	LBS	OZS	METHOD
Quick blend	1	4)	
Salt		3/4)	Cream together till light
Malted milk powder		6)	
Melted chocolate	1	8)	Add and stir in
Milk	1	8)	Add and stir in
Sugar	5	)	stir in. Mix till smooth.

Yield: 10 lb.

MAPLE CREAM ICING.

INGREDIENTS	LBS	OZS	METHOD
Brown sugar	3	12)	
Liquid milk	1	12)	heat to boiling temp. Cook to 70' to 75'
Salt		3/4)	
Quick blend	1	14)	whip together. Add above syrup, gradually. Continue beating about 5 minutes.
Maple flavor		1/4)	
Fondant	3	12)	Add and whip lightly about 10 minutes.

SUMMER CREAMED ICING

Quick blend	2	)	
Fondant	10	)	Cream for 5 minujtes at medium speed
Salt		1/2)	
Flavor (as desired)		)	
Boiled merangue	5	)	

White cream icing

INGREDIENTS	LBS	OZS		METHOD
Fondant	4	8	)	
Sugar	6		)	
Quick blend	1	2	)	Put all ingredients in bowl at one time. Cream 8 to ten minutes.
Egg whites	1	4	)	
Salt		1/2	)	

Flavor as desired

Note: Any flavor, color or prepared crushed fruit may be used.

BOILED MERINGUE OR MARSHMALLOW

Sugar	5	—	)	
Cream of tarter		1/4	)	
Water	1	8	)	Boil to 245° F.
Egg whites	2		)	Beat to soft peak, add above syrup slowly, beating all the while.
Sugar		8	)	

MARSHMALLOW CREAM ICING

Fondant	5		)	
Quick blend	1	2	)	Cream till light at 2nd speed.
Salt		1/2	)	
Flavor as desired			)	Add and continue creaming for 5 minutes.
Boiled meringue	2	8	)	

ROYAL ICING

Sugar	5		)	
Egg white	1		)	Cream until light and cover with wet cloth.
Cream of tartar		1	)	

CHOCOLATE FUDGE

Fondant	3	12	)	
Vanilla (as Desired)			)	
Salt same			)	Place in mixing bowl.
Bitter chocolate melted	1	4	)	Melt, add and mix smooth.
Quick blend		8	))	
Warm water		6	)	add slowlys and mix smooth.

GINGERBREAD

INGREDIENTS	LBS	OZS		METHOD
Sugar	2		)	Scale all dry ingredients into
Salt		2	)	mixing bowl and on low speed,
Soda		1	)	using cake paddle blend together.
Baking powder		2	)	Add shortening and water and on
Cake flour	5		)	low speed mix for five minutes
Cinnamon		2	)	scraping down twice.
Ginger		2	)	
All spice		1	)	
Powdered milk		8	)	
Water	2	8	)	
Cake shortening	2	4	)	
Voltex	2		)	Mix together in stainless steel
Grandma molasses	8		)	bowl then add to above in three
Water	1		)	parts. Continue mixing on low
				speed for four minujtes scraping
				down twice.

Scale into sheet pans and bake at 375°. Also good for cup cakes.

EGG WHITE MERINGUE

Egg whites (1 qt)	2		)	Place 2 lbs of egg whites in mixing bowl of machine. Beat on 2nd speed with wire whip.
				Important: Do not add sugar and do not beat at high speed.
Sugar	3	8	)	Mix 3 lbs of water to sugar and egg stabilizeer and place in
Egg white stabilizer		3	)	boiler. Stir well with a spoon or wire whip and bring to a boil
Water	3		)	Allow to boil for 2 or 3 min. Remove from fire.

When egg whites are beaten to medium dry stiffness, (Pulling away from side of bowl), continue to beat at 2nd speed, add the cooked mixture very slowly in a heavy thread like stream.

Pies with meringue should be brouned in 425° to 450° oven.

Allow the machine to continue beating the whites for about a minute after all the cooked mix has been added.

Note: It is unnecessary to brown off pies in a slow oven. Doing so dries out the meringue topping, causing it to shrink and become tough. With this formula, you can brown them quickly, leaving the pies in only long enough to brown as desired.

GERMAN CHOCOLATE CAKE

YIELD: 3 double layer cakes

CAKE

5 cups cake flour
4 cups sugar
2 cups shortening
8 eggs
2 cups buttermilk
2 teaspoons soda
2 pkg. German chocolate
1 cup boiling water
1/4 teaspoon salt
2 tsp. vanilla

METHOD:

Cream sugar and shortening, add 1 1/2 cups buttermilk, and 4 cups of the flour alternately. Then add beaten egg yolks. Add soda to the 1/2 cup buttermilk left and put into mixture. Then add other cup of flour, melted chocolate (melted in boiling water) and vanilla. Last, fold in the stiffly beaten egg whites. Bake at 350° for about 25 minutes.

FILLING

3 cups whipping cream
3 cups coconut
3 cups nuts
3 cups sugar
9 egg yolks
3 stocks oleo

METHOD:

Beat the egg yolks slightly, add sugar, cream, and oleo in pan. Cook over low heat until thick. Remove from fire and add nuts and coconut, beat until cool, and spread on cake.

CHAPTER VII

MISCELLANEOUS

SANDWICHES	Page	DRINKS	Page
Bacon & Egg	1	Fruit Punch	2
Chicken Salad	1	Lemonade	2
Ground Beef	1		
Ground Meat	1		
Ham and Cheese	1		
Pimento Cheese	1		
Pineapple Cream Cheese	1		
Potted Ham	1		

LIST HERE new recipes:

SANDWICHES

Pimento Cheese

Grate cheese. Put in beater, add a pinch of salt and some sweet milk. Beat until creamy. Add chopped sweet pickles and pimento.

Chicken Salad

Grind cooked chicken with just a little skin. Chop and add celery and boiled eggs, salt and pepper to taste. Mix with mayonnaise.

Ham and Cheese

Grind ends of a piece of boiled ham, a piece of longhorn cheese, chopped celery, green peppers and onion. Mix together and add mayonnaise.

Ground Beef

Grind roast beef, chopped pickles (sweet), pimento, green peppers and boiled eggs, salt and mayonnaise.

Potted Ham

Open cans of potted ham. Chop sweet pickles and boiled eggs, add to the ham and mix with mayonnaise.

Ground Meat

Grind ends and scraps of different sandwich meat. Chop sweet pickles and boiled eggs. Mix together with mayonnaise.

Bacon and Egg

Fry bacon and chop real fine. Use boiled eggs in proportion to bacon and chop them. Mix together with mayonnaise.

Pineapple Cream Cheese

Grate cheese, beat well, add pinch of salt and chopped pineapple, a little juice. Serve on nut bread.

DRINKS

LEMONADE:

8 lemons
4 oranges to one gallon
1 cup sugar

FRUIT PUNCH:

Use juices from canned fruit for fruit punch.

ADDENDUM A

Joe O. Luby's WWII Naval Operations

Leyte Island Operation – October 1944

THE BATTLE OF LEYTE GULF IS CONSIDERED to have been the largest naval battle of World War II and, by some criteria, possibly the largest naval battle in history with over 200,000 naval personnel involved. It was fought in waters near the Philippine islands of Leyte, Samar, and Luzon from October 23-26, 1944, between combined American and Australian forces and the Imperial Japanese Navy (IJN). The initiative was part of the invasion of Leyte, which aimed to isolate Japan from the countries it had occupied in Southeast Asia which were a vital source of industrial and oil supplies.

The Battle of Leyte Gulf secured the beachheads of the U.S. Sixth Army on Leyte against attack from the sea. However, much hard fighting would be required before the island was completely in Allied hands at the end of December 1944. The Battle of Leyte on land was fought in tandem with an air and sea campaign in which the Japanese reinforced and resupplied their troops on Leyte while the Allies attempted to interdict them and establish air-sea superiority.

The Imperial Japanese Navy suffered its greatest loss of ships and crew ever. Its failure to dislodge the Allied invaders from

ADDENDUM A

Leyte meant the inevitable loss of the Philippines, which, in turn, meant Japan would be all but cut off from its occupied territories in Southeast Asia. These territories provided resources that were vital to Japan, in particular the oil needed for her ships and aircraft. This problem was compounded because the shipyards and sources of manufactured goods, such as ammunition, were in Japan itself.

The following events were taken from my father's confidential activity reports sent to the Commanders of the various Task Groups of the Seventh Fleet under which he served.

```
                        U.S.S. LCI(G) 340
                        Fleet Post Office
                        San Francisco, Calif.

CONFIDENTIAL                                          20 October 1944

From:       Commanding Officer, LCI(G) 340
To:         Commander in Chief U.S. Fleet
Via:        (1) Commander Task Unit 78.2.3
            (2) Commander Task Group 78.2
            (3) Commander Task Group 78
                (Commander SEVENTH Amphibious Force)
            (4) Commander SEVENTH Fleet

Subject:    Action Report-
            LEYTE Operation

Reference:  (a) Article 97416, U.S. Navy
                Regulations, 1920
            (b) Com7thPhib Conf. Ltr. FE25/A16-3(3) su. 0212 of
                17 February 1944.

    1.      On 20 October 1944 this ship as a part of the San
Ricardo Attack Group, Task Group 78.2, assisted in establishing
the Landing Force on Leyte Island. This force consisted of seven
APA's, two AP's, two AKA's, five DD's, three P.C.'s, one SC six
LCI(R)'s, two LCI(G)'s, One ATF, and two beach party units. This
ship as a part of the close covering fire support group in company
with other LCI(R)'s, mission was to accompany the leading boat
waves and support the landing on White Beach from H-5 minutes to
H hour. Rocket ships were to be abreast and stationed about 400
- 500 yards apart with one ship on each flank of the boat wave and
three inside the lane. The sixth to be stationed 500 yards on
right flank to cover narrow neck of land leading to Tacloban Air
Strip. Each ship's responsibility to cover one-fifth of the beach
(400 yards). Support the landing with rockets and automatic weap-
ons, covering the beach thoroughly with rocket fire to a depth of
three hundred yards, and additional salvos to a depth of 800 yards.
Upon completion of rocket bombardment proceed at slow speed and
strafe with automatic weapons, air strip area. (Pertaining only
to ships of the right flank). Upon completion of strafing run re-
maine on flanks and reload forward rocket launchers to standby to
engage targets of opportunity.
```

October 20, 1944, Dad's ship was attached to the San Ricardo Attack Group of the Seventh Fleet and assisted in establishing the landing force on Leyte Island. At 6:20 AM they spotted several Japanese planes as they moved shoreward. 9:57 AM, they fired eleven salvos of forty-four rockets each and received return fire from the beach. Over the next few days along with several other

ADDENDUM A

ships in the attack group they monitored the area. Several enemy planes were spotted and fired upon.

October 24th at 8:47 A.M., a Japanese twin-engine bomber flew toward their ship low and fast. They shot off the tail section, and the plane went straight up. They continued firing bursts into the fuselage until the plane rolled over, dropped into the water burning, and sank.

```
0847    Enemy twin Engine Bomber (Dinah or Sally?) shot down by this ship.
        Plane flew in very low and fast approximatly 800 yards off star-
        board beam.  Nos. 1, 2 & 3 20 M/M , No. 2 50cal., and 40 M/M
        shot off tail assembly from bomber causing plane to go straight up
        and while in this position 50 cal. and 40 M/M bursts were fired in
        plane's fuslage.  Plane rolled over and dropped into water burning
        and sank.
```

October 25th from 5:00 in the morning until 4:47 in the afternoon, they remained in the area. During this time, a Navy fighter shot down a twin-engine bomber, and other ships opened fire on other dive bombers. One was shot down, and another was hit but didn't go down. Dad's ship fired on another dive bomber, which dropped its bombs, none of which landed near their ship. At 5:38 P.M., they received a message to proceed to the vicinity of the USS Blue Ridge, and at 6:48 P.M., they, along with several other ships, were ordered to rescue US Naval survivors form *DD's* (destroyers) and *CVE* (aircraft carriers).

October 26 at 4:46 P.M., they sighted and picked up a Japanese pilot. He was stripped, searched, given medical attention, food, and water, and placed under guard.

```
        26 October 1944

1646    Sighted lone survivor in water, proceeded to investigate.

1657    Reached survivor and identified him as Japaneese.  Reported to
        PC 623 and were given orders to make rescue.

1700    Rescued survivor from water.  Man taken aboard, stripped of cloth-
        ing, and searched, all papers and valuables taken in custody by
        Commanding Officer.  Survivor given medical attention, food, and
        water, then placed under guard.  Approximate position of rescue
        Lat. 11°34.5' N., Long. 125°57'30" E.
```

October 27 at 1:22 P.M., they picked up a lone Naval survivor from *USS Gambier Bay CVE 73*, and thirty-two minutes later they rescued survivors from seven life rafts. By 7:30 P.M., they had rescued 110 US Naval survivors from *CVE 73*. Many were badly wounded and given medical attention. They also rescued another 15 US Naval survivors from *USS DD 557* who were also badly wounded.

27 October 1944

0122 Picked up lone US Naval survivor from CVE 73. Was taken aboard given immediate medical attention, dry clothing, food, and drink.

0156 Commenced rescue of survivors from seven life rafts that were secured together.

0247 Completed rescue, taking aboard approximately 110 US Naval survivors from CVE 73. Several survivors were badly wounded and were given all medical attention that this ship was able to give. Every effort was made to give all men dry clothing, food, and drink. All ship's bunking facilities, both officers' and men's were turned over to survivors. Though cooking facilities were inadequate hot meals were served. No bodies were taken aboard.

0356 Sighted single life raft and proceeded to rescue survivors.

0630 Effected rescue of 15 US Naval survivors from DD 557. Large percentage of men badly wounded. Given immediate medical attention, food, drink, dry clothing, and berthing space.

1008 Sighted one enemy twin engine bomber (Sally?) flying low astern of convoy, distance approximately 2,000 yards. All hands went to general quarters. Plane did not attack, no guns fired.

1010 Proceeded on course to return to Leyte Island.

ADDENDUM A

Gambier Bay CVE 73, the only American aircraft carrier sunk by enemy surface gunfire during World War II

CVE73 rescue operation on October 27, 1944, in the Leyte Island Conflict

World War II Fletcher-class destroyer USS Johnston (DD 557) which was lost at the Battle off Samar, part of the Battle of Leyte Gulf, on Oct. 25, 1944

Led by Cmdr. Ernest Evans, a Native American from Oklahoma, the crew of the *USS Johnston*, outgunned and outmanned, charged into a massive line of Japanese warships in order to protect the American landing force attempting to liberate the Philippine Islands.[19]

Noticing the Japanese ships were targeting escort carrier Gambier Bay (CVE-73), Evans gave the order to "commence firing on that

---

19   https://www.history.navy.mil/news-and-events/news/2021/wreckage-confirmed-as-heroic-uss-johnston--dd-557-.html

ADDENDUM A

cruiser, draw her fire on us and away from Gambier Bay." One by one, the Johnston took on Japanese destroyers, although the ship had no torpedoes and limited firepower. After two-and-a-half hours, the *USS Johnston*—dead in the water—was surrounded by enemy ships. At 9:45 a.m., Evans gave the order to abandon ship. Twenty-five minutes later, the destroyer rolled over and began to sink.[20]

Of the crew of 327, only 141 survived. Commanding Officer Cmdr. Ernest Evans was awarded a posthumous Medal of Honor, the first Native American in the U.S. Navy and one of only two destroyer captains in WWII to be so honored.[21]

October 28, they were assigned as a fire-fighting ship and prepared to give immediate assistance to burning ships or fires on the beach. No remarks were logged for the next two days.

October 31 at 6:21 P.M., ship and shore batteries opened fire on Japanese bomber. Noted fire on the beach was believed to be started either by enemy plane or ship's AA fire. 6:48 They received orders to proceed and beach to windward of fire. At 7:26 fire party went ashore and continued extinguishing the fire until it was completely out at 2:15 the next morning.

---

20   ibid
21   ibid

```
31 October 1944:
1631  Set Condition I
1637  Made preparations for getting underway.
1641  Underway, and steaming in fire-fighting sector - SW transport area.
1821  Ship and shore batteries opened fire on Japanese bomber (type un-
      known). Noted fire on beach believed to be started either by enemy
      plane or ship's AA fire.
1822  Proceeded to vicinity of fire.
1848  Received orders to proceed and beach to windward of fire.
1923  Dropped stern anchor on way into beach. Long scope of cable out.
1925  Beached in approximate position Lat. 11° 12' 12" N. Long. 125°
      01' 30" E.
1926  Fire party went ashore with hose.
1931  Received word to start fire pump and put pressure on hose. Pressure
      immediately given. This is an oil fire and 50 gallon drums of oil
      are continually exploding. All fire-fighting ships are being used.
      U.S.S. LCI(G) 341 is on our starboard side and U.S.S. LCI(G) 74 is
      on our port side.
2030  Fire is still large.
2100  Fire fighters getting fire under control.
2130  Fire is rapidly being extinguished.
2159  Fire completely out.
```

The "South Force" comprised of the *U.S. Army 38th Infantry Division, 151st Regimental Combat Team* (151st RCT) embarked at Olongapo aboard destroyers from *U.S. Navy Task Group 78.3* (TG 78.3) in Subic Bay. They proceeded southward for an amphibious landing bound for Mariveles to liberate the southern end of the Bataan Peninsula in order to secure the flank of Manila Bay and ahead of operations to liberate Corregidor. In preparation for the battle, as part of task force 78.3, Dad's ship along with three other LCIs and two LCSs cleared beaches and transported and protected the first phase of the landing force. The ships stretched out in intervals of 350 yards each with responsibility for strafing their section of the beach in the formation.

ADDENDUM A

Zambales Operation - January 29, 1945

```
                    U.S.S. LCI(G) 340
                    Fleet Post Office
                    San Francisco, Calif.

                                        29 January 1945

From:    Commanding Officer, USS. LCI(G) 340.
To:      Commander in Chief, U.S. Fleet.
Via:     (1) Commander Task Unit 78.3.8
         (2) Commander Task Group 78.3
         (3) Commander SEVENTH Amphibious.Force.
         (4) Commander SEVENTH Fleet.

Subject: Action Report - ZAMBALES Operation.

    1.     The mission of Task Force 78.3 was to transport, pro-
tect and land the Landing Force, together with it's supplies and
equipment in the ZAMBALES Area and support the landing by air pro-
tection and close gunfire in order to block hostile retirement into
BATAAN Peninsula. This command, as a part of the inshore support
unit on RED Beach, formed as follows: 200 yards inshore of the Line
of Departure (LD 4,000 yards from beach) in the following order from
North to South, LCI(R) 337, LCS(L) 8, LCI(R) 340, LCS(L) 48, LCI(R)
338, and LCS(L) 7. The interval between ships 350 yards. The mis-
sion of this unit as first wave approaches the line of departure,
support ships will form 300 yards forward of waves and proceed with
them to the beach. Support the landing with Rocket, 3"/50 and 40MM
fire, each ship being responsible for that section of beach which
corresponds to his position in the formation. Cover the beaches
and flanks thoroughly to a depth of 400 yards. After Rockets have
been launched support ships will permit the first waves to pass
through them and then take stations on the extreme flanks. Reload
and remain on the flanks to engage targets of opportunity.
```

Grande Island, Subic Bay – January 30, 1945

Dad's ship was ordered to clear the beaches for the infantry as they prepared to seize Grand Island.

```
                    U.S.S. LCI(G) 340
                    c/o Fleet Post Office
                    San Francisco, Calif.

                                        30 January 1945

From:       Commanding Officer, USS. LCI(R) 340.
To:         Commander in Chief U.S. Fleet.
Via:        (1) Commander Task Unit 78.3.8
            (2) Commander Task Group 78.3
            (3) Commander SEVENTH Amphibious Force
            (4) Commander SEVENTH Fleet.

Subject:    Action Report - GRANDE ISLAND Operation.

        1.     The mission of this operation was to transport, pro-
tect, and land the landing force, together with limited supplies
and equipment on GRANDE ISLAND, SUBIC BAY, and support the landing
by close gunfire, in order to seize GRANDE ISLAND. This command
operated as a part of the inshore fire support unit. Task Unit
78.3.8. The mission of the LCI(R)'s was to proceed ahead of the
landing assault wave, and support the landing with rocket and 40
MM fire. Each LCI(R) being responsible for that section of the
beach corresponding to his position in formation. Upon completion
of fire permit leading waves to pass through to beach, then pro-
ceed to vicinity of control vessel well clear of boat lane. Rocket
ships formed on line of departure inshore of control vessel in the
following order from left to right: LCI(R) 340, 338, 337,341.
Course from line of departure to beach 180° (T), speed seven knots.
```

Phase I - Mariveles Bay Operation – February 15, 1945

Phase II - Corregidor to open the entrance to Manilla Bay– February 16, 1945

The mission of the task force was to transport, protect, and land the landing force together with its equipment and supplies at Mariveles Bay. In the second phase, they were to support the landing to open the entrance to Manila Bay.

ADDENDUM A

```
                    U.S.S. LCI(G) 340
                    c/o Fleet Post Office
                    San Francisco, Calif.

C-O-N-F-I-D-E-N-T-I-A-L                              18 February 1945

From:       Commanding Officer, U.S.S. LCI(R) 340.
To:         Commander in Chief U.S. Fleet.
Via:        (1) Commander Task Unit 78.3.8
            (2) Commander Task Group 78.3
            (3) Commander SEVENTH Amphibious Force.
            (4) Commander SEVENTH Fleet.

Subject:    Action Report - MARIVELES BAY OPERATION

    1.      The mission of this operation was to transport, protect,
and land the landing force together with its equipment and supplies
at MARIVELES BAY on 15 February 1945, with a subsequent operation
on CORREGIDOR on D plus one; and support the landing by close gun-
fire in order to open the entrance to MANILA BAY. This operation
consisted of two phases namely, PHASE I (MARIVELES BAY), PHASE II
(CORREGIDOR). This Command operated as a part of Task Unit 78.3.8.
This unit was composed of the following ships: USS LCS(L)(3), 48,
7,8,26,49,27, USS LCI(R) 340,341,338,337,225, and 226, PHASE I.
The mission of this task unit was to provide close inshore fire
support for the landing force with Rockets, 40 MM, 20 MM, and 50 Cal.
gunfire. This command stationed with the USS LCI(R) 338 and 341
proceeded to assigned stations 200 yards inshore of line of approach
on right flank of boat lane. LCI(R)'s took stations abreast from
right to left in the following order 340, 341, 338. The target area
for this unit was the area between the PANIKIAN River and TICTIC,
between which was believed to be a strong ENEMY troop encampment.
Upon execution of the boat wave signal ships proceed on course 000°
speed 7 knots toward objective area - laying down rocket barrage
penetrating 900 yards inland. Upon completion of rocket firing lay
to and cover flanks thoroughly with automatic weapons fire.

PHASE II
This operation visualized a landing on CORREGIDOR at H - Hour plus
two hours, D plus one Day. This command stationed with the USS
LCI(R) 341, 338, and 337 was assigned stations 500 yards east of
right flank of boat lane, when by executing a column left movement
when 3,000 yards from beach deploy into line abreast and equalize
spacing over the front between San Jose Point and Ordnance Point, a
distance of about 1100 yards. Upon execution of boat wave signal
proceed in following orders from right to left 338, 340, 341, and
337, into beach giving close inshore fire support with Rockets, 40
MM, 20 MM, and 50 cal. gunfire. Cover shore line and cliffs east
of boat lane. Remain in general area to engage targets of opportun-
ity.
```

On February 15 at 8:30 in the morning, all hands went to battle stations. 9:20 they entered Mariveles Bay. From 9:50 AM until 6:00 PM they opened fire with their 40 MM gun at various targets and fired twelve salvos of rockets. Then, they started firing on the cliffs behind the shorelines. During this time, at about 10:30 AM, the *USS LSM 169* exploded and was on fire. At 1:00 in the morning, Dad's ship anchored on the west side of Mariveles Harbor, and around 3:00 in the morning, they witnessed several ships exploding and burning. Dad's ship was hit forward and aft by shell fired during nights action.

On February 16, at approximately 0320, the Flotilla was attacked by about 30 suicide boats and by heavy shore-based gunfire that appeared to come from Cabello Island. In a matter of minutes, LCSs 7, 26, and 49, after receiving multiple hits, were sunk with the loss of around 75 lives, with many more wounded. LCS 27 managed to sink four suicide boats before the fifth blew up along the port side causing extensive damage and resulting in flooding. The ship was saved from sinking by beaching it in Mariveles Bay. Pharmacist Mate, First Class George Oliver Turner, and Seaman First Class William Dudley Whaley were killed as a result of the action. A large percentage of the crew was wounded. The more seriously wounded and the dead were taken off. LCS 27 was out of action for the landings, which took place on Corregidor later that day.[22]

---

22   http://www.navsource.org/archives/10/05/050027h.htm

ADDENDUM A

```
16 February 1945:
0001-Anchored on West side of MARIVELES HARBOR IN assigned anchorage.
0304-Screening ships under attack by enemy surface craft.  One ship
     of screen exploded and burning.  All hands to battle stations.
0307-Second ship in screen exploded and began burning.
0310-Third ship in screen exploded and began burning.
0330-This ship hit forward and aft by shell fire during nights action.
0412-Underway awaiting orders from CTU 78.3.8.
0440-Departed from Bay area in accordance with orders from CTU 78.3.8.
0450-Steaming on various courses in sector assigned by CTU 78.3.8.
0737-Re-entered MARIVELES BAY.
0741-Anchored awaiting sortie orders for PHASE II  CTG 78.3 operation.
0812-Underway steaming on right flank of boat lane enroute to land-
     ing beach on CORREGIDOR.  All hands went to battle stations.
0839-First contingent of para-troopers landing on CORREGIDOR.
```

On February 16 at 4:00 in the morning, were ordered to depart bay. At 7:30 the next morning and under orders, they reentered Mariveles Bay where at 8:30 they watched as paratroopers landed on Corregidor.

LANDING BY PARACHUTE ON CORREGIDOR, 15 FEB. 1945.   U S Army Photo 159-2

At 10:00, Dad's boat came under fire and began firing salvos of rockets. At 10:30, their mast was shot down by enemy shell fire, and they had numerous shrapnel holes from enemy machine gun fire. The mast was severed fourteen feet from the top.

Image Caption: Bill Freeman in LCI(R)-340 in the early morning of 16 February 1945 at Mariveles harbor, Bataan, shortly after suicide boats hit 4 LCS's resulting in the sinking of three and beaching of one.

Two hours later, while firing rockets on Corregidor, LCI(R)-340's mast was shot away, and numerous small arms fire-pelted the ship.[23] After the operation, Dad's boat moored alongside LCI (R) 337 shown below to assess their damage. During the operation, LCI 340 had fired 624 rockets and 1547 rounds from its guns and sustained only minor damage.

---

23   http://www.navsource.org/archives/10/15/150340e.htm

ADDENDUM A

1138-Moored alongside USS LCI(R) 337 to inspect damage.

1808-In column returning to MARIVELES BAY area.

1652-Laying to off MARIVELES BAY. Awaiting formation of convoy to Subic Bay.

1951-Departed from MARIVELES and CORREGIDOR Area in convoy to Subic Bay.

    3.   Following types ammunition expended:

PHASE I
```
    4.5" Rockets....................486
    40   MM.........................405
    20   MM.........................420
    50   Cal........................412
```

PHASE II
```
    4.5" Rockets....................138
    40   MM.........................310
    20   MM.........................  0
    50   Cal........................  0
```

    4.   This ship received the following battle damage from shell fire - Hits in bulwark foward port side, hits on gun tub aft port side (40 MM ?), Mast shot off (3"?), and numerous hits by 50 caliber. No serious damage effected. Damage inflicted on enemy unknown.

    5.   All officers and men preformed their duties in a most commendable manner. Ens. D.E. Rees, 393289, USNR; Williams, S.L., S1c, 894-02-028, USNR, and Sampson, B.L., RM3c, 868-73-59, USNR, received minor wounds from shrapnel.

                                            Joe O. Luby
                                            Lt.(jg) USNR
                                            Commanding

Lubang Island Operation – March 2, 1945

From February 28, 1945, to March 1, 1945, a task force from the U.S. Navy 7th Fleet, including destroyers USS Saufley (DD-465) and USS Gass, escorted the LCIs and LCMs that landed the U.S. Army 21st Infantry, 1st Battalion, which made an unopposed landing of a reconnaissance force on Lubang Island. The defending Japanese fled into the interior. Dad's ship, along with six LCIs, one LSM, four LCI(R)s, a destroyer, and destroyer escort were tasked with providing close in fire support for landing our troops. Along with LCI (G) 341, his ship was assigned stations inside the entrance to Port Tilic located on the north side of Labang Island where they lay down rocket barrage on the village of Tilic.

Zamboanga Operation – March 10, 1945

The mission of the attack group, reinforced of the Eighth U.S. Army, was to transport, protect, land, and firmly establish on the shore the 41ˢᵗ Infantry Division. They were to extend control over Basilan Strait and the northern Celebes Sea, denying movement of enemy forces to the Zamboanga Area, and to establish Naval facilities at Zamboanga in order to support future operations to reoccupy the southern Philippine Archipelago. The support staff consisted of five LCI (R)s, two LCI (Mortar) ships.

> "We have landed near Zamboanga on the southwestern-most tip of Mindanao.... The bulk of the enemy garrison, caught off guard, has fled to the hills in disorder. We now control the entire length of the western shores of the Philippine Islands from the northwestern tip of Luzon to the southwestern tip of Mindanao, a distance of approximately 800 miles. The blockade of the South China Sea and the consequent cutting off of the Japanese conquests to the south is intensifying."[24]

---

24   General Douglas McArthur, March 12, 1945

```
                    U.S.S. LCI(G) 340
                    c/o Fleet Post Office
                    San Francisco, Calif.

                                           14 March 1945

C-O-N-F-I-D-E-N-T-I-A-L

From:       Commanding Officer USS LCI(R) 340.
To:         Commander in Chief U.S. Fleet.
Via:        (1) Commander Task Unit 78.1.32.
            (2) Commander Task Unit 78.1.3.
            (3) Commander Task Group 78.1.
            (4) Commander SEVENTH Amphibious.
            (5) Commander SEVENTH Fleet.

Subject:    Action Report - ZAMBOANGA Operation.

Reference:  (a) Article 874l6, U.S. Navy Regulations, 1920.
            (b) Com7thPhib conf. ltr. FE25/A16-3(5) ser. 0212 of
                17 February 1944.

       1.      This operation visualized an amphibious landing on the
southern tip of the ZAMBOANGA PENINSULA. The mission of this attack
group being to transport, protect, land and firmly establish on
shore the 41st. Infantry Division, Reinforced of the EIGHTH U.S. Army.
Extend our control over BASILAN STRAIT and the northern CELEBES SEA,
denying movement of enemy forces to the ZAMBOANGA Area, and to estab-
lish Naval facilities at ZAMBOANGA in order to support future operat-
ions to reoccupy the southern PHILIPPINE ARCHIPELAGO. This command
operated with the LCI Support Craft Unit, CTU 78.1.32, consisting of
five LCI (Rocket) ships and two LCI (Mortar) ships, under the comm-
and Support Craft Unit, CTU 78.1.3. Target date, J - day 10 March
1945, H - hour 0915 Item. The Support Craft Unit assignment on the
assualt, was to take stations 500 yards inshore of line of departure
move forward toward beach ahead of first assault wave, supporting
its movement with all weapons which will bear on target area. Com-
mence rocket barrage when within range of target area, adjusting fire
to extend over a period of three minutes, in order to cover an area
from 200 to 600 yards inland. Close beach as far as safe navigation
permits and continue to fire with all weapons until first assault
wave passes through support lane, at which time close fire and re-
tire to flanks, reload rocket launchers, and standby to support
freindly forces advancing down flanks of beach-head.
```

CEBU Island Operation - March 26, 1945

Along with several other LCIs, the crews strafed the landing beaches in preparation for US troops to land. At 11:40 on the morning of March 27, 1945, they docked at pier and landed guerrillas.

ADDENDUM A

Joe O. Luby - Commendations awarded to the men aboard LCI 340 (G)

File No. FE25/P15(1)
Serial No. 01583

SEVENTH AMPHIBIOUS FORCE
Fleet Post Office
San Francisco, California

C-O-N-F-I-D-E-N-T-I-A-L

18 NOV 1944

From: Commander SEVENTH Amphibious Force.
To : Commanding Officer, U.S.S. LCI(R) 340.
Via : (1) Commander LCI Flotillas.
(2) Commander LCI Group TWENTY.

Subject: Letter of Commendation.

1. Commander SEVENTH Amphibious Force takes pleasure in commending the commanding officer, officers and men of the U.S.S. LCI(R) 340 for their outstanding performance of duty in rescuing many survivors of ships sunk by enemy action during the recent amphibious operations at Leyte, Philippine Islands.

2. The initiative and resourcefulness displayed by all hands while subject to enemy air attacks off the east coast of Samar during the rescue operations were outstanding. It has been most gratifying to receive reports of the untiring efforts of the officers and men and their splendid attitude of cooperation in caring for the survivors and providing them with the necessary medical attention and clothing.

3. In recognition of this meritorious service, it is directed that a copy of this letter of commendation be attached to the next fitness report of each officer and that appropriate entry be made in the service record of each enlisted man.

D. E. BARBEY.

Leyte, Philippine Islands

NAVAL SPEEDLETTER

File or Serial No. FE25-GF1/P15
128

Date 24 February 1945

SPEEDLETTER
TO: COMMANDER LCI(R) GR. 20; LCI(R)s 225, 226, 337, 338, 340, 341; LCS(L)s 7, 8, 26, 27, 48, 49; PC 1119, PC 1133

Use in lieu of despatches, telegrams, teletypes, and mailgrams when appropriate.
Do not handle through Communication Offices.
Despatch phraseology may be used.
Use size No. 9 window envelopes when appropriate and available.
If used for classified matter handle as prescribed in U. S. Navy Regs., Arts. 75½ and 76.
Upon receipt EXPEDITE HANDLING and DELIVERY as much as possible.

COMMANDER LCS(L) FLOTILLA ONE WISHES TO COMMEND THE OFFICERS AND MEN WHO SERVED UNDER HIS COMMAND FOR THEIR GALLANT WORK IN ACTION AGAINST THE ENEMY AT CORREGIDOR ISLAND ON THE 16TH OF FEBRUARY 1945 X A COPY OF THIS COMMENDATION IS TO BE ATTACHED TO THE NEXT REPORT OF FITNESS OF THE OFFICERS CONCERNED AND A NOTATION MADE IN THE SERVICE RECORDS OF THE MEN

Copies To
CHIEF OF NAVAL PERSONNEL
COMMANDER SEVENTH FLEET
COMMANDER SEVENTH AMPHIBIOUS FORCE
CTG 78.3

Signature and Title
R. E. ARISON, CAPTAIN, USN
COMMANDER LCS (L) FLOTILLA ONE
c/o FLEET POST OFFICE
SAN FRANCISCO, CALIFORNIA

ATTENTION ADDRESSEE: Address reply exactly as indicated on right.

Corregidor Island

ADDENDUM A

	Commander LCI (L) Flotilla Seven
FE25/P15 Serial: 00117	Seventh Amphibious Force Fleet Post Office San Francisco, California

S E C R E T   17 March 1945.

From: Commander Task Unit 78.9.7.
        (Commander LCI Flotillas, SEVENTH Amphibious Force)
To: Lt.(jg) J.O. LUBY, U.S. Naval Reserve.

Subject: Commendation.

    1.   The following letter was received from the Commanding General, 24th Infantry Division, U.S. Army, and is quoted for information.

    "On behalf of my division and particularly the 1st Battalion, 21st Infantry, I desire to express our sincere appreciation for the skillful assistance and willing cooperation rendered by Task Unit 78.9.7 in the assault on LUBANG ISLAND. Much enemy ammunition and fuel was destroyed by the preliminary bombardment and the enemy was completely routed from the landing area.

    Through the superior performance of your Task Force it was possible to land our troops and supplies without loss of any personnel or material and carry out an operation which completely destroyed a Japanese Q-boat base, a radar station and a radio station, thus securing the western exits to San Bernardino Strait and Verde Island Passage.

    The technical ability of Captain McGee and the attitude and performance of his officers and men in carrying out this mission is indicative of a well trained and disciplined unit and reflects great credit upon the service to which they belong.

    /s/ R. B. WOODRUFF"

    2.   Commander Task Unit 78.9.7 takes pleasure in commending you for the outstanding performance of your Rocket ship that took part in the LUBANG ISLAND operation. The able manner in which your ship was handled and made ready to provide close gunfire support if required reflects credit upon you. Your excellent work contributed to the success of the operation.

H. F. MC GEE

Copy to:
  BuPers
  ComLCSFlot1

Lubang Island

www.ingramcontent.com/pod-product-compliance
Lightning Source LLC
Chambersburg PA
CBHW040624240426
43666CB00020BA/2908